About the Author

LOUIS FERRANTE was born and raised in Queens, New York. *Unlocked* is his first book.

UNLOCKED

THE LIFE AND CRIMES OF A MAFIA INSIDER

LOUIS FERRANTE

HARPER

NEW YORK · LONDON · TORONTO · SYDNEY

HARPER

A portion of the royalties from this book will be donated to the Moshe ben Abraham Foundation.

A hardcover edition of this book was published in 2008 by HarperCollins Publishers.

HarperCollins books may be purchased for educational, business, or sales promotional use. For information please write: Special Markets Department, HarperCollins Publishers, 10 East 53rd Street, New York, NY 10022.

FIRST HARPER PAPERBACK PUBLISHED 2009.

Designed by Renato Stanisic

Library of Congress Cataloging-in-Publication Data is available upon request.

ISBN 978-0-06-113386-2

09 10 11 12 13   ID/RRD   10 9 8 7 6 5 4 3 2 1

TO MY MOTHER, JO ANN

There is no man, however wise, who has not at some period of his youth said things, or lived a life, the memory of which is so unpleasant to him that he would gladly expunge it. And yet he ought not entirely to regret it, because he cannot be certain that he has indeed become a wise man—so far as it is possible for any of us to be wise—unless he has passed through all the fatuous or unwholesome incarnations by which that ultimate stage must be preceded.

—Marcel Proust

AUTHOR'S NOTE

The story of my criminal life is well documented, due to the diligent efforts of law enforcement and meticulous filing of FBI documents. Government informants and criminal court records also constitute a wealth of material.

The following is my story, told by me. The names and certain identifying facts have been changed to protect the innocent, and conceal the guilty. Any similarities are unintended.

PART I

THE STREETS

I LIKE BURGERS AND FRIES

I leaned down, dropped a knee into his chest, and pressed my gun into his forehead right between the eyes.

"Don't kill me, I have a wife and kid."

"Do what I say an' you'll see 'em again."

He was large, big-boned, had a red beard, like a lumberjack. He was six inches away from death, the length of my gun barrel. If he flipped out, or my finger twitched, I'd have a dead body under me.

"It's a robbery. I want your truck, not your life."

"No!" he screamed. "I don't wanna die!"

He knocked the back of his head against the metal floor and swung his meaty arms, batting at the gun. His knuckles grazed my chin. I pushed his arms away, then jammed the barrel of the gun into his mouth. "You don't wanna die, huh? Then shut the fuck up!"

He shook his head. His teeth scraped against the steel, his lips sealed around the muzzle. He had to taste the weapon to know he didn't like it.

I let the steel sit between his teeth. When I pulled the gun back, he looked disappointed. The gun controlled him. He didn't trust himself to behave without it. I think he wanted me to shove it back in his mouth, to save his life.

"Turn over."

"Don't . . . shoot . . . me," he gasped. His coffee breath blasted me in the face. He was afraid to turn over, afraid I'd finish him off execution style.

"Do as I say an' you'll be home for dinner."

He twisted his broad shoulders in the cramped aisle, squeezing his eyes shut.

Once he was on his stomach, I reached into my jacket pocket and pulled out a roll of duct tape.

His wide back stretched his Snearco Tool shirt as he wrapped his hands around the back of his head. I didn't tell him to do this; either he'd seen it on TV or was shielding himself from a bullet.

"Put 'em behine your back," I said. "An' press your wrists together."

I placed my gun on a shelf against the wall. I spun the tape around his wrists, then tore it with my teeth.

He let out a long breath and lay still. He wanted to live.

I lifted his head off the floor by his hair, taped his mouth, then gently lowered his head to the side so he wouldn't crush his nose.

About an hour before I grabbed this guy, my crew and I had parked on a street lined with auto body shops. We smoked cigarettes and told jokes until this poor stiff swung his tool truck up onto the curb and parked.

His sliding passenger door was open, like most delivery trucks during the summer.

"I got this," I said to my friends as I jumped out of the car.

I felt a rush of adrenaline. The driver was alone, busy with paperwork when I climbed the steps on the passenger side.

"Can I take a look around, I wanna buy some tools."

He was startled at first, but quickly relaxed, probably hoped to open a new account.

"Sure," he said.

I looked down the narrow walkway. Giant toolboxes weighing a ton and standing as high as my chest sat along the walls. On the racks above me were ratchets, screwdrivers, hammers, and wrenches. The toolboxes were worth five to ten grand apiece; everything in the truck was worth over a hundred.

I pointed to tools, asked some prices.

When he looked away for a second, I whipped out a big bright .357 Magnum and pointed it at his head.

I don't know if he fell to the floor before or after I ordered him to lie down, but I stood over him as he looked up at me.

After I taped him up, I went to the doorway of the truck and waved to my friends, then went back to work.

I lifted him to his knees.

The name tag stitched into the chest pocket of his shirt read "Matthew."

"Matty," I said, "don't be afraid. I only want what's in your truck. This shit's insured, no?"

I knew it was, but wanted to reassure him that he was losing nothing.

He nodded. Sweat ran down his freckled forehead.

"We're gonna take the truck somewhere, then let you go. We'll call the cops, tell 'em where we leave ya, okay?"

The Catalano brothers climbed aboard. Chucky jumped behind the wheel and started the engine while Freddy stared at the tools.

I slid by Freddy to greet Chucky up front.

"Lift your ass." I pushed Chucky forward and pulled a red pillow out from under him as he took us into midday traffic.

"Gimme a hand," I said, sliding by Freddy again. He followed.

"Listen, Matty, we'll be on the road awhile. We're gonna prop ya up against the back door. I'll stick this cushion unda ya, so you don't break your ass on the bumps."

Freddy and I lifted Matthew and dragged him to the back, where we put him on the pillow.

Once under way, driving on noisy, congested streets, I pulled the tape off Matthew's mouth. Red bristles from his beard stuck to the glue.

"I saw a bottled water up front," I said. "Wanna sip?"

"Please," said Matthew, calmer now.

I put the bottle to his mouth so he could drink, then snatched a promo towel off a rack, wet it, and wiped down his face. I squeezed some drops over his head.

"Thanks," he said.

"No problem. Listen, Matt, there ain't gonna be nothin' left but a tin can when we're done wit' this thing. Anythin' you need, personal shit?"

"The pictures pinned to the visor, my wife and kid, can you put them in my shirt pocket?"

"Sure."

Up front, I looked out at the road. Cars, cabs, and buses wove in and out of lanes around us. Cops didn't know what we were up to, even as we drove alongside them. I patted Chucky on the shoulder, admiring his cool behind the wheel.

I returned with Matthew's pictures, slipped them into his pocket.

"I'm sure they're beautiful, I didn't look at 'em."

"They are," he said. "Take a look, they're my whole life."

"You'll be wit' 'em t'night. They won't even know nothin' happened to ya, 'less you tell 'em yaself."

"Good," he said, "my wife's a real worrier."

Freddy and I held on to the racks like commuters on an overcrowded subway. Freddy pointed to tools, and asked Matthew prices, already counting our money.

"Speaking of prices, would you guys mind if I asked for that metal folder up front? It's stuffed in the dash. It'll help me get everything straight when I sit down with the insurance company."

"I'll give it to you now, so we don't forget."

I wedged the folder under his arm.

We were driving from Queens, through Manhattan, and into Jersey. The Catalano brothers had an uncle who owned an auto body shop. He agreed to pay for the load beforehand.

Along the ride we made small talk.

Eventually Matthew felt comfortable enough to ask us personal questions.

"You got a girlfriend?" he asked me.

"Yeah," I lied, "good girl, comes from a good home. I hope to marry her someday." In reality, I was screwing some hole I met in a nightclub. I gave him the answer he was looking for.

"You in school?" he asked Freddy, a sixth-grade dropout.

I gave Freddy a kick.

"Yeah," Freddy answered, "I graduate this year. I'm the student council." He meant to say he was on the student council.

We carried on like this through Queens.

As Chucky paid the toll into Manhattan, Matthew let out a roar. Freddy slapped a hand over his mouth. "Shut the fuck up," he whispered, "or I'll waste you right here."

"What the fuck's goin' on?" hollered Chucky, checking his side-view mirrors as we pulled away from the tollbooth, merging with traffic.

"The toll guy hear 'im?" I shouted up front.

"I think we're all right," said Chucky. "It's loud out there. We'll know in a minute."

"What the fuck was that?" I asked.

"He says his leg cramped up," Freddy said.

"I didn't know we were going through a toll, I swear," said Matthew.

Freddy apologized for being rough.

We made it through Manhattan without any problems. Me, Freddy, and Matthew continued to bullshit as we entered the Holland Tunnel. By now, Matthew thought he was our friend.

"Hey, fellas," he said, "you're real nice guys, and you got your whole lives ahead of you. Don't you think this stuff will catch up with you someday?"

Tunnel lights flicked by along the walls. I saw the outline of his face in the dark. I didn't answer, didn't really understand his question. Good thing. I was ignorant enough to resent him for casting a black cloud over my future.

Years later, I'd sit in prison, raucous violence teeming around me, loneliness eating away at my heart, and I'd remember Matthew, and what he said to us that day.

I took Matthew's driver's license. "We know where you live. Tell the cops niggers robbed ya, an' you'll never see us again."

Freddy put tape over Matthew's eyes and walked him out into a deserted lot in an industrial area, ten minutes from our drop.

"Matty," I said, "don't move. We'll be right across the street, watchin'
you. When we're done unloadin', we'll let you go, okay?"

"Thanks," he said. For the conversation, for carefully walking him
down the steps, for sparing his life, I don't know. "Good luck," he added.

"I liked that guy," I said as we drove away.

I was seventeen years old. I liked girls. I liked fist fighting. I liked to
drive fast cars. I liked hamburgers and french fries. I liked playing stickball
in the school yard. And I'd just realized that I liked to hijack trucks.

Not everyone knows it, but the most famous Mob bosses weren't
born into "the Life." They started out as petty thieves, graduating to
bigger crimes as years passed.

Thomas "Three Finger Brown" Lucchese, the founder of the
Lucchese family, was once pinched for auto theft. He went on to run
Manhattan's multibillion-dollar garment center.

Charles "Lucky" Luciano was ten years old when he was arrested for
shoplifting.

The New Orleans boss Carlos Marcello, known for his feud with
RFK, took a pinch for armed robbery before he was twenty.

Vito Genovese, the namesake for the Genovese family, was stopped
by a beat cop as he was about to pull a stickup at age twenty.

And Carmine Galante, a Bonanno family boss, was also twenty when
he was nabbed as he was about to hold up a truck in Williamsburg,
Brooklyn.

Twenty years before my own career began, my boss, John Gotti, hijacked trucks from the same airport as me. Like the rest of these bosses,
he was also in his twenties.

A kid with big balls and no brains can go from flat broke to fat
pockets with one good stickup. It's the quickest money on the street.

Soon, the kid will get the attention of mobsters.

This is how Luciano, Genovese, and Gotti began their careers.

This is how I began mine.

I GOT SOMETHIN' GOOD

I'd been hijacking trucks for a few years. By now, I was the "go to" guy if anyone had a tip on a load.

I was playing cards in a social club in Ozone Park when I got a beep from Eddie. I folded my cards, left my money, cigar smoke, and cursing behind, and went outside to use my cell phone.

"What's up?"

"I got somethin' good."

"Can it wait?"

"I guess." He sounded disappointed.

"Then call me tomorrow." I hung up and went back inside, in time for a new deal.

I knew Eddie my whole life. He was one of those losers you find in every neighborhood: old hairstyles, outdated clothing, blasting music from old muscle cars as they cruise up and down the block.

He hung out in school yards, downing six-packs and smoking joints. Sometime in his early twenties, his mother started charging him rent for his basement bedroom. He hustled dime bags, scratched out enough to keep his mom quiet and still hang out.

I met Eddie the next day.

"I got a friend who hauls loads outta Kennedy. He wants to give one up."

"What's he haulin', an' how much of it?" I asked. "Find out if anyone's ridin' shotgun, an' if there's any trackin' equipment on the truck. An' tell 'im he gets ten percent of my take, which has to be worth it for him to lose his job, since they'll probably hook 'im up to a lie detector an' fire 'im if he fails. Call me after youse talk."

A day later, I saw Eddie at Bagel Bite. He pulled me aside.

"He's haulin' shit from Silk Secrets, worth a half mil."

"You tole 'im he can lose his job?"

"Yeah, he jus' passed the fire test, so he's quittin' after the score, they'll never get to lie-wire him up. It'll look like the robbery shook 'im up an' he's too scared to go back to work. I can pick the truck up an' drive it wherever you want."

I was already giving Eddie five percent for the tip, why not let him work for it? I agreed, and we arranged a date for the "give-up."

Pricey stuff gets shipped everywhere. Truck drivers out for a quick buck will turn to us. I tell them to leave their keys in the ignition and take a leak in a gas station. When they come out, the truck's gone. Some ask me to tie them up and leave them somewhere to make it look good. Give-ups—the easiest jobs, all planned out. The truck is unloaded and abandoned, and the fence has the haul before the driver even reports it stolen.

The morning of the score I ate a bowl of Cocoa Pebbles. Twenty minutes later, I was in Maspeth, Queens. I drove into Sergio's body shop. Noise everywhere: loud compressors, dent pullers popping out sheet metal, spray guns hissing, and lump hammers banging away at fenders.

I spotted Sergio yelling at a half dozen Mexicans, "Drag that jack over here," "Get a dolly block an' bang out that dent," "You gotta pull out the grille before you fix the radiator."

I walked up behind him as he stuffed himself into a car trunk; his dusty pants slid down to show the crack of his ass. I tapped him on the back. He twisted his head around and asked, "Truck's here?" He was chomping on a soggy Macanudo.

"Not yet." I looked at my watch. "How do you breathe in there wit' ail that smoke?"

"Better than all these chemicals." He waved an arm around.

I helped him out of the trunk. We walked into his office. His desk was cluttered with parts lists, chewed cigar butts, promo pens for supply stores, and naked women sprawled across free business calendars. I sat and flipped through a calendar while Sergio hollered into the phone. I was admiring June or July when my cell phone rang.

The excited voice on the other end said, "I got it."

"I'm waitin'." I hung up, cutting Eddie short before he said too much.

Ten minutes later my truck growled around the turn, bucking; Eddie shifted like shit. He nearly ran me down when I walked out into the street to wave him into the driveway.

He rolled down the window. "I'm loaded." He smiled. "She barely moves."

"Can you squeeze through or you want me to do it?" I nodded toward the narrow garage just as the truck coughed and stalled.

"Shit!" Eddie stepped on the clutch, tried to restart the engine. Instead, he set off a piercing siren.

"Fuck, the alarm!" he moaned.

I opened his door and saw the alarm pad attached to the dashboard. "You got the code?"

"I couldn't remember it, so he told me not to shut off the engine."

Pens were stuck in the visor, and crumpled McDonald's bags on the floor. I don't know why he didn't write it down, but it didn't matter now as traffic backed up the block.

Drivers honked their horns. I tried to calm them as a blue-and-white turned the corner and inched up behind the last car. A moment later, another car turned into the block, keeping the cops from backing out to avoid the jam.

"Stay calm," I told Eddie. I ran inside. Sergio was already rounding up the Mexicans to push the truck. I stripped off my sweatshirt down to my wife-beater, smeared grease on my pants, and smudged my face. I snatched a cigar stub from an ash-filled hubcap, bit down on it, and sprinted outside.

Sergio leaned into the passenger window of the first car and apologized to the pissed-off driver, while I waved to the others.

The Mexicans finally shoved the truck up the ramp and into the shop.

Traffic sped by. Drivers threw me the finger or lowered their windows to curse. The cop car stopped in front of the shop. I saluted them as I took the cigar out of my mouth. "Sorry for the wait, Officers."

The truck siren was still blasting behind me. I pointed at a rusty ding in the squad car's right front fender. "We should fix that. Why don't youse drop it off one day?"

"It's the city's, we don't give a fuck," said the cop in the passenger seat before his partner punched the pedal, speeding off.

Maybe they thought nothing was wrong; broken car alarms blast all over the city. Maybe they couldn't be bothered, with Dunkin' Donuts a block away.

I raced inside and closed the shop's gate behind me. Three Mexicans were under the hood of the truck, hacking at anything that could hide a siren.

Sergio lay across the front seat, chopping at the dashboard with a tire iron. Broken plastic flew everywhere.

Eddie was picking his nose.

"I found it!" Sergio yelled.

I looked over his shoulder and saw a blinking red light on a small black box bolted into the cowl. He smashed at it with the tire iron until it went dead.

"Let's move," I said, "in case this thing's got trackin'."

Sergio clipped the padlock on the cargo door. I swung it open and we both smiled at boxes piled high and packed tight.

While Sergio's all-purpose Mexicans emptied the truck, I flipped open a pocketknife and cut into a box to peek inside. I pulled out a clear plastic package holding a shit, no-name brassiere with hard cone cups. What the fuck is this? Josie, my seventy-five-year-old grandmother, wore them on my porch in the summer.

She'd sit with an iced coffee in one hand, fanning herself with the other. I'd tell her, "Go inside, you're embarrassin' me."

"Oh, what's the difference," she'd say. "Same shit girls wear at the beach, like a bikini."

My friends never let me live this down.

Now I had a truckload of Josie's bikinis.

To be sure, I dug through the boxes, and found more of the same.

Sergio managed to start the truck as the Mexicans finished unloading. I followed him in my car as he drove it out of the shop and ditched it in a weeded lot a few miles away. On our way back, I told him what we got.

"You're shittin' me."

"Wish I was."

Back at the shop, the Mexicans were goofing around wearing brassieres. One swung around the pole of a car lift like a topless dancer, another pretended to hump his buddy from behind as he held a bra around the guy's chest. Sergio ordered them back to work after I handed each a C-note.

I found the manifest sheet. I'd intercepted a quarter of a million bras on their way to a low-end chain store.

Of course, my fence didn't want them. "I'll take a dozen thirty-six Ds for my mother-in-law."

"Stop fuckin' aroun'," I said.

"Well, whatta you want me to do wit' 'em? My mother-in-law's tight as a crab's ass, an' cheap as she is, she wouldn't wear this crap. You want the sample back?"

"Throw it in the garbage."

I showed the bras to a couple of other fences. They laughed their asses off. One told me to give them to Sally Potatoes, a 450-pound capo. "He's about ready for them," the fence said.

When I finally told Sergio to dump them and chalk it up as a loss, he mentioned a friend in Brooklyn.

"He owns dollar stores, he'll take a thousand at a clip."

"It's not worth the aggravation," I told Sergio. "Tell 'im take the whole lot, an' he owes us a favor. In fact, we'll owe *him* for gettin' rid of our trash."

I broke the news to Eddie. Eddie told the driver, who apologized for the screwup.

In the meantime, Sergio needed room in his shop and had moved the boxes to his uncle's warehouse. It was raided the following day. Everything was taken away by the feds.

"What'd they pinch your uncle for?" I asked Sergio.

"Stolen parts or counterfeit money, I dunno. My mother's supposed to talk to my aunt tonight. They'll probably charge 'im wit' the load, too."

A couple of weeks later, I was getting ready to go out when my house phone rang about eight p.m. My caller ID showed a Queens area code with a Howard Beach exchange. I was sure it was the friend I was meeting that night.

I picked up the phone. "Hello."

"I'm callin' about the load," some guy said, in a hoarse, "tough guy" voice.

"Stop playin', you gettin' ready or what?"

"The load from JFK, you got the manifest sheet?"

"You're fuckin' nuts! I'm leavin' my house in five minutes."

My bra heist was the joke of the week. I was sure my friend was pranking me.

A minute later, my phone rang again.

"Hey," I said, "you serious yet?"

"Yeah, I'm serious. You don't hang up on me when I ask a question! I want the manifest sheet from that load outta JFK."

My friends wouldn't go this far. It might be the FBI trying to push my buttons, get me to talk. I took down three trucks in the last month. They could've been investigating any one of these hijackings.

"I dunno what you're talkin' about."

"Yeah, you do!" said the mysterious caller.

"No, I don't. An' who the fuck are you anyway?"

"I'm wit' Joe C. an' he wants his load or his money!"

"Fuck you and your friend Joe C.!" I slammed the phone down.

I called my friend Vinny, who lived in Howard Beach, and reeled off the number that appeared on my caller ID. "It's from your area, ring a bell?"

"Not wit' me," he said, "but I know a girl who fucked everyone in the neighborhood, she'll know it. I'll call you right back."

He did. "He's not a cop," said Vinny. "He runs wit' a crew in Bensonhurst, spends most of his time there."

"That's all she knew?"

"An' he's a good fuck, if you're interested."

"Thanks." I hung up and dialed the number. "Hey, punk, let's meet over by you, I know where you're from. I'm on my way."

"Meet me on the boulevard, behind L and S Auto, an' don't forget that fuckin' list!" He hung up.

I called my friend to change our plans. "Somethin' came up, meet me by Plaza Pizza."

I reached under my bed and stuffed a .38 Special into the waistband of my pants. I raced in and out of traffic, got to Plaza's lot, and pulled in beside my friend's Lincoln. He raised his hands. "What's up?"

I jumped out of my car, into his, and told him the story.

"You packin'?" I asked when I finished.

"Of course, I heard it in your voice."

"Watch my back in case someone's lookin' to clip me. I'm meetin' him alone, jus' stay in the car an' come out blastin' if you hear shots."

"Why not send word through the proper channels, handle this the right way?"

"I'm too hot, I can't wait. This punk called my house twice."

The rear parking lot of L & S Auto Supply was unlit. I'm sure that's why he chose this spot.

My friend made a U-turn and pointed his headlights into the lot. We spotted an average-sized guy pacing, arms crossed.

"Looks like he's by himself," I said. "Watch the entrance."

I got out of the car and walked into the lot. I kept my eyes on his hands, in case he pulled a gun. I stared into his mug when we were inches apart, close because it was dark, and to see who had bigger balls.

He screamed at me, spraying spit in my face. All I saw was teeth opening and closing in the darkness. I cocked back and nailed him in the jaw with a right. He stumbled, then swung back. We were brawling.

His fists were like bricks, so I tackled him to the ground, where I bit his face. He screamed as I tore a chunk from his cheek. As I spit it out, my friend pulled me off him.

"That's enough, Louie, let's get the fuck outta here."

"This ain't over, muthafucka!" he screamed from the pavement as I walked away. I turned back and reached for my piece, but my pal grabbed my arm. Besides, the gun was stuck in my crotch, caught in my Jockey underwear.

"Lucky you didn't shoot ya balls off," my friend said, once we were in the car, speeding away.

I took the gun out of my pants as he handed me a napkin to clean the blood off my face.

I showered and borrowed a shirt at his house.

"I think you should put this on record," my buddy said, "in case somethin' comes of it."

"I'll stop by the club tomorrow an' tell John."

"Why not t'night? That guy was fucked up, who's he wit' anyhow?"

"Vinny said he's wit' a crew from Bensonhurst, claimed a Joe C. sent 'im when he called my house."

"Joe C. from the Luccheses?"

"I don't know, why?"

"'Cause they jus' made him actin' boss."

Most mobsters sleep 'til noon, so when I say, "Early the next morning, I got a phone call," I mean around twelve-thirty, one o'clock.

"Big Paulie wants you by the club. Come now."

"I'm on my way."

I knew why Paulie wanted to see me. I got there fast.

"Joe C.'s lookin' for ya head," said Paulie, "claims he sent someone to give you a message las' night an' you an' ya buddies put 'im in the hospital."

"The guy blabbed Joe's name on my phone, so I doubted he was for real. An' nobody touched the guy but me. I had one friend wit' me who pulled me off 'im or I mighta killed 'im."

"You been to enougha these things, you can go alone," he said. "Tell Joe I couldn't make it, I gotta go to a wake tonight. Be real respectful 'cause I ain't supposed to send you alone. But don't let 'im bully you either."

Joe C. was acting boss of the Lucchese family, with all due power and respect. The real boss was serving five life sentences in maximum security.

I met Joe C. at a small restaurant on Cross Bay Boulevard. I rolled up in a Corvette convertible and found a spot on the street.

A guy from my crew came along as a silent witness. We waited on the sidewalk as a black Caddy parked behind my car. A barrel-chested guy in his forties hopped out of the driver's side. An older man used the door frame to lift himself out of the passenger seat.

"Hi, Joe." I shook the passenger's hand, and we exchanged kisses on our cheeks. I'd never seen Joe, but knew I had the right guy. He was in his mid-sixties, diamond-face Rolex, pinky ring, and a way about him that said, "I'm the boss." He looked like Scorsese's fashion consultant from *Goodfellas* dressed him. I wore a black T-shirt, blue jeans, and a baseball cap.

"Where's Paulie?" Joe asked, as his lackey closed the car door for him.

"He apologized but couldn't make it. He had a wake. He tole me I can speak for myself."

Joe shook his head, and looked at his friend; both seemed insulted.

Too damn bad. I lost any respect for this phony old fuck when I found out the telephone tough guy was his friend.

We walked into the place. A couple of older guys at the bar sucked up to Joe until a pretty young hostess seated us at a booth in the back. It looked like our fathers were taking us to dinner.

Joe and his friend ordered black coffee with a shot of Sambuca. My friend and I ordered sodas. When the waiter left, Joe leaned in with that typical 1930s gangster snarl. "The truck driver you fucked is wit' me, says you owe 'im fifty Gs. An' when I send somebody to confront you in my name, you raise a hand to him, let alone jump 'im wit' a buncha goons an' put 'im in the hospital? An' I heard you said, 'Fuck Joe C.' "

He leaned back and crossed his arms, a smug look on his face; his friend finally stopped nodding along.

The guy I beat up must've told Joe, "I got jumped by a bunch of goons." I guess it sounds better than, "I got my ass kicked trying to bully a kid half my size."

Joe was an opportunist. The truck driver sold his story to someone, probably the chooch sitting next to Joe. And Joe signed on, convinced there was money to be made. Joe didn't give a shit about the driver, he wanted a piece of the action.

Since I had Paulie's blessing, and Joe was letting me speak on his level, I leaned in as he'd done.

"First off, if the truck driver's wit' you, why did he come to me? Second, your messenger called me on my home phone, hollerin' about a manifes' sheet. He said your name, but I know a few Joe C.'s, never figurin' that a schmuck who blabs on the phone could be wit' a guy big as you."

He sank into his seat, probably thinking about biting the guy's other cheek.

"When we met," I continued, "he started off by screamin' at me. That's not how we do things. Yeah, I cracked 'im first, but only after he spit in my face. An' no one jumped in. My friend saved his ass, dragged me off 'im. As for the load, it's gone, taken by the law when they swarmed the joint where they was bein' stored. None of us made a nickel, an' I'm hopin' my friend's uncle stands up, or we still might take a pinch. If the driver, my driver, your driver, whoever's driver, gave the right info, I'd've offed the load right away. Instead, I was stuck wit' five hundred boxes of shit brassieres I couldn't sell as slingshots."

Joe folded his hands on the table. He stared at the dummy next to him, who I was sure conned him into appearing on the driver's behalf.

Joe dismissed the beef with, "I hope everythin' works out all right for your friend's uncle, an' tell Big Paulie everythin' was squashed."

He nearly shoved his friend off the seat getting out of the booth. I'd have given anything to hear them on their way home.

In my fifth or sixth year in prison, I was sitting in the yard reading a book. I looked up and saw a frail old man straggle onto the compound, a little stooped over. Italians bumped into each other trying to greet him, even blacks and Hispanics after they found out who he was.

This ass kissing went on several days. I laughed to myself, watching grown men make idiots of themselves. I knew the geezer but had no reason to close my book and say hello. He belonged to my past, a past I was still paying for, but my mind was elsewhere. I couldn't be bothered.

One sunny day, I took off my shirt and began reading in the yard. The old man broke away from his gang and came over to me. "You don't remember me?"

"Sure I do, how you been?" I got up, thinking, Shit, this guy's going to want to bullshit about the old days, and I'm in no mood.

"Hangin' in there." He shrugged his shoulders. "Wanna walk?"

"Okay."

He only talked about his wife and a son who'd killed himself, though he didn't say when it happened or how old the boy had been. He was a man who'd given up.

"Sometimes things have a funny way of workin' themselves out," I said, trying to prop him up. "I know the feelin', it sucks. I also faced a life bid, but got off with thirteen years."

"That's life for me," he said, "I'm an old man."

I rested a hand on his shoulder. "Joe, what can we do, it was the life we chose." I think I quoted an old Mob movie.

I looked at Joe and knew exactly what he'd do, but I kept it to myself since you don't label a man a rat, especially a godfather, unless you got proof.

I kept my distance from Joe until I was shipped from that jail.

About two years after our walk in the yard, I landed in a prison high up in the Adirondack Mountains. I called a friend to say hello. He accepted the charges, eager to break news. "You see today's paper?"

"No, it won't reach my block 'til tomorrow."

"Joe C. went bad, they're pinchin' everybody."

My only surprise was that Joe didn't sing sooner. How'd he fool so many men for so long? I found myself asking this question about more and more guys as years went by.

JIMMY THE JEWELER

Where did I off a load of swag?

When I was young, starting out, I sold loads to Barry the Brokester, Umberto "Bert the Zip," the Count, and Billy Brains (because he had none).

No one had any problem dealing with a kid. My word was good. I delivered.

When I got older, Uncle Jimmy fenced nearly every load I stole.

Jimmy was Sneaker Pete's uncle, not mine. Still, I called him "Uncle Jimmy" out of respect.

The first thing I brought Jimmy were traveler's checks. I busted open a safe in Brooklyn and found seventy-five hundred dollars' worth folded up in a rubber band. I never traveled anywhere, so I didn't know traveler's checks from Monopoly money.

They were numbered; I wasn't sure if they were on a hot sheet. I called Sneaker Pete. He tossed around the idea of cashing them at his bank. "I'll say some towel-head walked in off the street an' bought sneakers."

"Seventy-five hundred worth? May as well rob the bank, since they'll hit the buzzer unda the counter as you sit there bullshittin' wit' that stupid grin you always make when you lie."

"You're right, let's go see my uncle."

Pete and I were on the corner of Forty-seventh and Sixth, Manhattan's jewelry district, when Uncle Jimmy hustled toward us.

"Nice to meet ya, kid." He shook my hand.

We ducked into a coffee shop. Jimmy sat across from me in a button-down shirt, chest hairs sprouting over his open collar. He had sharp brown eyes and heavy black brows. Gucci sunglasses rested on a thick head of blown-out hair.

I showed him the traveler's checks.

"How much you got?"

"Seventy-five hundred."

"You take five grand?"

"Sure."

He handed me the wad under the table, then slipped the checks into his pocket as he slid out of the booth. "I'm in a hurry." He threw a twenty on the table for the coffee he never drank.

They called him Jimmy the Jeweler, even though he never owned a jewelry store. Jimmy was always in a rush, but always cool. He wore five-hundred-dollar hand-painted ties, and a different watch every day. Diamond cufflinks and an ice cube on his pinky. He stuck his feet in a mold to have shoes custom-made.

It's said that every major jewel heist in the world sooner or later ends up in Manhattan's jewelry district. Gold is melted down, diamonds recycled, every last trace of a heist disappears.

The district had its share of thieves, but only four or five "heavy movers," guys who knew everyone and could fence anything. They were in competition but got along. Jimmy was one of them.

Pete heard stories about Jimmy. "He masterminded heists in Europe."

"No shit?"

"For real. He even escaped Swissland on a glider, landed in Italy. Greaseballs hid 'im in the mountains 'til things cooled down."

Jimmy wasn't a wiseguy. He was a half-breed, so he couldn't get made. He looked full Italian, spoke it, sung it, cooked it, and could've fooled any family into giving him a button by adding a vowel to the end of his name. But Jimmy was straight up, no bullshit. That's how he made his reputation.

Jimmy lived in a ritzy apartment in midtown. In his office, he had a big oak desk. In the top drawer was a sheet of paper taped to a piece of cardboard and covered in cellophane. It was a list of nicknames, across from each was a phone number. Every load I brought Jimmy went to someone on this list.

After hearing what I had, Jimmy would put on reading glasses, run a finger down the list, stop on a name, and make a phone call.

"It's me, the Jeweler," he'd say, "let's meet for coffee."

He'd hang up and give me and Pete a wink.

"That list's worth a million bucks," Pete once said after we left Jimmy's apartment.

"Not wit'out your uncle's voice on the other end."

Jimmy's word was worth a mil, not his list. If Jimmy told me there was fifty large waiting for me, it was money in the bank. When he handed me money, I'd tuck it away without counting it. How could I? He never looked inside my trucks.

Sometimes, Jimmy paid up front. This was unheard of on the streets, since anything might happen; hijackers get pinched, loads get confiscated. But when I told Jimmy I had something valuable, he'd disappear into his bedroom and come out with cash. He'd hand me thirty or forty grand, like he was giving a kid a dollar.

Jimmy was so fair that I couldn't think of being otherwise with him. He was a class act, and brought the best out of me.

Jimmy and I had no contracts, no lawyers, no bill of sale; a handshake sealed the deal. Try that in the straight world.

I knew how much Jimmy trusted me when he waved me into his bedroom, moved a throw rug, and lifted a floorboard. He opened a steel box stuffed with bills, and handed me a bundle.

On our way home, I told Pete what I saw.

"Let's rob 'im," he blurted.

"He's your uncle, you bum. Besides, who's gonna buy our nex' load?"

He laughed, but I saw his wheels turning; Sneaker Pete was a greedy motherfucker, greediest man I'd ever met.

I was around famous mobsters every day, but I admired Jimmy more. Jimmy ran alone, didn't need a Mob to make him tough. He took no orders, gave none, and reported to no one.

In a world in which fear and muscle rule, Uncle Jimmy never even threatened anyone. He was respected because of his word. And everyone liked him.

HEY, KID, YOU HIT THIS GUY IN BED?

I was meeting Bobby Butterballs for lunch. Six months back, I lent Bobby ten grand to open a cocktail lounge in Flushing. Business was good; time to pay me back.

I walked into his place early and saw a few old drunks at the bar; worn faces, missing teeth, and raspy voices. Someone was telling stale jokes. The others stared at a silent television with sports scores and highlights. I knew daytime drunks drink their checks—pension, disability, welfare—so I bought them a round.

The bartender, Timmy McLaughlin, pushed my money back at me. I shook his hand.

"Is Butter aroun'?" I asked.

"He's on his way. Have a seat, I'll get you a menu."

I left my money on the bar and sat at a table.

Timmy was a neighborhood kid who tended bar part-time while school was out. His mother died of cancer a few years back. My own mother, her close friend, was now dying the same slow death. Although me and Timmy didn't see much of each other, the pain of watching our mothers die tightened us.

Timmy sighed as two husky, rough-looking men returned from the restroom. They looked lit, maybe did a line; one rubbed his nose. They wore dirty jeans and work boots. I took them for construction workers done for the day, too numbed up to return to work. They stood at the bar, yelling about baseball, scooping up pretzels, and shoving them in their mouths.

Real fucking animals, I said to myself. If that's what work does to you, I'm glad I never had a job.

Just as it seemed the two would come to blows, one threw a pretzel nugget at an old man sitting a couple of chairs away. It ricocheted off his balding head. The two jerks broke into hysterics as the old man muttered something. Just for that, they hit him with another nugget. The old man swiped his money off the bar and split, cursing through false teeth that swished around in his mouth. The chief bully started to throw pretzels at the other drunks as his sidekick laughed up a storm, playing Ed McMahon to his Johnny Carson.

When an old woman finally got hit, Timmy said, "Relax, guys," then glanced over at me for help.

The bully reached his arm across the bar and smashed the bowl into Timmy's chest. "Shut the fuck up, an' gimme more pretzels."

I walked up to them; both stood a foot over my head. I slid a twenty on the bar between them. "Hey, fellas, forget the pretzels, drinks are on me. Enjoy yourselves." I didn't think I could buy them off, but I gave it a shot.

"Fuck you!" said the bully. "How 'bout I bend you like a fuckin' pretzel? Wanna go outside?"

For a moment, I hesitated. Would fighting them inside or out make a difference?

"Sure." I turned for the door.

My Lincoln was parked out front. I had a nickel-plated .45 automatic under my front passenger seat, and a Louisville Slugger in the trunk. I had seconds to choose my weapon.

The block was busy, and .45 shots sound like cannonballs. If someone IDs me or my plate, I'm doing twenty-five to life for a pretzel, fifty if I take them both out. I popped the trunk.

I was already practicing my swing when they stumbled from the bar. I stepped onto the sidewalk like I was stepping up to the plate.

"You're a big guy, you don't expect me to fight fair." I gave the bully a chance to back down.

"I'm gonna shove that bat up your ass!" He came at me.

I leaned in and swung at his head with everything I had. The impact lifted him into the air; his feet were level with his ears before he slammed onto the pavement and skidded on his back. I stood over him. Blood poured from a pulpy hole in the middle of his forehead.

"Shit, I killed him."

I spun back for his friend; he's got to go too, or he'll be pointing me out in a lineup.

He was running away as fast as he could. Some friend.

I tossed the bat back into my trunk and covered my rear license plate with an oil rag. I had to get rid of my gun, my bat, my car, and myself. I drove to Little Paulie's house. He answered the door in boxer shorts and a wife-beater.

He stared down at my shirt, splattered with blood. "Who'd you kill?"

I told him what happened, borrowed a few grand, a change of clothes, another car, and took it on the lam.

"You did what you hadda do" were his parting words as I pulled out of his driveway.

I went over the episode a thousand times while I drove, creating a manslaughter defense in my mind, counting on Timmy McLaughlin, a good college boy, as my star witness.

I thought of ways to break the news to my family, and imagined how old I'd be after five, ten, or fifteen years in prison.

When I spotted a highway cop, I paid closer attention to the rules of the road, while telling myself that even if I was wanted, I couldn't be connected with the car I was driving.

I was still pumped up. My hands trembled holding the wheel. When someone cut me off or sped by recklessly, I shouted things like, "You know what I jus' did?" and "You want a beatin' too?" I was channeling nervous energy when all I wanted to do was get somewhere safe with no more trouble for the day.

I checked into the Radisson on Long Island's East End under a phony name. I called home to tell my family I'd be vacationing in the

Hamptons with some friends for the next couple of weeks. I'd stay put and wait to hear if I left a body behind, then figure out my next move.

That night I watched the local news, relieved to see no mention of what I'd done. I slept like a rock, confident no one knew where I was.

The next morning I ate a king's breakfast in the hotel, then drove a few miles to a public phone. I called Little Paulie.

"Hear anythin'?"

"Word on the street is that some bar bully in Flushin' had the shit beat out of him but lived, an' no one knows who done it."

Timmy kept quiet. I waited a few days, then went home to my normal routine.

I forgot the whole thing until late one night, two months later, I got a phone call from Butterballs. "Detectives know it was you. They asked me to tell you to turn yourself in. They wanna put you in a lineup."

I knew right away Butter gave me up. Detectives don't make courtesy calls to friends of suspects with polite requests. Since my batting practice, Butter was avoiding me. He knew if I went to prison, he wouldn't have to pay me my ten grand. Besides, the cops were threatening to yank his liquor license if he didn't talk. He was a nice rat, eased his conscience with a phone call.

I had choices.

I could either take it on the hop, or roll the dice in a lineup. By now, my mother had only weeks to live; I couldn't leave her. If I turned myself in and blew the lineup, I'd be booked, processed, and back home on bail in days. I could hold off a trial date for months. My mother would never know about the pinch.

I mulled it over with my crew.

"Let's get ridda the troublemaker before he picks you out," said Botz.

"I don't even know who he is," I said.

"We'll take 'im out in fronta the precinct," Botz suggested. "All you gotta do is point 'im out."

"That's great in Hollywood, not in real life," I said. "Sit tight, we'll get 'im later if he picks me."

Tony Botz was crazy. *Pazzo* means "crazy" in Italian. When we said it fast, it came out sounding like Botz.

The next morning, I arrived at the office of Richard Piccola, a local attorney who'd just passed the bar, the test that pre-pardons men for a life of crime. He asked me for seven hundred. I gave him cash.

We ate breakfast at a diner, then went to the 109th Precinct in Queens.

We climbed the dingy staircase to the second floor. Piccola introduced himself to the case detective, a big, brawny cop with black hair, a necktie already hanging low on his chest at ten a.m., and a cup of coffee in his hand. The doughnuts were on his desk.

"This shouldn't take long," he said. "Even if he picks ya, you'll be out this afternoon, maybe tomorrow."

Minutes later, I sat behind a two-way mirror with four cops, all with mustaches and blue T-shirts. Piccola threw a fit since I was clean-shaven and my shirt was white. He ranted phrases like, "Duh, who doesn't belong?" and, "My client's too young to grow a mustache!"

"Take it easy," said the detective. He found a clean-shaven cop, and instead of giving me a matching shirt, he picked up a drop cloth where some men had been painting, telling us to hold it up to our necks.

The cop to my left elbowed me with a chuckle. "Hey, kid, you hit this guy in bed?"

We all laughed. A tap on the window. A minute or so passed as I acted like a cop irritated with this detail. Another tap and we left the room.

"The dummy didn't pick ya!" Piccola greeted me with a hug on the other side.

"Really?" I couldn't believe it. I was prepared for the worst, sure I was off to prison.

Piccola signed some papers as the detective told us how even he hated this bully. "The prick and his family pressed us to charge someone with attempted murder, otherwise this complaint would've been lost. This bum's got a shitload of his own assaults, even threw his girlfriend's old man down a flight of stairs, and now he calls us when someone cracks his own cantaloupe. He even admitted to threatening you before you clobbered him. If the guy stuck the bat up your ass like he said, you think he would've walked in here and told us?"

"I dunno. I didn't do it."

Piccola beamed, and put his arm around me.

"Listen, kid, the lineup's done." The detective leaned back in a wooden chair that bent on a creaky spring; his fat belly strained the buttons on his coffee-stained shirt. "He didn't pick ya, an' I sure as hell don't want ya. I'm jus' wonderin' if my snitch was good. My word of honor, it dies here, did ya hit him?"

I hesitated, didn't trust him, but it seemed he hated the bully more than me. "Not hard enough."

He winked and smiled before Piccola and I headed for the door.

My crew took me to dinner, and I returned home to care for my mother. A month later, angels carried her away. She died in my arms.

CHUMP CHANGE

Funzi knew this kid, Carlos Ruiz.

Ruiz lived in a second-floor apartment above a corner pub in Corona, Queens. His landlord, who owned the entire block, increased Ruiz's rent after Ruiz got hit with a double whammy: his wife got pregnant, and he lost his job.

Ruiz called Funzi looking for help. "I'm fucked," he said. "I'm outta work, an' expectin' a baby. You know lotsa people, can you help me find a cheapa place? I'll owe you big time."

"I ain't no real estate broker but I'll ask aroun'," Funzi said.

A few days later, Ruiz was carrying groceries home when he spotted two men inside the foyer leading up to his apartment. Only Ruiz and his landlord had a key. He walked to a pay phone and called Funzi.

"Yo, man, that muthafuckin' lan'lord put some thugs in my hallway. I can beat the shit out of them right now, but my girl be pregnant, she upstairs. I can't have her gettin' all scared an' shit, maybe somethin' happen to my baby."

"Go have a drink down the block an' cool down, I'm on it."

Funzi hung up and called me. I listened to the story. "His landlord sounds like a dirty muthafucka."

That night, I canceled dinner with friends and found Ruiz's landlord sitting in the bar he owned under Ruiz's apartment. As we drank two bottled Buds, I got my point across; he gave Ruiz a break on the rent, even hired him as a bar-back. He also promised new appliances within the month. I never met Ruiz, didn't have to. He thanked me through Funzi.

About a year later, I was licking a chocolate-chip ice in front of Corona Ice King when Funzi said, "Oh, shit, I forgot to tell ya what happened yesterday. Remember that kid Carlos we helped when his wife was pregnant an' his landlord was throwin' 'im out?"

"Yeah, Ruiz, he had a boy, right?"

"Uh-huh. He called me las' night. He's got a new job drivin' coin trucks, goes aroun' to apartment buildin's pickin' up change from washers an' dryers. I tole 'im I wanna hit 'im, he said, 'No shit, poppy, that's why I'm callin' you.' "

"What can we get, a hundred apiece an' some slugs?"

"I thought the same thing, but they stuff the truck wit' like fifteen, twenty grand by the enda the day. We don't even need a fence."

"He alone?"

"No, he rides wit' anutter guy who ain't in on it, but says the guy's a real shit pants, scared of his own shadow."

"So it's a halfa stickup. We got a lotta shit goin' on, hold off for now."

I wanted the job, but I felt like I'd be going backward. I dealt with coins as a kid. Me and my friends would cut the heads off parking meters with a pipe cutter. We'd sledgehammer the meters open in my buddy's garage. Inside each meter was a small plastic cup that never held more than five or six bucks in change, a big score for us back then.

A couple of years later, we graduated to gumball machines.

This old wop named Toto owned a candy route. He had machines in fifty supermarkets, did real well for himself. He owned the biggest house on the block, with marble lions on his porch. In our neighborhood, the more gaudy statues you could stuff on your tiny property, the more money you had to piss away. The rest of us couldn't scratch out enough to pay Sammy the Albanian to fix the cracks in our stoops.

Me and my friend Pee Wee would steal a pickup and drive around looking for machines that didn't belong to Toto. We'd pull up in front of a supermarket or drug store, and Pee Wee would go in and ask for the manager.

"We're from the candy company," he'd say, "here to remove your ole chipped machines an' replace 'em wit' nice new ones tomorrow."

Pee Wee was a good bullshit artist. The managers would hand him the keys or unlock the chain for us. Some managers even helped us load the machines onto our truck.

Toto paid us a hundred bucks a machine, and gave us the change inside as a bonus.

One day, me and Pee Wee were stealing machines in Jackson Heights when a two-hundred-year-old Spanish man walked out of a bodega, dropped into a police stance, and yelled, "Freeze!" He aimed a rusted Saturday night special at me.

"Put that gun away, ole-timer, you're watchin' too much *Baretta*." I pushed the barrel aside with my finger.

"You don't know me." He aimed the gun at me again.

What he meant was, "You don't know who the fuck I am."

I got the message.

"I know you, you're one bad muthafucka, everyone knows you."

He smiled. I cringed, more from his rotted teeth than from the gun. While I talked him out of killing me, Pee Wee started the truck. I jumped in and we took off.

We didn't know if he was Colombian Mafia, or just some crazy old bastard. Either way, Pee Wee shit his pants and quit on me. I was done with chump change—until now.

After a weasel meter maid gave me a ticket as I dug through my pockets for a quarter, I told Funzi to get ahold of Ruiz.

I met Ruiz for the first time when me and Funzi went to his apartment to talk about the job. He answered the door holding a cute baby with chubby cheeks and jet-black hair. "What up, son?"

"Nothin' much, came by to bullshit," said Funzi.

"Come in an' sit down. Wanna drink?"

"I'm good," I said. I sat on the couch, crushing a rubber toy that squeaked under my ass.

The baby started to cry; next came the smell of shit, and then the baby smiled. Ruiz kept talking while he spread a blanket out on the floor, his son under his arm. He laid the boy down and began changing him.

"My wife went shoppin', so we can talk."

"Funzi told me about your job." I got to the point.

"Least I can do for you after helpin' me back then. Easy score, I'ma call you this week, maybe tomorrow, late, when my truck's nice and fat. You can take me uptown, near Harlem."

"How much?" I asked.

"Maybe twenty."

"We're on."

"You don't need no real gun. My partner'll shit if he sees a water pistol an' you threaten to squirt 'im."

"Done," said Funzi, stacking the last ring onto the pole of a toy.

I didn't know if Funzi meant the score was as good as done, or he was proud to finish the baby's game.

When Toys Galore opened in the morning, Funzi ran in and bought a water gun. We drove into Manhattan, had lunch in Little Italy with some friends, then made our way uptown, toward Harlem. As planned, Ruiz beeped us from a pay phone. Instead of his phone number, he punched cross streets into my pager. We were close by.

When we got there, I saw a coin company logo on the door of a stretch van, double-parked in front of a high-rise. I drove by, noticed the driver alone, drumming his hands on the wheel, listening to music.

I circled the block and pulled over about a hundred feet behind the van.

"I'll follow you," I said as Funzi got out and walked toward the van.

Just as Funzi neared the rear of the van, Ruiz walked out of a building.

"Wait up!" yelled Ruiz, struggling with a bag.

I honked my horn, to get Funzi's attention. He walked past the van, looking straight ahead, turned the corner, and was out of sight.

I stayed put, watching Ruiz.

Ruiz went up to the van, dropped the heavy bag to the floor, swung open a hatch, and hoisted the bag in.

I sped off to look for Funzi. He shot out into the street when he saw me coming.

"Your horn, right?" he asked, getting in.

"Ruiz waved us off. He popped outta nowhere."

"Sonofabitch! I had 'im."

"Easy, I'll go aroun' the block, see what's up. Take the gun outta your pants. If you snap it, it won't squirt."

I spotted the van two blocks down and followed it until the driver double-parked in front of another building. I pulled in behind them.

Ruiz hopped out and walked to the back doors. He held up two fingers behind his head.

"A peace sign?" said Funzi. "What the fuck does that mean?"

"He's got two stops left," I answered.

"He made us wait for another fuckin' bag of change, is he kiddin' me? The guy was mine."

"Them bags add up," I said.

Minutes later, Ruiz strolled out of a building with another bag. He dumped it into the chute, waved one finger behind him, then got in.

Further down the block, Ruiz went in and out of another building, dumped another bag into the chute, then waved his arms like he was clearing us for takeoff on an aircraft carrier.

Funzi jumped out and tucked his toy gun into his jeans.

Ruiz climbed into the van as Funzi bum-rushed the driver's side, swung open the door, and flashed his gun.

The area was busy, but no one seemed to notice or care.

Ruiz threw up his hands. "Please, don't kill us, take the truck, jus' leave us alone. You know my son, Hector." He meant to say, "I got a baby at home."

The driver panicked, pushed Funzi out of the way, and ran toward my car. He flung himself onto my hood, screaming, "Help! Help! I'm gettin' robbed!"

Ah, shit, I thought, he's got the right one.

I lowered my window.

"Calm down," I said. "What happened?"

He rolled off my hood and yelled into my face, "I jus' got robbed! A gun! A gun! He hadda gun!"

"I'll get 'im!" I sped off after the van.

I watched him shrink in my rearview mirror as Funzi drove the van around the corner on two wheels. Ruiz waved, laughing, as I flew by. He didn't care if anyone saw him.

I followed Funzi out of Manhattan, covering his ass, in case cops picked up his tail.

"You was bottomin' out like crazy," I said to Funzi after we pulled into Sergio's shop. "Sparks were flyin' off the bumper."

"I know, I'm loaded."

I swung open the back doors. A large steel box the size of an old steamer trunk was welded into the floor.

Sergio clipped the padlock and opened it. A pile of canvas bags.

"If only they were bills," I bitched.

"Be happy they ain't pennies." Sergio was always positive.

Me and Funzi piled the bags into our cars.

"Get goin'," said Sergio, "I'll dump the van."

We drove to Funzi's house and spent the night in his garage counting change. We counted over fifteen grand with a handy little change counter I found in the van. We left a few full bags in our trunks when we finally called it quits.

The next morning, I called some businessmen I knew. The biggest amount anyone would take off me was a few hundred bucks. Not worth the hassle. I wanted to cash out. I called a fence.

"I'll give you seventy cents on the dollar and keep them for my kid."

"Gimme eighty cents, an' you're fulla shit, your wife tole me you never gave your kid a dime."

"Seventy-five?"

"You pickin' 'em up?"

"Sure."

"Deal."

"Why not do it again?" Funzi suggested as I handed him his cash. "These trucks are all over the place. We can look for 'em anytime an' anywhere."

I didn't like to repeat a crime. A year earlier, this guy from my neighborhood stuck up the same movie theater twice before getting pinched. The cops were waiting for him.

"A real nigger crime," I said at the time, as if my guinea crimes were any brighter.

Anyway, a week later, Funzi and I drove to College Point and hit a second truck.

Two weeks after that, we hit a third in Bayside.

My fence was beating me up, dropping his exchange rate ten percent with each load. By the third, I said, "I'd rather dump 'em in the slots in Atlantic City."

This gave me an idea.

Three hours later, me and Funzi pulled a wheelie down the Atlantic City Expressway with a trunkload of coins.

It was ten p.m. when we saw lights from the casinos.

"We'll cash a coupla grand in each casino," I said. "Let's start at the Taj."

The Taj Mahal was Atlantic City's newest hotel and casino. Inside, areas were still under construction, but the tables were packed and the arms swinging on the slots; the important parts were up and running.

"I'm dead tired." I yawned. "Let's getta room."

"We're all booked," said the cute blonde behind the front desk.

I hit on her, made her laugh, but she said, "I got a boyfriend."

"I believe you're taken," I said, "but I don't believe all your rooms are. You savin' 'em for high rollers?"

She looked to her left and right, then slid a key under a sheet of paper and winked. "Fill this out."

"Thanks." I smiled.

We left the change in the car for the night, and took a private elevator up to a suite overlooking the ocean: Jacuzzi, wet bar, big-screen TV, the King Farouk Room.

"Wow," said Funzi, "that broad looked out."

I called the desk to thank her.

We conked out.

I dialed room service for breakfast. After we ate, we went to the parking garage and each took a bag from the trunk.

We left the garage and stepped onto an escalator that lowers gamblers into the casino.

I was holding my bag against my chest when I heard a *ding* below me. I looked down at my feet, then turned back toward Funzi, who was standing a step above me.

He shrugged. "Wasn't me."

"Me neither."

Ding . . . ding.

We looked down. Two coins were on the step between Funzi's feet. We looked up. Just as our eyes met, Funzi's bag broke open and five thousand quarters poured past me. Funzi gazed down at the empty bag in his hands, wondering if all that change could be put back in. He dropped the bag at the same time he scratched the idea.

An old woman in front of me looked down at the quarters, then at the landing quickly approaching, unsure if her feet could do the shuffle. I reached out an arm. "I got ya."

I braced her as the escalator came to a sudden halt, steps away from sure disaster. A woman who worked for the hotel had pushed the Emergency Stop button, sounding a loud buzzer.

The woman and I helped the old lady over the change piled up at our feet.

The buzzing and the coins attracted gamblers. They probably thought I put a quarter into the escalator and it paid out. Some picked up change and returned it to me. An older couple made off with a few bucks. Imagine me complaining to security, "Hey, stop those bums who just stole that money I stole!"

One woman pretended to help for about a minute, then asked, "Where were you playing?"

"Over there." I pointed.

"Which machine?"

"Number five," I lied. I didn't know if the machines were numbered. She ran off.

A hotel worker, on one knee, stared at a slug in the palm of his hand.

"We're pinched," I said to Funzi. I knew we were staring into a million cameras. I pictured security in a room upstairs watching this comedy unfold through monitors, laughing as they searched their computers for a recent coin heist in the Tri-state area.

I waited for them to approach and say, "Follow us."

It didn't happen.

I told Funzi to guard the money while I bought tote bags in the gift shop. We stuffed them and bounced out of the Taj, without checking out.

Of course we pushed our luck, hit nearly every casino along the boardwalk. Whenever I noticed slugs in the tray behind the cashier's window I'd say, "Oh, shucks, that mus' be from the little bag of change I started wit' this mornin'. I own candy machines."

After we cashed out, I gambled. I was playing with stolen money so I couldn't lose. I bet big, and won big.

We ate a steak dinner at Resorts and drove home.

A few weeks later, Botz and I were stopped at a traffic light near the Van Wyck Expressway when a coin truck pulled up beside us.

"Is that one of them trucks you an' Funz was hittin' like crazy?"

"I had enougha them things. If you want it, I'll follow ya, there's a gun unda the seat."

Botz tucked the gun into his pants, looked around for cops, got out of my car, opened the driver's door of the truck, and got in. Just like that, as casual as if he'd hopped in with a friend. That's how nutty we were.

I followed Botz onto the expressway. I wondered how he held the wheel and kept the two workers at bay. I slowed down behind him as he pulled onto the shoulder and let them out on the passenger side. They kissed the ground as I passed.

An hour later, we split a meatball hero at Paolo's Pizzeria, complaining that the bread was hard, while somewhere two poor bastards dealt with the trauma of a stickup.

Ruiz called Funzi the next day. "Yo, man, slow down, they got a sketch hangin' up at work, looks jus' like you."

"I didn't do the las' one," said Funzi, as if that mattered.

"Well, if that's your boy, I know what he look like too, his mug be hangin' nex' to yours."

We finally stopped.

A few months later, I was dating a girl named Laura. She was serious about school, worked in a hospital, even fed the homeless on weekends. She had no idea I was a criminal, but her mom did. Every time her mother saw my shiny black Mercedes in front of her house, she smirked and shook her head.

Laura and I were hanging out in her room one night when she pointed to a water cooler bottle in the corner, half filled with change. "How much you think I have saved? I've been filling it since my first Holy Communion."

Every coin truck I robbed crossed my mind. Each driver's face appeared in the bottle, from the guy who'd thrown himself onto my hood to the two who'd kissed the shoulder of the expressway. I saw myself counting change for days on end in Funzi's garage, and scooping up coins on an escalator. Over a hundred thousand dollars in quarters had passed through my hands. Manhattan, Queens, and Atlantic City.

"Don't think about it so hard, it's not that important. You save change too?" she asked.

"No, I cash mine in at the Taj Mahal." I gave myself a laugh.

"Wow!" Laura said. "No one I know even heard of the Taj Mahal. I'm studying India in school right now. My mom's so wrong about you, you're so interesting."

I LEFT MY GUNS IN SAN FRANCISCO

Street money. I had several cars, Rolex watches, even a Patek Philippe, which I pronounced "Patty Faleepi."

I'd drop ten grand at the tables in Atlantic City, pick up a five-hundred-dollar tab at a steakhouse, and hand out hundreds to anyone with a story.

I was doing good, but it wasn't enough. After all those coin trucks, I was literally tired of chump change.

I didn't want to end up like guys in my crew, still pulling bullshit robberies in their forties and fifties. I needed a big score, big enough to retire.

Armored cars.

They rolled up alongside me at every traffic light. They were double-parked on every corner. I even saw them in my sleep. I woke up one night coughing from the exhaust of an armored car as it sped away; a guard dangled a money bag at me through the back window.

Whenever I spotted a truck parked, I'd pull my car over and watch.

Three guards. The driver never got out of the truck. One guard carried the money, another looked around.

Older guards were relaxed, went through the motions, maybe glanced up or down the street, thumbs tucked in their holsters. Bored after years of the same shit. I didn't see them as a threat.

Younger guards were alert and ready for action, hands on their guns.

But if ambushed, I'd bet my ass they'd throw down their guns. And why shouldn't they? It's not their money.

Life's funny. If you really want something, it'll find you.

I was hanging out in the back of my friend's cigar store when Jackie walked in. "My buddy Carl jus' got a job workin' for an armored car company out in Cali, he wants to play."

"Let's go where we could talk." I threw an arm around him, and we walked out onto Rockaway Boulevard, leaving behind the aroma of expensive cigars for car fumes.

The block was hot, so we got in my car and headed for Huron Street in Greenpoint, Brooklyn, where the East River chops its way over to Manhattan Island.

I parked near an embankment where old wooden piers had fallen away and broken slabs of asphalt stuck out of the water. The rotted rear end of an old Plymouth jutted out of the drink, probably an insurance job.

We got out of the car and spoke above the sound of water lapping against the muddy bank.

"How good you know this guy?" I asked.

"We was in school together when we was kids, we got into a lotta fights, always watched each other's backs. He never let me down."

"He done anythin' on the streets?"

"Robbed a few cars when he was young. Joyrides. Not for money. That's about it."

I asked too many questions for Jackie to remember, so I said, "Find out everythin' there is to know an' get back to me."

Over the next few days, I blew off anyone who came to me with a tip.

I told a manager who wanted me to rob his supermarket, "Yeah, yeah, sounds good, I'll get back to ya." I even got arrogant when a cable guy told me he saw an open safe stuffed with cash while he was installing a cable box in the office of a "zillionaire."

"If it's such a good score," I told him, "why don't you do it yaself?"

I couldn't be bothered.

Jackie got back to me. The new info he told me didn't jibe. But it didn't matter. I'd already made up my mind that I was going to Cali.

Since I was a kid, I was thickheaded, and refused to quit whatever I'd started.

When I was sixteen, my friend Pudgy took a summer job at a storage company. Once a week, he'd walk four or five grand in cash to the bank, but he never knew when he was going until they handed him the envelope.

One night, drinking with me at a party, Pudgy had a bright idea. "I'll give you the envelope and say I was robbed."

"Gimme a call, I'll be happy to rob you."

Every week when I'd ask Pudgy, "What happened?" he'd give me another bullshit excuse: "Next week will be better" and "Let's wait till there's even more dough."

I don't think Pudgy realized what he'd gotten into until each week he had the envelope in his hand and it was time to dial me. He wanted to forget the whole thing—I didn't.

By late August, I was fed up; Pudgy's summer job was coming to an end. Monday, I stole a car near my house and drove it to the storage company. I waited across the street. No Pudgy. Tuesday, I did the same thing. I sat in the car, listening to the radio for about ten minutes before Pudgy strolled out into the afternoon sun, smiling, a fat yellow envelope tucked under his arm.

"You chubby little prick," I said to myself. I turned down the radio and drove behind him slowly as he walked two blocks to the bank. Just as he entered the bank's parking lot, I rolled up alongside him.

"Lou." He beamed, happy to bump into me. His face suddenly dropped as he looked down at the envelope and realized why I was there.

"Gimme the fuckin' envelope!" I reached out a hand from the car.

"It's not a good day." He stepped back, pressing it against his chest.

"I'll take it anyway."

"I promise, I'll call you next week, we'll score!"

I threw the car into park and jumped out. He looked torn between running and crying. I snatched the envelope and gave him a good slap.

Years later, I was still as stubborn. I refused to let go of this Cali heist, even though Jackie's info was sketchy.

I said to Jackie, "You still don't know shit."

"It's not me, it's Carl, I hang up scratchin' my head."

"At least I know it ain't a setup, 'cause the law could never be this stupid."

Jackie and Carl were smart enough to talk in riddles over the phone, but too dumb to understand each other. I decided to take my crew to Cali and speak to Carl myself.

For an armored car robbery, I needed one more crew member besides Jackie. I wanted the guy with the biggest balls for a gunslinging, daylight robbery.

I picked Botz for my third man. He was happy, told his girl, "We're headin' out west to look at property."

Me, Jackie, and Botz met over the next couple of weeks, bouncing around different diners in Queens. There was a lot to talk about. Cali wasn't our turf.

In New York, I could have a car stolen and delivered to me in minutes. In Cali, I'd have to steal one myself.

Besides using a hot car, I liked one crew member nearby behind the wheel of a "bumper car" listening to a police scanner.

A bumper car is legal, driven by a licensed driver. If something goes wrong during a robbery, like the cops speed down the block, or a hero driver intervenes, the bumper car will "bump" the car, or block off the street, allowing us to escape. Later, when my driver is questioned: "Sorry, Officer, my car stalled."

We couldn't register cars in California, and a bumper car with a New York plate near the crime scene was a tip-off for the cops. No bumper car.

In New York, if a robbery went bad, I knew a million places where I could lay low until the heat cooled down. Out west, we'd have nowhere to hide.

Despite these problems, I was still too cocky to back down, so sure we'd get the money that I told my crew before leaving New York, "Stay away from the tables when we hit Vegas on the way home. No big bets. I don't want any attention. If you gotta gamble, play the quarter slots."

Before 9/11, anyone could book a flight under a phony name. I had a friend book airline tickets for each of us, telling him, "We're goin' out west to collect money."

I put our guns, duct tape, two-way radios, police scanner, and ski masks into a cardboard box stuffed with newspaper, and shipped it UPS to Carl's house. When he received our box unopened, I packed my bags, changed my Rolex for a Timex, and headed for the airport.

Since I didn't want to leave any of our cars in long-term parking, my buddy who booked the flight drove us to the airport. He picked me up first, my crew along the way.

Botz slid into the backseat. He stunk of cologne. I held my nose. "Holy shit, whatchu break the bottle over ya head?"

We swung by Jackie's house next. He jumped in, also reeking.

"What the fuck is that smell?" I asked.

"My mother made macaroni wit' garlic an' oil. She always cooks for me when I go away."

We stunk up coach and arrived in San Francisco. We took a cab from the airport and checked into the Holiday Inn. I stopped Botz from flirting with one broad at the airport, another in the hotel lobby. I didn't want anyone to remember talking to a New York Italian. It took me a good ten minutes to explain to Botz that *we* had the accents here, not them.

In the room, we sprawled out on two double beds. Jackie channel surfed while he and Botz went back and forth about the expensive toys they'd buy after the heist. I thought of questions I wanted to ask Carl.

"Keep it down, the walls are thin," I whispered whenever the noise interrupted my thoughts.

I told Jackie, "Go to a pay phone an' call Carl."

When he got back, he told us, "We're meetin' him for dinner tomorrow night in Oakland. He don't wanna be seen wit' us aroun' town."

"I don't blame 'im," I said, "I don't wanna be seen wit' youse either."

The next day, we took in the sights. San Francisco was a clean city;

hilly roads and shiny trolleys, unlike New York's potholed streets and diesel-spewing buses. The surrounding water was clear, the air easier to breathe, and the people more polite. We were the perfect representatives from New York.

We ate lunch at a busy little restaurant along Fisherman's Wharf, then walked off the meal gazing out at "the Rock," isolated by the cold waters of San Francisco Bay.

"Let's visit Alcatraz," Jackie suggested.

"Youse go, not me," Botz said, "I ain't visitin' no jail before a heist, that shit's bad luck."

"Maybe nex' time," I said. "Let's stick to business for now."

That night, we met Carl at an Italian restaurant he'd never eaten in before, so no one would notice him.

I saw him across the room as we entered, the only man seated alone. He sipped a drink and broke off pieces of bread served on a wooden board, rewrapping the loaf in a white napkin each time he nibbled. He noticed Jackie and flashed a smile.

I shook his hand then pointed to the wrapped bread. "Good habit, always hide the evidence."

We all laughed and sat around the table making more stupid jokes, getting acquainted.

We ordered appetizers, and I began to pick his brain.

"There's three guards in every truck," Carl said, "two up front and one in the back. I can give you the routes, and show you the best places to hit them."

"How much we talkin'?" I asked.

"Loaded, 'bout a mil, mil and a half."

"You're givin' us your truck, right? This way we'll have two gunmen to deal wit' insteada three."

"No, I don't want anything to do with this." He must've forgotten that he was seated with us, spilling his guts, and our guns were in the trunk of his car.

"You buddy-buddy wit' anybody?" I asked. "Maybe some guy you drink wit' wants to make a quick buck, all he's gotta do is not reach for his piece when we hit the truck. I'm tryin' to gamble wit' better odds."

"No," he answered quickly, "I don't know these guys long, don't trust them."

I tried to get him to reconsider but he wouldn't budge.

"If this goes down, what's my end?" he finally asked.

I wondered how someone without any guts could have such balls.

By time the check came, I got as much out of Carl as I'd gotten out of complete strangers I'd met at a bar. Without him or a coworker on board, we'd be shooting from the hip. Dinner amounted to a learning seminar for those interested in pursuing a career as an armed guard.

When I paid the tab, Carl asked, "Can I leave the tip?"

"No, your tips are shitty," I said. He knew what I meant.

In the parking lot, we took the box of guns from Carl's trunk because he bitched, "I don't wanna carry them no more, I might get pulled over."

"You should get run over." I was disgusted, and didn't care if he heard.

We were quiet on the ride back to the hotel. I got out of the shower to find Botz and Jackie lying down. Botz's face was buried in a pillow. Jackie was staring at a silent TV, his jaw lower than mine.

"Let's do it," Botz said as he lifted his head. "We're already here. We got the guns. We can slip outta town an' no one'll ever know we was here."

Jackie agreed, then asked Botz to keep the Bible in the drawer, "So God can't see what we're doin'."

I lay down to think, a towel still around my waist. Before leaving New York, I thought Carl was in on it, figured three of us could do the job. Without Carl's direct involvement, I'd need an extra man, one of us for each of the three guards, plus a wheel man.

That night I phoned my alternate, Angelo. I spoke to his wife, who told me he broke his leg on his motorcycle and was laid up in the hospital.

I had two other crew members in mind. I ran them by Jackie and Botz, asked who they wanted to work with.

"Slippy's perfect," Botz said.

"He ain't one of the choices," I answered.

"But he's good."

We'd used Slippy before; quiet guy, big balls, moved fast, thought on his feet, did his job, got paid, and faded.

"Call him," I said.

Botz did. "Hop on a flight to San Fran, we'll pick you up at the airport. Somethin' big."

"I'm there." Slippy asked no questions, knew we were for real; he'd made money with us before. Next day we waited for him at the Pan Am terminal.

"What's up?" Slippy greeted us with sweaty handshakes. He was jumpy, rocking on his heels, not the man I remembered. "I rushed, so I couldn't get my shit," he said.

I pulled Botz aside. "What's he talkin' 'bout?"

"He gotta get straight," Botz said.

"What's that mean?"

"He needs a hitta dope. It puts him right, keeps him from gettin' sick."

"He's a junkie? You're fuckin' kiddin' me, send 'im home." I whipped out a wad of cash and licked my thumb to count.

"Louie." Botz leaned closer. "He don't get high, he needs it to function. He's a stand-up guy, my word. He done time an' don't give a fuck. He been locked up wit' my kid brother. Losin' the junk don't make 'im weak. My brother tole me he was in a cell screamin' an' cryin' for the shit, an' the cop said, 'If you talk, we'll send ya to meds.' Slippy said, 'Fuck you!' an' spit at 'im. So he ain't no rat. He'll piss an' shit himself when he's kickin', but he won't talk."

"Then my problem ain't wit' him, it's wit' you." I poked a finger into his chest. "You shoulda tole me, I'da called Fabio if it wasn't for his habit. We both know Fab's better than all of us."

"Look, Lou, I shoulda said somethin'. I like workin' wit' him, but I'll send 'im home if you want."

While Botz and I talked, Slippy stood several feet away, the airport crowd whirling by him from every direction. His head jutting forward, he rudely stared into people's eyes as they passed, paying special attention to men.

He suddenly launched himself at a forty-something man in a blue suit and necktie. He said something I couldn't hear. The man stopped, dropped his briefcase to the floor between his legs, and began pointing, as though helping a tourist with directions.

I was curious what this was about. Slippy hurried back to us. "We gotta hail a cab an' head downtown." He mumbled off a couple of cross streets.

"Whaddya ask 'im?" I asked Slippy.

"Where I can cop a bag."

"How'd ya know he'd know?"

"It's all in the eyes." He widened his own. "They never lie."

As angry as I was over Slippy's habit, I was impressed by his ability to home in on a neat, square-looking executive I'd have never taken for a junkie.

Botz took Slippy to cop. When they came back to the hotel room, Slippy appeared normal, besides rubbing his nose a bit.

"He's got enough shit to last 'im the month," Botz whispered to me as Slippy unpacked.

"What's wit' the fartin'," I asked, "is that the drugs?"

"No, the pizza. I took 'im for a slice afta he copped. I got 'em too. Mine stink but not that loud."

"I'm gonna watch 'im awhile, then decide," I said to Botz.

That night we had a drink in the hotel lounge before we went upstairs, where Botz brought Slippy up-to-date. Slippy sat in a chair, listening, taking it all in.

When Botz finished, Slippy asked, "So what the fuck is the plan?"

With this, I knew he was fine, sharper than the rest of us.

"We don't have one yet," I cut in, "we're gonna go over the routes an' see where's the best spot to hit one."

"We coulda did that in New York," Slippy reaffirmed his sanity. "There's more trucks there, and the dope's better." He scratched his neck, staring up at the ceiling. I rolled over and went to bed.

Next morning we bought a dent puller and a screwdriver from a local hardware store. We'd use them to steal a fast car on the day of the heist.

After breakfast, we found the army in full dress in the hotel lobby.

"What's up wit' the soldiers?" I asked a girl behind the front desk.

"Convention," she said, "and we're overbooked. Will you gentlemen be staying another day?"

"No," I said, "we'll check out in an hour."

"We'll go somewhere quieter," I told my crew.

Down the street, we checked into a "no-tell motel," a name we used back home to describe shabby motels for johns and cheaters. Shitty places with hourly rates, brown toilets, stained bedsheets, and a wood-paneled TV with the remote chained to a night table. The rooms stink of cigarettes. The air-conditioners are all noise. And the parking lot is always out of sight so guests can hide their cars—no-tell motel.

"We got no inside guy," I said as we ate lunch in Chinatown. "All Carl's willin' to tell us is the route an' the take. Other than that, we're on our own. If anyone wants out, you ain't gotta feel like a punk, jus' say so."

I glanced around the table. I felt I was letting them down.

"We'll watch these trucks a coupla weeks. I'll have everythin' down to a tee before we jump. If not, we're outta here, I'll give youse a G-note apiece to blow in Vegas, an' we'll head home. Chalk this up as a little vacation on me."

Botz toyed with chopsticks, shifting in his seat. He looked at Jackie and Slippy before saying, "I'm in."

"Me too, I'm good to go," said Jackie, slurping his wonton soup.

Slippy nodded yes, his mouth stuffed with fried noodles.

Back at the motel, our rooms were accessed from a second-story landing overlooking the rear parking lot.

The four of us bullshitted as we climbed the steps. "Hurry, I gotta take a leak," Jackie said as I jiggled the key in the lock. Botz and Slippy were behind us, leaning over the railing, when I suddenly heard one of them blurt, "Ah, fuck!"

"Get against the wall!"

"Don't fuckin' move, or I'll blow your fuckin' brains out!"

A SWAT team raced up the stairs from both sides, pointing guns at us. I spread my hands on the railing. Below, cops in bulletproof vests. Above, snipers on rooftops.

Guests peeped out between blinds, hoping this wasn't for them.

"We got 'em!" one of the guys said into a small speaker clipped to his shoulder. Other radios crackled with disjointed commands. More cars sped into the lot with flashing lights.

This was the first time I realized how dangerous I was.

"What's up?" I asked the officer cuffing me.

"We're taking you for a ride downtown, someone wants to talk to you."

The guns hidden in our room crossed my mind, but I only faced a year in the can for possession, then back on the streets.

Once we were cuffed, they marched us down into the parking lot and shoved us into cars. I was in a backseat with Jackie; we kept silent.

The fleet of unmarked sedans rolled out of the lot. The manager stood in front of the main office, hands on his hips, as if we ruined his motel's rep. "Asshole," said Jackie. "He shoulda bought a Seven-Eleven."

The cop in the front passenger seat turned around to talk to us through the grating. "You fellas are far from home, whaddya run outta banks to hit back east?"

I kicked Jackie to keep him quiet.

"Listen, guys, we're SFPD. The FBI's back at the station, they wanna ask a few questions, we're only bringin' you in."

A few minutes later, we were led into the precinct, where the cops put us in a holding pen.

"Want some sodas?" one of the cops asked.

"No, thanks, we jus' had lunch," I said politely, then found a spot on the bench free of gum and grime.

The cops had our real names. They called Jackie first. He was gone ten minutes.

"They got shit," he said when he got back. "They know we flew unda phony names an' that somethin's up, but that's it. They asked to search the room an' I said no, figurin' if they asked, I hadda choice."

This pumped up Botz, who suddenly couldn't wait to spar with the feds. He was taken out next.

"They know who we are, an' that we're up to no good, but that's it," he said when he came back.

Slippy went after Botz. When he came back, he said the same thing.

At last the bars swung open, and two cops told me to follow them.

I swaggered from the cell. What could they do to me?

For a year I slept on the floor beside my mother's bed. Lumps the size of softballs grew out of her head. I refused to let her waste away in a dark room. Each morning at dawn, I carried her downstairs to lie in the sun shining in through the front windows. She didn't have the strength to hold her head up so it rolled around on her shoulders like a bobble head with a broken spring. I carried her back to bed each night. Her bones became so brittle that I had to carry her while she sat in a chair. Still, I snapped her arm as I lifted her one morning. The doctors implanted a steel rod from elbow to shoulder, piling pain on top of pain. All because I wanted her to see and feel the sun. Now, what could these men do to me that hadn't already been done?

We entered a maze of desks, phones ringing, typewriters clicking, guys yelling; a reunion episode of *Barney Miller*.

I was led into a cubicle where a small Asian man sat at a neat desk. He was dressed in a white button-down shirt with a solid necktie. His sport jacket hung over the back of his chair. I knew right away he was a federal agent, clean-cut with a stick up his ass, unlike the loud slobs around him.

I'd seen plenty of agents in Queens, in front of social clubs, but never had a face-to-face with one.

"Hello, Mr. Ferrante," he began, his pen hovering over a white lined pad on which he'd scribbled some notes. It was weird hearing a complete stranger address me by name like he knew me my entire life.

"I've already spoken to your confederates." The word "confederate" made me think of the Civil War. I had no clue how it could relate to us, except we were rebels. "I'd like to ask you a few questions, you don't have to answer."

I was struck by his stylish hair and perfect English. The Asian immigrants in Flushing all had bowl haircuts and butchered the English language.

"First." He tapped his pen on the pad. "I understand you've flown out here under an assumed name."

"Is that against the law?" I asked. I should've kept my mouth shut, but what the hell.

"That depends, can you tell me why?"

"Yeah." I leaned back in my seat. "I wanted to get away, take a little vacation wit' nobody knowin'. Is that all right wit' you? What's this all about, anyway?"

"To be quite frank, it often happens that a crew of men travel from other states, sometimes New York, hold up a bank or two, then flee, leaving us clueless."

"Not for nothin', you think I flew across the country to stick up a bank wit' a million banks in my neighborhood?"

"I'm not saying you did, only suggesting that it happens."

"Well, it ain't happenin' wit' me."

"Did you know that one of your confederates has a warrant out for his arrest?"

"No, I didn't," I answered truthfully.

"I find that hard to believe."

"If you was runnin' from the law, would you go aroun' tellin' everybody?"

"I wouldn't be a fugitive."

"Then you're smarta than him."

He smiled.

"Do you mind if we search your room?" He became short with me.

"Yeah, I do."

"Why is that?"

"I don't like nobody goin' through my undawear."

"We won't touch your clothes."

"Nah, if you need my okay, I ain't givin' it."

I imagined agents back at the motel laying our guns out on the bed.

Legally, they may have needed a warrant, but I was damn sure they'd already searched the room.

"I know you paid for everyone's trip."

"So."

"Do you have a job?"

"I sell sneakers."

"You do well?"

"Not bad."

"You pay taxes?"

"Off the books."

"What are you going to do when you leave here?"

"I'm goin' straight home. You ruined my vacation, no sense in stickin' aroun' somewhere I ain't welcome."

The agent summoned a cop to put me back in the holding pen.

As I got up, I looked the agent in his eyes. We both knew the truth. He was doing his job. I was doing mine.

Back in the cage, my crew was laughing with a bum dressed in a long army jacket. His pants were torn at the knee, his boots opened at the toe, and he stank. There was more food stuck in his beard than I'd eaten for lunch.

"You mus' be Lou," he said as I entered, bars slamming behind me.

"Did Botz recruit you, too?" I asked, disgusted.

With cops nearby, Jackie and I pretended to be offended by the whole thing.

The bum began rocking in his seat, singing "Everybody Plays the Fool." Under his voice, I asked, "Whicha youse got the warrant back home?"

"Me," said Slippy.

"Why ya think they didn't pinch ya?"

"They still might."

"If they don't," I whispered, "it's 'cause they wanna watch us, see what we do nex'."

An hour or so later, we were released without apology.

"Can you fellas help a poor black man?" said the bum.

He might've been a plant; still, I slipped a twenty into his breast pocket. "Buy dinner, no booze."

"You Eyetalianos is good peeps, take care now."

The cops offered us a ride back to the motel.

"Thanks, we'll take a cab."

Outside, I took my first breath of fresh air after being stuck in a cage all afternoon.

I couldn't wait to skip town, but we couldn't leave the guns in the motel. A sure pinch. The feds would go back in the room after we left; I could see it now: "Well, look what the maid found."

I figured we'd all leave the room at the same time, but take off in different directions. The feds would be playing a game of three-card monte, trying to guess which one of us had the guns.

Slippy gave me a bad vibe when he said, "Let's keep the guns, lay low a week or two, then go ahead wit' the job."

"Are you fuckin' kiddin' me?" I asked.

"No, let's go for it."

"Is that the cops talkin'? If you ain't pinched when we get home, you're a dead man."

"It's a bullshit warrant."

"No such thing."

Around midnight, I watched our weapons sink like stones into San Francisco Bay, probably the only clean guns laid to rest beside a rusted arsenal of junked murder weapons dating back to the Gold Rush. I trashed the radios, the scanner, and the duffel bags I brought to carry the cash home.

"You ride with Slippy," I said to Botz. "I can't even look at 'im. I'm goin' home wit' Jackie."

As I drove over the Golden Gate Bridge with Jackie, I wanted to sink my teeth into the dash and chew. I called everyone a rat.

"It's that fuckin' guard!" I slammed my fist.

"It's that no-good junkie!" I slammed my fist.

"It's that smelly motel manager!" I slammed my fist.

Once I cooled down, I blamed myself, going over a list of mistakes.

I left my house without a plan.

I let Botz pick Slippy, a junkie, maybe a snitch.

Bad info. A strange city. A nomadic week. The list went on.

I was too arrogant to think I could fail. I acted like the kid I was, not the man I ordinarily pretended to be.

I'm sure the feds saved a few lives, including our own. I didn't see it this way.

It was all too much for my brain. I just wanted to go home and get laid.

I was home a week when I heard Slippy hadn't been pinched. I decided to pay him a visit with Tony the Twitch, a name he'd been given for the nervous twitch in his eyes. But he could shoot straight, the reason I brought him along.

Slippy rented a place on the first floor in a row of old, run-down garden apartments. It was five a.m. when I sent Tony in through an open window. He quietly opened the front door and let me in. Since there were no curtains, the outside lamppost cast a dim light on the place: a warped couch, chipped paint, beer bottles on the floor, and the smell of vomit.

We stepped softly, guns drawn.

In the bedroom, Tony spotted a man lying on a mattress, his head resting on a thin pillow with no pillowcase. Tony signaled to me. I went in.

Slippy was out cold, a threadbare blanket draped across his chest.

I crept up to him, put my .38 Special against his temple, and drew back the hammer. His eyes opened slowly, then rolled toward me even slower. He wasn't startled, as if I was his girlfriend waking him for breakfast.

"Look at me." He twisted his forearms, showing me his tracks. "You ain't gotta kill me, I'm killin' myself."

"Not fast enough," I said.

"I ain't a rat."

"You live like one."

"Don't make me one. Botz will tell ya, I go to jail when I gotta. Don't waste me, you're makin' a mistake."

"Are we?" Tony pressed the muzzle of his gun against Slippy's other temple.

"I really don't care if I die," said Slippy. "I got nothin' to live for anyhow, same reason I don't care when I get locked up."

"Who's the rat if it ain't you?" Tony asked.

"My roommate knew what I was up to. He drove me to the airport. I tole 'im I was goin' to Cali to do somethin' big wit' you guys, an' I'd hit 'im off when I got back. He thought we was hittin' a bank, that's why the feds kept sayin' a bank."

"Where is he?" I asked.

"He skipped. When I tole 'im I was gonna tell you that he knew everythin', he took off. I'da tole you sooner, but I was on a binge the last coupla days. He left all his junk behine. That's how I knew he was guilty. Us junkies don't leave our dope behine for nothin'."

"What's up wit' your warrant?" I asked.

"They been callin' my house every day, play my machine." He shifted his eyes toward the end table, covered with empty pill bottles and syringes. "They lef' five or six messages. I'm gonna turn myself in today. I jus' wanted to finish the shit my ex-roomie lef', get in my last hurrah knowin' I'll be kickin' in a cell."

I didn't play his answering machine. He was telling the truth.

"C'mon," I said to Tony. We tucked our guns away and left.

After this fiasco, the thought of Rice-A-Roni made me sick.

HOME SWEET HOME

One summer morning, my friend Augie's teenage sister, Anna, went bike riding. She was pedaling through Charles Park when two girls grabbed her long hair, pulled her off her bike, and stomped on her face. One nasty bitch broke a bottle over a bench and cut Anna's cheek.

Anna knew the girls, knew they didn't like her, but had done nothing to provoke them.

I was with Augie when his mother called him from the emergency room, where doctors were patching up his sister. He left in a cursing fit, headed straight for the park to look for the girls.

"I'll go wit' you," I said.

"To help beat up broads? Bad enough I'm doin' it."

I stayed behind.

Augie spotted the two bruisers laughing on a park bench, a few feet away from broken glass, blood spots, and his sister's bike. He ran up from behind and piped one over the head, *clunk*. The other girl ran. He caught her and dragged her along the pavement by her ponytail.

No one got involved. Joggers ran away, bicyclists pedaled their asses off. Eventually, someone called an ambulance, and the girls were rushed to the same hospital where Augie's mom and sister, still in the emergency room, enjoyed seeing them wheeled past.

Neither Anna nor the girls made a police report. They all bullshitted the doctors, claimed they'd fallen.

Anna was taught to keep her mouth shut. The men in her family were mobsters. They handled her problems, not the law.

The first girl Augie piped also grew up in a Mob family. She was the daughter of Larry Goggles, named for the thick prescription glasses he wore. Larry was a Genovese capo known for violence, a trait he apparently passed on to his daughter.

Before the day was up, Larry hopped into a car with two thugs, all three packing. They drove to Augie's house. Augie's mom had just returned from the hospital, and answered the door in a housedress.

As Augie sat in Gino's Pizzeria telling me what he did to the girls, Augie's mom took a shotgun out of the hall closet and pumped a round into the chamber.

"Get the fuck off my porch!" she shouted at the three screaming wiseguys looking for Augie.

"Your fuckin' son is dead!" said Larry. "Make his funeral arrangements."

With that, they got into their car and left. She put the shotgun back in the closet next to the vacuum, and dialed one of her brothers.

Augie's mom was no stranger to the Life. Her late father was a capo, the Bonanno rep for Kennedy Airport. Her brothers were wiseguys in the same borgata.

Since mothers and daughters were involved, the men from each family quickly arranged a sit-down.

The next day, I drove Augie to a motel on Cross Bay Boulevard. He met one of his uncles, Vinnie Bo Peep, in the lot.

"Stay in the car," Vinnie told Augie. "If he sees you, he'll go nuts. You'll fuck up any shot I got of straightenin' this thing out."

Vinnie disappeared into a room. Augie waited in the car with me and played with the radio.

"I wonder what's goin' on inside," I said after a few minutes.

"I could give a fuck. Those bitches acted like men, so I treated them like men. I'd do it again. Fuck them an' that fat, four-eyed fuck inside."

When Vinnie came out, he walked over to my car. "I got nowhere wit' this piece a shit. Take my nephew on the lam in case this hump breaks the rules an' looks to clip 'im."

Augie and I booked a shuttle from the Marine Air Terminal at La Guardia. We landed in Atlantic City less than an hour later. We drank Coronas and played blackjack, picked up two cocktail waitresses, who met us after their shift, and waited for the captains from each family to meet and decide if Augie would be handed over or excused.

At the time, Augie was on the list to get made.

"I hope this don't fuck up my shot," he said.

"He's lookin' to whack ya, that might fuck it up."

At the next sit, Larry brought a witness who said Augie knew the girl he'd piped was Larry's daughter, even before he hit her. This put Augie in the wrong; he should've gone straight to Larry.

In the end, the capos agreed that Augie was dead wrong to pipe Larry's daughter, but Larry also broke the rules by going to Augie's house and disrespecting Augie's mother. They squashed the beef.

Larry's fuckup saved Augie's life. The home is sacred, off limits.

Because the home is sacred, I turned down any job that involved a house—almost any job.

One day, this bookmaker Franky Stitches came to me. "Louie, this dentist who bets wit' me keeps fallin' behine. I tole 'im to catch up b'fore I make 'im work on his own teet'. He asked if he can work off his bill wit' a tip, says his brutter owns a truckin' company. Want the job?"

"A dentist?" I wondered if I could get my teeth cleaned as part of the deal.

Favors were part of our world. You could make twenty grand with a guy, but if he sells fifty-cent goldfish, you can't help but ask him for one in a plastic bag. We all did this.

Criminals want to get without having to give. When stealing becomes your job, a goldfish for free is more gratifying than a pile of stolen jewels, because somehow you worked for the jewels, the fish was on the arm.

"Yeah," said Franky, "a dentist. He went to college up at Villa

Roma"—he meant Villanova—"where he started bettin' football tickets. Now he bets five grand a game, baseball, football, even hockey. Who the fuck bets hockey?"

I met with the dentist, a smart man who made me wish I had more doctors giving me tips. He gave us a tip on a clothing truck.

My crew did the job, everyone made money, and the dentist cleared his bill.

The following morning, the dentist paged me. I called him back from a pay phone.

"I have another tip, it's a house," he said, like it was a big real estate investment. "There's a hundred grand in cash underneath the dryer in the basement."

"I don't do homes," I told him. "Stop bettin' football, or start liftin' some gold fillin's when your patients are unda."

"But the house is empty. The old woman who lives there is in the hospital. Her husband's dead. He owned a candy store for fifty years, an all-cash business. They saved every penny. When she passes on the cops will sweep the house and find it."

He was trying to tempt me, figured everyone in the Mob hates cops.

"She tole you all this unda the gas?"

"No, she's not my patient. Let's just say I heard."

"Nah, not for me, find somebody else."

"I'm sorry to hear that. Would you please give me the number to someone in your crew?"

"If it ain't for me, it ain't for them!" I hung up with him and got in my car.

Sitting in traffic, I gave it more thought.

I had widowed aunts who hoarded money. Aunt Rosie was loaded but still gave me a two-dollar handkerchief for my birthday, the same gift for Christmas, only a different color. I'd blow my nose in them once, then throw them out.

Aunt Carmella had a half mil in the bank. When the color tube on her twenty-year-old TV blew, my cousin Enzo offered to drive her to Newmark & Lewis, help her pick out a new set. She refused to touch the bank. "What for?" she asked as she cut the bar code off a cereal box. "I only watch *The Honeymooners* and *I Love Lucy*, both are in black and white."

I lay in bed that night, thinking it through. With the old lady in the hospital, there'd be nobody home. Was this a loophole? If the old woman was anything like my aunts, she'd never touch her stash, go to her grave never knowing it was missing.

I called the dentist back. The house was in Newark. I made Funzi drive me.

I picked a hot night. Air conditioners hummed in neighbors' windows, blocking out street noise.

I walked through a narrow side yard, kicked in the back door, stepped inside, and turned on a flashlight. I was in the kitchen. I looked for the basement stairwell. I opened a closet door, a pantry door, then swung open another door to find this little old lady standing in front of me, in a nightgown and cap. She clutched at her heart, gasping.

"Oh, shit!" I was more nervous than she was. I patted her on the shoulder, swore I'd never hurt her. I walked her over to the table and pulled out a chair. I switched on the kitchen light as she sat down.

I should've run, but I wanted to comfort her. She reminded me of my grandmother.

"Sorry." I shrugged my shoulders.

When her breathing returned to normal, she looked me in the eye and said, "My no-good junkie bastard grandson sent ya, huh?"

"Yeah." Better she thought I was like family than a complete stranger.

"There's lemonade in the fridge, the glasses are over the sink."

"No, thanks."

"Pour me a glass." She sounded annoyed.

I poured us each a glass then sat across from her. "You all right?"

"How much he tell ya I got, ten, twenty grand?"

"He said there's a hundred unda your dryer downstairs."

"A hundred?" She chuckled. "Next week, he'll tell you bums it's a million. There's nothing down there, you can check, first door on ya left, right behind you."

"My grandmother wrapped a G-note in foil, kept it in the freezer."

"Ya rob her, too? There's some Tupperwares of sauce and a bluefish my son caught. He's a bum too, asked me to cook it for him."

"So where's the money?" I figured I'm already here.

"You want a cigarette?" She reached across the table for her pack. I noticed a hospital band on her wrist. She lit two and we smoked.

"You look like such a nice boy. Why you want to rob an old lady? Can't you get a job?"

"I want your money so I can get outta here. My friend's waitin' down the block."

"Ask him to come in, I'll put on a pot of coffee."

By now, this old woman was playing me. I beat up a thousand men, but couldn't twist a hair on her forearm—and she knew it.

I never searched the basement; instead I apologized for the broken door, even gave her a little hug good-bye, which she accepted.

She was standing under the porch light, smoking another cigarette, when we drove past her house on our way out of the block.

I told the dentist to lose my number, warned Franky to beware of him, and never ever went near a home again.

BARRY THE BROKESTER

I grew up with a tough kid named Danny; he fought a lot, stabbed a few guys. He started carrying a gun when he was fifteen. He'd walk around the neighborhood showing it off. As kids, we were tight. Eventually, Danny became a drug dealer. I got in with the Mob.

Danny dealt drugs with black and Spanish gangs. He spoke their slang.

One night, I bumped into Danny in front of a dance club.

We were bullshitting on the sidewalk when a pimped-out minivan with chrome rims pulled up to the curb. A Spanish kid with thin sideburns and a goatee poked his head out of the passenger window. "Yo, shorty!"

I didn't recognize him. I picked up the conversation with Danny.

"Yo, shorty!" he yelled again, pinching my Napoleon nerve.

"Who the fuck you callin' shorty?" I reached for my gun.

Danny grabbed my arm as the van sped off.

"You hear those muthafuckas?" I put my gun away. "He called me shorty twice, two muthafuckin' times."

"Easy, Lou, cool it. Homeboy wasn't talkin' to you, he be yellin' at them girls. We call pretty girls shorties."

Behind me, a group of Spanish girls giggled at my stupidity.

I couldn't keep up with Danny's lingo, couldn't understand half of what he said.

I saw less and less of him.

Then one day Danny paged me.

"Yo, Lou, I gots a truck fulla appliances, gotta dump it," he huffed into the phone, like the law was on his ass.

"Where you wanna meet?"

"Can you swing by my crib?"

"I'll be there in ten."

A truck was idling on the corner when I turned into his block. I parked behind it, got out, and saw Danny smiling in the side-view mirror. I stood on the runner. "When'd you start hijackin'?"

"Today." He looked at his watch. "'Bout a half hour ago. I was wit' my boy, 'bout to dump this yayo when I swung my ride aroun' this block an' some punk-ass nigga up an' lef' his truck. When he dip out the project, I said yo what up, move that shit. Muthafucka threw me the finga, went back inside. I wanted to smoke 'im, but I say ta ma man, yo dog, I'ma vick that truck. I did, an' here I am."

I jumped off the running board and looked around for cops. I walked to the back of the truck, swung open the cargo door, and climbed up. First-rate appliances. I could move them anywhere. I thought of Barry the Brokester.

With a swag load on the street, I had to move quick.

I called Barry.

"Come over," he said, "I'm waitin'."

At one time, Barry was my number-one fence. I gave him first shot at everything I had. But Barry was a weasel, and I stopped using him. I only called him now because I promised him my next load; I was keeping my word.

When I first met Barry he was in his mid-thirties, I was in my teens.

He had a shylock book. He heard I was a tough kid and wanted me to collect some debts. I made good money chasing his stiffs.

He also owned a chain of video stores. He got his father a job running the projector in a movie theater. On premiere night, the old man would set up a videocamera beside the projector, record the movie, and give Barry the tape.

Barry had dozens of VCRs in his basement, stacked on shelves, across a pool table, even on the couch. Tangled wires were everywhere. He'd use the hot copy his old man made for him to knock off tapes and sell the bootlegs all over the country. The clarity sucked; sometimes you heard whispering, even cheap sex in the back aisles, but nobody gave a shit. Everyone likes to see a movie first, and the price was right. Barry made a killing.

When Blockbuster busted up the small guys on the block, Barry's video stores went under. He took a shot at nightclubs. By then, I was running with the Mob, and Barry's stock in me was starting to pay off. He called me in to protect his nightclubs. I ran off thugs who tried to shake him down until everyone knew he was with me.

By right, I was owed a protection fee for my troubles, but Barry wouldn't go for cork. "I'm flat broke, barely makin' ends meet," was his favorite tune, and that's how he got the name Barry the Brokester.

Whenever me and my friends stopped by Barry's nightclub, he offered us free drinks. "No, thanks." He gave us passes to the VIP room—worthless. He even introduced me to his hottest shot girl, and threw me the keys to his office.

"She likes you," he whispered in my ear.

Her blow jobs were great but not worth the five hundred a week he was trying to save by doing me this favor.

Under my protection, Barry built up his shylock book, and opened up two more nightclubs, and never paid street taxes.

He finally pushed his luck when he got into the Joker Poker business. Joker Poker routes are Mob business.

The machines are in stores, bars, and pizzerias. They look like arcade games. A gambler inserts a bill, and registers credits on the screen. He pushes a button to bet from the bank, and is dealt an electronic poker hand. It's like playing a slot machine. Most people lose because the odds are in the machine's favor.

If a player wins, and wants to cash out, he calls over the store owner, who checks the tally on the screen, then pays cash out of his pocket, or dips into the sales register.

When the owner of the machine makes his routine stop, he opens the machine and slides out a plastic bin stuffed with bills. He counts the cash in the bin, then hits a button on the machine to check what the owner laid out, reimburses him, and the two split what's left.

Men have been killed over a prime spot. In some neighborhoods, as soon as a storefront is rented, the tenant is approached by one hood after another, each offering a "loan" to secure the spot.

A store owner can get ten, even twenty grand in front money when he needs it most. The store owner's weekly share gets deducted until the debt is paid.

My goombah, Tony Pork Chop, asked me to put a machine in the back of his pork store. It did so well, Tony moved his meat freezer to make room for more.

After a few weeks, Tony traded his white, bloodstained overcoats for designer sweat suits, and his meat cleaver for a fat cigar. He set up a table in the back with hot food, coffee, and doughnuts, and hired a girl to serve drinks and hand out cigarettes. He installed a satellite antenna on the roof, and aired the races so he could take action. He cashed pension checks for old men and women who dumped the money back into his machines.

Meanwhile, the sausages in his display cases turned green, the bracioles grew hair, and the artichoke jars collected an inch of dust. I could've cracked someone's head open with a loaf of semolina.

"Tony, what the fuck is goin' on here?" I asked him one day when I found him in the corner of his store, wearing dark sunglasses and counting money.

"Ah, who gives a shit about meat, I do ten times better wit' these machines."

"What happened to 'Hi, Mrs. Rolofini, what can I do for you today?'"

"She's in the back, too." He smiled.

"Tony, wit'out the store as a front, we're runnin' a casino, an' we ain't got a gamin' license."

Tony was eventually fined, then arrested. He blew the spot and we lost the machines.

Barry was smarter than Tony. He was low-key and kept up a good front.

Barry knew plenty of crooked store owners from his pirate movie days, and built up a sweet route. He never told me, afraid I'd muscle in on his action. I only found out Barry had machines all over the boroughs when a Bonanno soldier from Brooklyn took over a luncheonette where Barry had his machines.

The place was a gold mine, five machines lined up against the back wall raking in over ten grand a week. Waitresses took orders and delivered meals straight to the machines. There was spit all over the screens from people cursing the cards with food in their mouths.

The Bonanno guy gave Barry a chance before he moved in. But instead of telling me about the beef so I could straighten it out, Barry bullshitted the Bonanno guy, "I'm with someone, but I can't say who."

He hoped the wiseguy would give up, but a wiseguy will give up his wife before he gives up a ten-thousand-dollar spot.

The wiseguy spared Barry, but took Barry's machines out of the joint, and replaced them with his own.

"Tell that muthafucka to call me if he wants his machines back," the wiseguy told the luncheonette owner, who had no say in the matter. "Better yet, have his imaginary friend gimme a ring."

When Barry showed up to empty his machines, they were gone. The owner gave him the message. Barry called me and we met.

"Remember I told you about those machines I have?" He had the balls to act like I knew but might've forgotten.

"You shoulda called me sooner." I shook my head. "You had months to tell me about this; I coulda straightened it out. Now, it'll come to a sit-down an' I'll lose."

This happens all the time. A guy's got a good thing, and keeps it to himself. He only calls for muscle when he's lost it and wants it back. It could be a gambling book, a small skim, or a hook at the airport for swag, anything.

When it's too late, he searches for a wiseguy to back him, a friend of a friend, his wife's cousin, a childhood pal he hasn't seen in years, anyone.

If the wiseguy is desperate or greedy, he'll sign on and arrange a sit. But it's a tough win, since nothing was "put on record" before the sit.

"Can't help ya," I told Barry. "You never coughed up a dime, an' I never kicked a nickel upstairs. Who's gonna take my back if it goes higher?"

He looked at me like I'd let him down.

"Put your spots on record, so this don't happen again."

"I have no other spots." He refused to come clean.

I left him and called a friend of mine who worked for Barry. It was as easy as this: "Where's Barry's poker spots?"

"Which one, the three in Queens, the two in Staten Island, the two in Brooklyn, or the one in the Bronx? I helped him carry the machines in."

"Gimme the Bronx address."

Next day, I sent Tony the Twitch to a cabstand on Tremont Avenue off the Cross Bronx Expressway. He walked in and told the dispatcher to "shut the fuck up if you know what's good for you," dumped the machines on their sides, then gave him a number. "Tell the prick who owns these to call me!"

Tony called me on his way home. "Done."

Barry called me, minutes later.

"Hey, what's up?" I answered.

"Listen, Lou, I just got a new spot in the Bronx, dropped my machines off this morning. I was planning to give you a ring tonight, to let you know. Can you believe this shit? I already had a problem. The family men, you know who I mean, they want to speak with me. Can you take care of it?"

His voice cracked, a nervous wreck.

"I'll see what I can do. I'm glad you tole me right away. Did Ton—they leave you a number?" Like an idiot, I almost asked, "Did Tony leave you his number?"

He read off Tony's number to me.

I met with Barry that night.

"I took care of it," I told him. "Any other spots I should know about?"

"No, I lost my other spot, and this one didn't make anything yet, I just got it."

I handed him a scrap of paper with a list of his locations. He turned beet red.

"Why can't we share?" I asked. "You need me more than I need you. Fork over a few hundred a week, I kick a piece upstairs, everyone's happy, an' you get rich."

It was killing him, I could see it in his eyes.

We were standing in Arby's parking lot on Queens Boulevard. His legs went weak. He leaned against a car, and stared down at the paper. I think he wanted to swallow it and start our conversation over.

"I'm flat broke, barely makin' ends meet."

"Don't be cheap. Gimme the few bucks, keep things runnin' smooth. This way, if somethin' happens, I don't look bad, you don't look bad. I'll give you a truck once in a while, you'll make back double what it'll cost ya. That's my word: you'll get a load from me here an' there, like the ole days."

Barry never agreed, but he started to pay. He cried the blues so much I told him to leave the envelope with Funzi.

Over the next few months, I straightened out a couple of ridiculous beefs for Barry, figured he was looking for trouble just to get his money's worth.

Because I promised Barry a load, I called him with Danny's appliance truck.

Once Barry had the goods, he chiseled me down, made me nuts. I almost took the load back.

Danny got so aggravated, he wanted to pay Barry a visit. I talked Danny out of it. "Don't blame 'im, it's my fault for usin' him."

Barry was lucky. Another hood would've handled him differently.

The poker route would've ended with Barry being invited to dinner.

The last thing he'd have seen was a bowl of spaghetti. His wife would've reported him missing. And the killer would've taken over his route.

As for the load of appliances, Barry would've been told to pay top dollar, or he would've ended up in one of the refrigerators.

Barry was a real winner. Last anyone heard he was living in a mansion in Beverly Hills. Before that, a penthouse in Vegas. I just hope he's not in a barrel at the bottom of the East River.

"Ah salute Barry, wherever you are."

SORRY, YOU'RE OVER YOUR LIMIT

Sonny was a knock-around guy with the Colombos. He ran a high-priced geisha house in Bay Ridge, Brooklyn, a block from the Belt Parkway. He rented a vacant warehouse and hired his wife's beautician to decorate.

"She's got pizzazz," he said. I think he just wanted to nail her.

From the outside, the geisha house was an old red brick building. Inside, plush carpets, leather couches, and a dozen cubicles along the walls, each with a bed, dressing table, and mirror.

The girls were snuck in from Asia. They lay around on sofas, waiting to be picked by a client.

Sonny had big-shot clients; actors, stockbrokers, CEOs, and mobsters hobnobbed in the locker room and soaked in the same Jacuzzi.

Sonny blew money on exotic pets. Against one wall of the sitting room was a large saltwater fish tank; against the opposite wall was a bigger tank with two snapper turtles and a crocodile.

I bought credit cards from Sonny. One day, I was sitting on the couch waiting for him when one of the girls tugged at my wrist. "Sneaky fuck."

"I no pay." I pulled my hand away.

"You no pay." She pointed to her room. "Sneaky fuck."

I looked her up and down: sexy eyes, smooth skin, shiny black hair, and fake tits poking through a tight pink shirt. I shrugged my shoulders. "Why not?" We went to her room.

I once walked into the geisha house and saw blood on the walls. Two kids who worked for Sonny were on their knees rolling up the carpet; two more were wiping down the leather couch. The water in the mop bucket was red. It was a Mob murder with the cleanup crew in full swing.

"Shit, bad timing." I turned for the door.

A kid carrying a bottle of ammonia walked by, shaking his head. "The fuckin' turtles ate the croc las' night."

"Get the fuck outta here!" I said before I spotted Sonny coming toward me.

"Imagine this shit?" said Sonny. "My fuckin' two-thousand-dollar turtles ate my five-thousand-dollar croc. The broads were beepin' me all night. They said the turtles were fuckin' wit' each other when the croc got involved. Then the turtles turned on the croc." He sighed. "Maybe it's my fault, I shoulda bought a bigga tank. Maybe that's why them poor melanzanes kill each other, we cram them into little projects, they're on top of each other."

"A shame." I put on a sympathetic face. "Any plastic?"

"Yeah, I got two on my head."

Sonny lifted his wig and pulled out an AmEx and a Visa. He said if he was pinched and patted down, cops wouldn't find them there.

But this hiding spot had other risks.

One time, three cards flew off Sonny's head, across Victory Boulevard. I was supposed to meet Sonny at his geisha house earlier that day, but got stuck in heavy traffic on the Belt Parkway.

"Come to my house," Sonny said when I phoned to say I was running late.

That evening Sonny and his wife had tickets for a show.

I pulled into Sonny's driveway as he and his wife came out onto the porch to greet another couple getting out of a stretch limo. As the five of us met on the sidewalk, a landscaper walked out of their backyard; his leaf blower drowned out our voices.

Sonny yelled at the guy, "Shut that shit off!"

We all said hello, then Sonny held his hand out in front of the land-scaper. "That shit's powerful, give it a rip."

The landscaper switched on the blower and shot Sonny's hairpiece clean off his head. It whirled around like a leaf in the wind. Credit cards flew everywhere.

We all laughed, except the landscaper, who knew Sonny was Mafia. Sonny's wife peed herself and went back in the house to change. I scooped up the cards, slipped them into my pocket, and left.

For years, I made big wood with Sonny's "dupes," phony credit cards with real numbers. He sold them to me for a hundred bucks apiece. Sonny had salespeople in retail stores on the take, boosting charge card receipts. He'd stamp the stolen card numbers onto his dupes. They looked phony, so I couldn't pass them off just anywhere. They were only good where I knew a business owner willing to phone in the sale.

I'd visit a jeweler who was in on the scam, and buy a Rolex. If the watch retailed for five grand, I'd tell him to hit the card for ten. I left with the watch. He made money. Both of us happy.

Mikey Schnozzola owned a leather warehouse. I rolled a rack of leather coats up to his counter. I counted ten and told him, "Charge me for twenty."

He smiled when he hung up the phone; the purchase was approved.

That day, I gave a coat to every friend I bumped into. I pulled over on Linden Boulevard when I saw the Catalano brothers. They were trying on coats in the street, right out of my trunk.

If I knew a guy who sold stuff I didn't want, like Paulie Flowers, I'd work out a cash split. I'd show up at his flower shop and tell him, "Hit my card for four grand. Keep two, an' gimme two when you get paid." He'd tell the card company that he delivered arrangements to a wedding, and send them a phony bill of sale, and that was that.

I had a good long run.

I had closets full of designer clothes, and a jewelry box stuffed like a pirate's chest.

I was generous with other people's money. I bought rims and tires for friends' cars, marbled one friend's bathroom, and finished another's basement. I shopped, dined, and stayed in fancy hotels—and never had a problem. Until I got involved with Ricky.

Ricky was a small-time hustler with his hands in every shit-ass scheme. He'd use my name to bail himself out of bullshit beefs with local clowns. I liked him, so I didn't mind.

I once found a note under my wiper blade: "Louie call Ricky."

I tucked it in my visor and forgot about it until two days later, when I pulled down the visor and it fell in my lap. I called. He wanted to meet.

Ricky slipped into my car.

"Some guy's inta me for fifty big ones," he said.

"Really? Let's walk."

We got out of my car.

Ricky wanted me to collect "dead money," money written off as impossible to collect because the debtor is a deadbeat. The going rate for collecting dead money on the street is fifty percent; if I collect ten grand for someone, I keep five.

Collecting money was easy for me.

A week earlier, I collected twenty grand from a guy who owned a dress company in the garment center. I threatened to hang him out the window. He paid, even though his office was on the first floor.

When people think the Mob has walked off the big screen into their living rooms, they pay. One deadbeat lost his nerve just hearing that I drove a black Lincoln.

Before I stopped bothering with Barry the Brokester, he recommended me to a doctor who owned radiology machines all over the city.

"My partner robbed me," said the doctor. "He sunk our business then offered to buy me out dirt cheap. He was so slick with the books, I'll certainly lose if I take him to court."

"I'll get ya money."

"Will you whack him too?"

"Take it easy, Doc." I rested my hand on his shoulder. "You're watchin' too many movies. Besides, ain't you supposed to be savin' people?"

"But he said he's in the Mafia. What if he kills me first?"

"Don't worry, Doc, only a jerk-off would talk like that, he's fulla shit. We don't use the word 'Mafia.' I'll get ya money."

I called the doctor's partner, a real wiseass.

"Who the fuck are you, and who the hell gave you my number?"

I hate "telephone tough guys" who threaten you from a thousand miles away, but I kept my cool, and got him to agree to meet me that night.

"Only so you never call me again!" he said.

Before we hung up, he asked, "What kind of car will you be driving so I recognize you in my parking lot?"

"A black Lincoln."

"Oh, how apropos."

"What the fuck does that mean?" I got confused and lost my cool. "Don't get smart wit' me! Jus' make sure you're there!" I slammed the phone down.

Since I was a kid, I had a bad habit of taking a swing at people when they said things I didn't get, in a tone I didn't like.

Later, I bumped into some friends and asked them what "apropos" meant.

"I don't know."

"No fuckin' clue."

"Sounds like a wisenheimer to me. Can I take a ride wit' you?"

This man's fate rested on what I believed the meaning of "apropos" to be by six p.m.

An ex-girlfriend called me to get together "for a quickie," saving his ass. I swung by her house.

After we fooled around she cracked her gum and asked, "Why the rush, whatchu doin' tonight?"

"What's 'apropos' mean?"

"I'm proud of you, you're expanding your vocabulary. Appropriate, like if I were to say to you, 'When you walk away from me after sex, that's apropos.' In other words, it fits the way you treat me."

"How 'bout if I said to somebody I'm supposed to meet tonight, 'Look for me, I'll be drivin' a black Lincoln,' an' he says, 'Oh, how apropos.' "

"It just means that people would associate a black Lincoln with the Mafia, and the guy must know you're in the Mafia. It's not an insult." She knew I had a complex.

I met the guy in his lot. He walked over to my car. His smirk and strut meant trouble. I squeezed the door handle, ready to jump out and fight, but his shaky voice told me he was just so used to fucking people and getting away with it that he couldn't lose the attitude.

"Nice car," he said. "Wait here, I'll be right back." He went into his office and returned with a brown paper bag.

"You don't have to count it." He leaned into the car. "If it's not all there, you'll be back to break my legs, right?"

I had the money, and more than enough of him. I raised the power window, almost on his nose, and pulled away.

Even people who welsh on bets, screw their landlords, and hang up on bill collectors pay the Mob.

So Ricky told me he's owed fifty large from some half-ass hood Tony Varro. Ricky and Tony opened phony businesses under fake names. After getting approved to accept charge cards, they'd "bang out" forty or fifty grand with dupes, get paid, then split, leaving behind a vacant store.

"Tony tole me he don't wanna do it no more," Ricky whined, like the love of his life gave up sex. "So I tole Tony, 'Fine, jus' pay me the las' fifty you owe me an' we're even.' But he swore he never got paid. I tole him to show me the bank account but he won't. I taught him the scheme, an' I bet my ass he's still doin' it, but he musta figured why split the scratch if he could do it wit'out me? Hope you don't mind, but I said it was your money. I called you ten times las' week but couldn't get aholda ya. That's why I lef' the note. I was givin' you half if he paid me, but he didn't give a fuck about you either, he still ain't payin'.'"

"If I'da known it was fifty Gs, I'da called ya back. You're always callin' me for peanuts."

Aside from phony businesses, Tony Varro owned a car wash. The following afternoon, I drove Ricky to his place.

When we pulled into the lot, Ricky pointed out Tony, who was barking orders at workers. I backed into a spot. Ricky got out. I lowered my window, then killed the engine so I could listen. Ricky reached out to shake Tony's hand, but Tony left him hanging.

Here we go, I said to myself.

Tony's mouth moved, rapid fire, "Why'd you . . . I don't give a . . . too bad . . . fuck off . . ."

I heard enough to know it wasn't going well.

I got out of my car and walked over to them. Tony toned down his tough talk, not sure, if I was with Ricky, that I'd let him get away with it.

"Everythin' all right?" I asked.

"Yeah," Ricky said, "no problem here."

"Look," said Tony, his eyes shifting between us, "I'll get ya your money, but it'll take time. Like I said, they never paid me, but I'll still come up wit' it."

"Nice place," I said.

"Thanks, I'm in big debt, though. I borrowed through the nose to open it up. But I'll make it work, I know this business inside out."

"I seen you aroun' but can't remember where. You got another car wash?"

"Yeah . . . yeah, I do. Two towns over. It's doin' bad, worse than this one, no money comin' in."

"You borrowed to open that, too?"

"Yeah, I did, I'm in double debt with that place."

"This place looks like it's doin' good."

"Lucky I break even."

"Well, don't get into debt wit' us!" I got nasty. "If you owe Ricky money, pay it. If not, show 'im why, an' he'll walk away, I'll make sure of it. Capisce?"

"Yeah, gabeach."

"Good. Let's go," I said to Ricky, and we left.

A week or so later, I was driving down Main Street and spotted Ricky coming out of the German deli with a sandwich bag. I tapped my horn and pulled over. He shook his head and threw up his arms.

"Nothin' yet?" I asked, as he leaned into my window.

"Not a dime. Every day he bullshits me, says he's got paperwork showin' the charges were denied. Every time I ask to see it, he's got another excuse. Meanwhile, I heard he jus' bought a house in the Hamptons, an' picked up a Porsche to zip aroun' in, 'cause he only wants to use his new Beemer on weekends."

"This guy's hot shit. New house, new cars, new businesses, an' no paperwork."

"He talks to me like I'm stupid," said Ricky.

"You are stupid, we can't get mad at 'im for that. An' what about me? He still don't give a fuck who I am, even afta I talked to 'im."

"Says he asked a buddy about you, an' the guy tole 'im you're close wit' the Gottis, but his buddy claims he's close wit' 'em too."

"Who's his buddy, he mention a name?"

"Nope."

"I don't believe 'im, more of his bullshit. He figures if we're bluffin', we'll back off. You ever tell 'im I was close wit' the Gottis?"

"I did," Ricky reluctantly admitted, lowering his head.

"That's how he knew. He's probably a rat. I ain't goin' back, I'll send a coupla guys to break 'im up. People get aholda money faster from the hospital."

Ricky called me less than an hour later from a pay phone. "I jus' heard from Tony. He's got a tip, wants to know if we're interested. A tire guy he does business wit' got a safe in the back of his store. Tony swears there's at least a hundred large in it. No guns, no alarms. He said he don't want nothin', jus' wants to even up wit' us."

I should've said no, but I was a sucker for a good score.

I no longer did the work myself, so I gave the job to Botz and Juney. If the take was what Tony said, me and Ricky could split fifty, and Botz and Juney could split the other fifty.

Juney scoped out the place. He liked the setup and decided to hit the store before closing, if no customers were inside.

The night of the robbery, Botz and Juney walked into the store and drew guns. They locked the employees in a back room, searched the safe, and left.

I was playing cards at a friend's house when my beeper went off. "Gotta go." I pushed my winnings into the pot. "Split it up."

I spoke to Botz, both of us on pay phones.

"Nothin' in the safe," he said, "but we got the strongbox. The owner told us to take it when he saw how pissed we were. It's the size of a shoebox."

"Get to the point. What's in it?"

"I don't know, figured we'd open it together. Where you wanna meet?"

"By Sergio's garage. I'm on my way."

I knew Sergio would be there; he chopped cars all night.

Opening a safe or a strongbox is like playing *Let's Make a Deal* with Monty Hall. I'd get as excited as those idiots in ridiculous costumes, choosing Curtain Number One.

When I knocked, Sergio cracked open the steel door to his shop, looked up and down the street, then let me in.

"What's up wit' that?" I brushed past him. "Ya think I'd bring heat?"

"Not you. Juney was bangin' on my door like a fuckin' maniac while I was cuttin' a car in the back. I'm hopin' the bulls don't pull up. Heckle and Jeckle are waitin' for ya in my office."

Botz and Juney were sitting on opposite sides of Sergio's desk, both staring at the metal box like they were figuring out how to dismantle a bomb. A cigarette burned in an ashtray. They didn't notice me at the door.

"I bet ya five grand it's over a hundred." Juney rubbed the stubble on his chin. "We had two hundred in a shoppin' bag las' year, an' it wasn't that heavy."

"What about the metal box," said Botz, "it's gotta weigh somethin'. Ten Gs says it's between fifty an' seventy-five."

I walked in.

Juney looked up at me. "Hey, paesan, how much ya think is in here?"

"Youse got the key?"

They looked at each other like "Oh, shit, we forgot to ask."

"He didn't have one," answered Botz.

I shook my head. "Jus' open it."

Botz had a tire iron and a flathead screwdriver on his lap. He started wrestling with the box, knocking stuff off Sergio's desk.

"Harder than I thought." He broke for a breath before trying again.

"Lemme call Sergio," I said, "he'll open anythin'."

"I got this," Botz insisted as Juney snickered.

Botz finally pried it open. We all hovered over the desk; three heads banged into each other, six hands shuffled through the dented box: one gold Indian head, two five-hundred-dollar bonds, and some snapshots, probably the owner's family.

"Fuck! . . . Shit!" Botz and Juney said in sync.

Life has a funny way of waking a sleeping conscience. Showing you pictures of your victim's family is one of them. I felt horrible for about two seconds, then said, "Unfuckin'believable! An' there was nothin' in the safe?"

"Nothin'!" Juney said. "It was the size of a refrigerator, not even locked. The shelves were used to store ole ledgers. I ripped through it anyhow."

"That filthy bastard bullshitted Ricky again. He gave us this tip to get us off his back."

I called Ricky. "It's done. Nothin'!"

"You're kiddin' me," said Ricky. "I know Tony's a bullshitter, but I can't believe he went this far."

"I can't believe I fell for it."

"He's still at his place. I spoke to him a little while ago, said he's workin' late. I'll call him."

"No, don't, we'll drop in."

Botz and Juney jumped in with me, both still packing.

The whole ride, they went on and on about what they wanted to do to Tony once we got there. I got so tired of listening to them. "If youse hurt Tony half as much as youse are hurtin' my ears, he's in trouble."

I pulled up to Tony's car wash. Late-night workers were waxing cars under a tent. I drove in and we jumped out.

"Where's Tony?" I asked, hoping someone spoke English.

A guy pointed under a car where shiny patent-leather shoes hung off the edge of a creeper. I grabbed the guy by the ankles and slid him out. It was Tony, dressed for an affair, tux and bow tie.

"Hi, Lou."

"The safe was filled with shit, like you."

"You did it? Already?" he asked.

"Surprised, huh? You see these guys?" I pointed to Botz and Juney behind me. "They jus' risked their asses so you can live in a mansion an' not pay bills. Is that the Porsche you jus' bought?"

"It's not mine, it's my wife's . . . she borrowed the money for it."

"From who, you?"

"No, her parents."

"It doesn't end wit' you, gimme the keys."

"I don't have them."

His jacket was hanging over a chair. I searched the pockets.

Tony shit when he heard the keys jingle. "Oh, you mean those keys," he said.

"Here." I threw them to Juney. "See if it starts."

Juney slid into the seat and started the engine, which sounded like a rocket. He smiled and fixed the mirrors like he just won the car on a game show.

"I'm takin' the car," I said. "Pay what you owe, an' you get it back. Ricky says you got paperwork that proves you never got paid. Show it to him an' you'll never see us again."

Juney drove the Porsche to Brooklyn. I had him park the car in a friend's garage, asked him to store it for us.

On the way home, Ricky called my phone. "That prick Tony jus' called me. I heard about the car. He says that tough-guy friend of his wants you to return it. Says if you don't, you're a dead man."

"Oh, really." I hung up, drove home, and went to sleep. If Tony said I was a dead man, I'll probably live forever.

Ricky found me the following day. "I got another call from Tony, says his friend wants to know when you're bringin' the car back."

"He calls you a lot now; he knows how to dial when somebody owes him somethin'. Who's his friend?"

"Rallo. Johnny Rallo."

"Never hearda him. If Tony's got a real guy behind 'im, an' I doubt he does, we'll get paid. He'll never beat us at the table. Ask where Rallo's from, what crew he's wit'."

Ricky called Tony in front of me. He hung up and said, "Rallo's wit' Artie the Hair-Do, hearda him?"

"No shit, wish I'da known. Artie's a capo from my borgata, like a father to me. We can't lose, he'll never rule against me. Besides, we're in the right. Tony fucked you outta money, won't show us paperwork, an' two of my crew jus' put themselves out for a bullshit tip. He's got some pair bringin' all this out, I'd rather lose the car if I was him."

I left Ricky, believing we'd finally get paid.

Artie the Hair-Do was a gangster for over forty years. I never heard a bad word spoken about him. Artie's father, an old-timer from the Crazy Joe Gallo days, ran Manhattan's Little Italy for the Gambino family.

Artie was a tall, handsome man. In his prime, singers and actresses chased him.

Now in his sixties, Artie had a long street life behind him. He was in the infamous Gambino group photo with Castellano; he knew Sinatra and Jimmy Roselli.

Artie owned two restaurants and a café in Little Italy where all the stars ate. He was close with priests and politicians, as friendly with them as he was with us. He smoked twenty-dollar cigars and always gave me two when I saw him.

"Give one to your father," he'd say.

My dad smoked Dutch Masters; the whole box didn't cost twenty bucks. I'd thank Artie and give both cigars to my father.

I went to meet Artie downtown.

Manhattan is broken up into wards. A year earlier, I was opening a nightclub in the fourth ward, not far from Artie's social club. It was disrespectful to swing open the doors under his nose without telling him. Besides, if I had a problem with local cops or thugs, Artie would take care of it.

"I love you, Louie," he said, after hearing about my latest venture.

"You're such a good kid. I jus' wish you wasn't so wild. Why not open a Kenny Rogers Chicken joint, you spin the chickens on a nice rotisserie wit' giant flames undaneath." He spun a hand in the air. "I got the hook. I can get you a franchise. You'll have your own territory, like the Bronx. Open five or six joints, an' you're makin' a killin'."

I had a brief nightmare of myself in a chicken suit, Kenny Rogers singing "The Coward of the County" in the background while a little fat kid barked an order at me.

"You'd rather be aroun' the broads," he said, reading my face. "Everyone drinkin' an' dancin', right?"

"Yeah, of course."

"I'll warn ya now, nightclubs are a real pain in the ass, I owned enough of 'em to know. Who broke a bottle over whose head. Who stabbed who. The cops'll be there every night."

I opened the place. I owned two clubs before I realized Artie was right, and wished I owned a chicken joint.

Today, I was here to ask Artie about Johnny Rallo.

"I hear he's from Nyack." I filled Artie in. "Says he's wit' you. Know 'im?"

"The name rings a bell, but he ain't wit' me. Lemme ask my son, he lives in Nyack."

Artie called a waiter, asked him to run across the street to Artie's other restaurant and get his son Marco. While waiting, I played with the silverware, thinking, once again, Tony bullshitted me, this time about his connections, and once again I'd fallen for it. I was sure, even if Tony believed his own shit, that Johnny Rallo was lying to Tony. This made sense since liars hang out together. Who else would believe them?

Marco came over and said hello. After he and I exchanged a kiss and a handshake, I mentioned Rallo.

Marco's face grew bitter. "He's a cold-blooded killer, stay away from 'im."

"So he ain't wit' you?"

"Hell no. He runs wit' a buncha crazies upstate, they kidnap drug dealers. A few disappeared, even afta they was ransomed. He ain't all there. He shot a guy at a gas station for drippin' gas on his car. Another poor bastard insulted his girl at work. Rallo sat on the side of this guy's house for hours, shot 'im five times when he left for work. A real fuckin' nut. An' it ain't the first time he's throwin' me or my father's name aroun'. Las' time I sent a coupla guys to confront 'im. He denied it. I let 'im off the hook, figurin' he got the message, but it don't surprise me he's doin' it again. Don't sleep on 'im, Louie."

"You want me to take care of it?" asked Artie, puffing on a seven-inch cigar.

"No." I shook my head. "I'll take care of it."

"Watch yaself."

I drove home over the Manhattan Bridge, thinking things out. If Johnny Rallo had real connections with Artie the Hair-Do, I'd have easily straightened this out. Artie would've held a sit with me and Johnny. Each of us would've told our story, and Artie would've ruled.

If Artie told Rallo, "Have Tony pay the fifty," that would've been that. Rallo and Tony would've come up with it.

The fact that Rallo said he was with Artie, but wasn't, proved his insanity. Artie could find himself at the center of a police investigation because some bean shooter like Rallo used his name. You can't go around saying you're "with" someone if you're not. Otherwise, every wannabe gangster would extort people, claiming to be with John Gotti or Chin Gigante. Throwing around names is a dangerous habit on the street, you can wind up hurt or dead. Although Marco let Johnny Rallo off the hook for running his mouth, the Mob usually comes down hard on that shit.

Johnny Rallo was a loose cannon. If I was smarter, I'd have given Tony back his car, scratched the debt, and forgotten the whole thing. But my instinct was to fight. I knew what I had to do.

I went to Ricky's house, pretending I didn't have a spine. "Get aholda Tony. Tell 'im, 'Louie wants no problems wit' either a youse, he wants to give back your car an' personally apologize to Johnny for offendin' 'im.'"

I didn't let Ricky in on my plans, but he knew me too well to believe I was serious. Tony didn't. I stood next to Ricky when he called, repeating my words to Tony.

Tony toughened up his voice, taking charge of the conversation. "You tell Louie he's lucky he's not dead already, an' I can't wait to see 'im apologize after he hands me back my keys. And tell *your* friend Louie, if *my* friend Johnny wants to charge 'im for the days I didn't have my car, shut up an' pay up, if he knows what's good for 'im."

Ricky said, "I'll tell him."

"By the way," Tony added, before hanging up, "even if I got your money, and it so happens I do, you ain't gettin' it now, you're fucked."

The meeting was set for midnight where the Porsche was being stored. After I moved the car from my friend's garage, me, Angelo, and Funzi sat down on crates where it had been. We had a view of the dimly lit street through a hole in one of the garage door panels.

We parked a truck on each corner, at opposite ends of the street. Jackie was behind the wheel of one truck, Juney the other, both laying low on the seats. We all had walkie-talkies. When the car carrying Tony and Johnny rolled to a stop, Jackie would block off one end of the street, Juney the other, trapping Johnny and preventing innocent people from getting in the way.

Inside the garage we passed the time bragging about old fights and showing off scars. We talked about girls we'd slept with, or wanted to sleep with, the Colombo war, and how we hoped it would turn out. We talked about new scores we wanted to pull off. Funzi suggested we rent office space above a check-cashing place on Woodhaven Boulevard and cut our way through the ceiling one night.

Around midnight, a dark Mercedes stopped in front of the garage. The passenger read addresses. I watched as he got out for a closer look. I saw a shotgun upright, leaning against the seat.

Suddenly, I heard gears grind and an engine rumble; Juney blocked off the street in front of the car.

The driver of the Benz panicked, and punched his pedal in reverse. The passenger tried to dive back into the car, but the open car door slammed him to the ground. He rolled on the asphalt; a handgun slid away from him. The car sped away, tires smoking.

We pulled open the garage door and threw wild shots up the street at the car. The driver got away, nearly crashing into Jackie, who drove his truck into position too late.

The street burned with the smell of rubber and gunpowder. Smoke clouded the air like fog at the docks.

Tony lay near the curb. I walked over to him.

"You all right?" I barely heard my own voice, deaf from the shots.

He stared up at me, his face pale white. "You gonna kill me?" He trembled, certain I would.

"No, I'm not a killer. Tell your friend Johnny we play wit' guns, too."

I kicked Tony's gun to the curb and walked away.

Juney moved too fast, Jackie too slow.

Next day, I was summoned to Little Italy. Marco greeted me. "Johnny sent word las' night through some clown I know. He musta asked aroun', says he knows who you are, an' wants no problems. I don't think he'll use me or my father's name again. You musta did some job on 'im. What was it over?"

"Credit cards."

"Over his limit, huh?" He chuckled.

Johnny Rallo was later convicted of multiple murders in the notorious "Comanche Case."

In the pen, I was introduced to the leader of the Comanche Crew, who was serving six life sentences. After he heard my story, he was pissed that Rallo got away. He'd just learned from his attorneys that Rallo had escaped once again, this time from prison. Rallo was released after helping prosecutors take down half of Nyack. His crimes were forgiven, he was relocated, and given a new identity.

Three to one, Johnny Rallo's the friendly neighbor of a nice American family in the Midwest, probably plotting to kill the son for riding a bicycle over his front lawn.

WHATTA WE, IN THE FLOWER BUSINESS?

Every ski season, city kids head north to Hunter Mountain, New York. They chip in, rent a chalet, and cram every inch of it with sleeping bags.

Juney had a kid brother named Chris, a high school senior. He was a good kid, respectful, easygoing, a happy drunk who was fun to be around. Chris was handsome. Some guys in the neighborhood resented him because he scored well with the girls.

One year, the gang didn't tell Chris about their winter rental. Chris felt left out. He mentioned it to me when we bumped into each other on the street.

"The last thing a buncha drunken desperados want aroun' them in a party house is a girl-getter like you," I told him. "They're jealous. It's not an insult, take it as a compliment."

He looked at his reflection in my car window. "You're right. Fuck them."

Chris slept with every girl in the neighborhood, but had a steady, Margie. Margie's friends also rented a house near Hunter Mountain. She was invited but chose to stay home with Chris.

The wild week came and everyone left for the mountains except Chris and Margie. The two got drunk, got laid, then got bored, and hopped into Margie's beat-up Volkswagen and drove upstate.

"We'll sleep by my friend's place," Margie told Chris.

They pulled into town three hours later and went to the Crazy Moose, where Margie's friends hung out. When the club emptied, Margie asked her friend Kathy, "Can me and Chris stay by your place?"

"You can, but Chris can't, no boys allowed," said Kathy. "Chris, why don't you stay with the guys and leave Margie with us. We'll all meet for breakfast in the morning."

"I don't want to leave Chris," said Margie.

"Where are the guys?" Chris asked Kathy. "We'll crash there."

Kathy rattled off directions to Ray's house.

Ray was older than Chris and the rest of the gang; the house was rented in his name.

Chris drove drunk while Margie navigated.

"Wait here," Chris told Margie as they parked in front of the house.

He went up to the porch and knocked on the door.

After a few minutes of banging, Ray opened the door. "Beat it, punk!" he told Chris.

"C'mon, no jokes, we got nowhere to stay." Chris pointed to Margie in the car. "I already gotta girl, you ain't gotta worry about me. It's freezing out here."

"Too fuckin' bad, you shoulda rented a place."

"Nobody asked me."

"Then go get a room."

"Gimme a break, you can't find a room up here this week. Lemme in, I'll owe you big time."

"Fuck you!" Ray slammed the door in Chris's face.

Margie heard the commotion and walked up to Chris.

"How much you got?" Chris asked her as he dug into his pockets and counted his money. "I got eighty bucks."

"I think I have twenty."

Chris banged on the door till Ray swung it open.

Chris waved the cash. "I got a hundred bucks. Can we sleep in the basement?"

Ray slapped the bills out of Chris's hand and pushed him down the steps. Chris fell in the snow. Margie screamed as everyone rushed to the door to egg Ray on. Ray pushed Margie aside and beat the shit out of Chris.

When Chris lay still, Ray turned and walked into the house. Margie cried while the drunks picked up the loose bills and moped inside; the entertainment was over.

Margie helped Chris into her car and drove home, blasting the radio to keep her awake. Chris lay across the backseat, whimpering.

Next day, I got a call from Juney. After he told me the story in a nutshell, he said, "That muthafuckin' Ray is dead."

I wanted to hear the whole story, so Juney took me to see Chris.

Chris lay in bed, holding his ribs. He recapped the entire weekend for us, even imitated Ray and Margie's voices.

Juney wanted to kill Ray. "I'll bury that fuckin' bastard in the lot behine my house."

"I gotta get him myself," Chris said.

Chris had a point. He lost his honor, not us, only he could get it back.

"I'm not sure if he can handle Ray," I whispered to Juney as we left. "But we'll let 'im try anyhow, it'll give 'im his face back. We'll get Ray later, the right way."

After a couple of weeks, everyone finally got bored with the same old story of how Chris drove all the way up to Hunter Mountain to get the shit beat out of him so he could turn around and drive home.

Everyone made a joke. "At least he went skiing," said one wiseass, "down a flight of steps."

Chris put up with this shit; he had a plan.

One night, Chris spotted Ray's car parked behind McLane's Tavern. He peeked in and saw Ray near the jukebox, holding a beer. He crouched behind a green Dumpster and waited. After the bartender hollered last call, Ray stumbled out.

Just as Ray stepped through the door, Chris slammed a tire iron into Ray's jaw. Ray fell over a pile of trash bags, and Chris went to work on him. When Ray passed out, Chris spit on him, ran to a pay phone, and called Juney.

"I got 'im good," he said.

"Don't go home," said Juney, "in case they're lookin' for ya. Wait for me in Kissena Park. I'll flash my lights, gimme ten minutes."

Juney picked up Chris and they drove to my house, where Chris told us the story.

"Good work. Feel better?" I knuckled his chin.

"Hope I didn't kill 'im." He started to worry.

"Any witnesses?" I asked.

"Someone was yelling, 'Call the police.' I think it was the bartender."

"Stash 'im in the Poconos," I told Juney. "Betcha there's cops at your door already."

I threw some clothes into a bag for them, handed them a few bills, and they left.

I drove by their house in the morning and spotted an unmarked car across the street. I looked up at the porch as I passed; a calling card was wedged in the screen door. One of the detectives in the unmarked must've left it.

I called Juney in Pennsylvania. "They're sittin' on your house. Who's Ray close wit'?"

"Dago Dom, he works at Mantucci's junkyard by Shea Stadium."

"Call you later."

Shea Stadium, home of the New York Mets, is a block away from Willets Point Boulevard, home to New York's filthiest junkyards.

I drove down the flooded street. My tires sank into potholes. A gypsy ran up to my car. "Yo, amigo, wanna buy some rims fo ya ride?" I waved him off. Another yelled into my window, "Ay, señor, I tint your windows while you wait." He pointed to some crates in a weeded lot. I guess he expected me to sit there while he worked, like the waiting area at Jiffy Lube. I waved him off, too.

I pulled into a gravel driveway and parked next to the junkyard's office, made of stacked rims. Forklifts plowed through the mud. Chained dogs barked at the noise. I got out of my car and hopped over oily puddles before I spotted Dago Dom ripping off a fender.

He saw me and ran, but his boots stuck in the mud.

"I ain't afta ya," I yelled.

"I got nothin' to do wit' that, I swear." He pressed a hand to his heart. "I tole Ray he was an asshole for fuckin' wit' Juney's brother."

"I ain't accusin' you a nuttin'." I approached him. "I came to ask how Ray's doin'."

"You did?" He was surprised. "He's all fucked up, still in the hospital. His jaw's wired up, and he got a thousand broken bones in 'is face. His nose is fucked up, too, it looks like this." He pressed his nose flat against his face.

"Go see 'im, an' tell 'im to call off the bulls. If he didn't call the cops in Hunter Mountain, he shouldn't call 'em now. If the DT car ain't gone by tomorrow, I'll finish what Chris started. Tell 'im I take this whole thing as an insult to myself. He shoulda never laid a hand on Juney's brother."

"Done," said Dom. "I'll visit 'im after work. I tole 'im he fucked up. I knew it."

"Get aholda me later."

Dom called me around seven that night. We met.

"I spoke to Ray," said Dom. "They got 'im on some heavy shit, wish I could get a hit of it for the weekend. Anyway, he says he's sorry for everythin'. He's droppin' the charges firs' thing in the mornin'. He tole me the only reason he pressed 'em was 'cause he got no insurance to pay the hospital bills. Someone tole 'im he could sue the bar if the cops did their thing first."

"Call me as soon as he talks to 'em so I can tell Chris to go home."

Next day, Dom called. "Ray said it's safe for Chris to go home. He's real sorry, like I said, he only did it 'cause he ain't got no insurance."

"Gimme his doctor bills, I'll see what I can do."

Chris came home. He looked and stank like shit, hadn't washed in days. He couldn't take the pressure of being a wanted man. He hugged, kissed, and thanked me.

A couple of weeks later, I was on to a million other things when I got word that Big Paulie wanted to see me. I went to his club.

"What's up?" I kissed him hello.

"One of our skippers wants to meet wit' you, says you owe 'im money."

"I don't owe nobody a dime, who is he?"

"DiGiovanni, Patsy DiGiovanni. Know 'im?"

"Never hearda him. There's a guy in my neighborhood wit' that las' name, but he breaks his ass, works construction, he ain't got nuttin' to do wit' us."

"Maybe he mixed you up wit' somebody. Here's his numba." He handed me a scrap of paper. "Arrange the meet, an' tell me what happened. I'm curious myself."

On the phone, DiGiovanni was brief. "I'm in Brooklyn," he said, "but wherever you wanna meet is fine."

We met outside a pizzeria in Queens, minutes from my house. He told me he'd be driving a black Eldorado with tinted windows. I watched one park. When I saw the driver get out wearing flashy gold and a steam-pressed sweat suit, I knew it was DiGiovanni.

"How was traffic?" I asked as we began to walk.

He ignored my question. "I'm here for a guy named Ray Bloom. Says your buddy almost beat him to death an' you said you was gonna pay his doctor bills. I'm goin' low when I say twenty grand, an' that's wit'out plastic surgeries. My wife does 'em, they ain't cheap. How fas' can you come up wit' this?"

I stopped in my tracks. It was a shakedown. Ray was close friends with the hardworking DiGiovanni from my neighborhood. That stiff must've scraped up someone in his family who was Mob. Ray had every right to hold me to my word. But he should've come to me himself, or sent Dago Dom. I'd have paid his damn doctor bills. It was the gavone he sent that bothered me. And I knew the pig was out for a cut. If he wasn't, he'd have been diplomatic, questioned my pledge, maybe asked what I thought was fair.

"You stickin' up for a rat?" I asked.

"He ain't no rat!"

"He called the cops on my friend."

"Yeah, but he dropped the charges."

"So he ain't a rat no more? Is that like, I'm only gay on weekends? He dropped 'em 'cause I threatened his life, he's still a rat."

"It only matters that he dropped 'em."

"Really? Why not take this upstairs." I was referring to the head of our family. "See what he thinks about defendin' a cop-caller, besides somebody goin' against his own for an outsider."

"Listen, between you an' me, your guy hit 'im wit' a tire iron, that ain't right."

"Whatta we, in the flower business? He's lucky he didn't shoot 'im dead."

DiGiovanni was wrong and knew it. He said and did nothing.

"You wanna take this higher?" I broke the silence. "Or we let it die here? Less embarrassment for everybody." I meant for him; I was being kind.

He looked disgusted, turned, and headed for his car.

"You sure Ray won't press them charges again, maybe this time on me?"

"You ain't gotta worry 'bout that." He dropped into the driver's seat, his fat ass screeched against the leather. "He's unda my command now, an' I ain't no rat!"

"Maybe 'cause you ain't been pinched yet," I said under my breath.

That evening, I went to dinner with friends. When the party broke up, I pulled aside a buddy who was leaving us to meet Paulie in the city. "When you see Paulie, tell 'im the DiGiovanni thing was a misunderstandin', an' I straightened it out."

DiGiovanni broke the rules by sticking up for a cop-caller. He knew he'd have lost the sit, maybe his life.

Every day, I met more and more DiGiovannis, wiseguys willing to break our rules for a quick buck.

I was so wrapped up in my bullshit life that I didn't realize I was rising in the Mafia at the same time the Mafia was in decline.

ATLAS

His name was Nino. I sat across from him in the Hillcrest Diner on Union Turnpike. He was a big guy with a fixed smile, mid- to late twenties, thick chestnut hair combed over his forehead, like Caesar. His muscular arms rested on the table in front of him. Occasionally, he looked out the window into the parking lot, probably on the lookout for cops. He downed his last gulp of juice and ordered a coffee.

A week earlier, Nino came by Juney's house to pick up Juney's sister, Maria. Juney didn't trust anybody who dated his sister. He gave Nino the third degree. When Nino told Juney what he did for a living, Juney ran out and called me from his car.

"You'll never believe what I jus' stumbled on in my livin' room. You gonna be home, I'm on my way."

When Juney got to my house, he clued me in, told me what Nino did for work.

"We gotta rob this guy," he said, "biggest give-up we'll ever get. I'll get to know 'im then ask if he's down."

"Don't wait too long, your sister'll be done wit' 'im soon, he'll be heartbroken, an' hate you jus' 'cause you look like her. Feel 'im out. Meantime, we'll find somebody who knows 'im."

Whenever we were about to make a move with somebody we didn't know, we'd check the guy out, find someone to vouch for him. Whether out of greed or stupidity, we'd accept any moron's, "He's okay."

Juney put feelers out, said he wasn't sure about this new guy dating his sister. He found out that some local guy, Freddie Spaghetti, had dated Nino's sister. Juney went to talk to Freddie.

"Know anythin' about Nino?" Juney asked.

"Great guy," said Freddie. "Comes from a real close family. His sister's a good girl. She's got more balls than mos' guys I know. She held my guns when I thought I was gettin' pinched for that bullshit assault on Bell Boulevard."

To us, if Nino's sister was stand-up, so was Nino.

I ordered a vanilla shake, turned to Nino and said, "Gimme the layout."

He slid his coffee aside and took a crayon out of a plastic cup next to the ketchup bottle. I put some quarters in the jukebox above the table to muffle our voices. Juney and I leaned forward, watching Nino draw on the back of a paper place mat.

"The front door is here, and the garage doors are here, they run on electric. At the end of the day, we park our trucks in rows, right up to the back wall. The office is here, and the vault," Nino said, choosing a different color crayon, "is here."

My eyes were fixed on this purple square, the little door to my dreams.

"The owner's name is Bob Hannaford. He stays late every night, usually locks the place up on his own. He parks his car across the street, a brown Buick Skylark."

"He's packin'?" I asked.

"A Glock. Nice piece. Keeps it right here." Nino tapped a hand on his right hip. "He showed it to me when he bought it, let me hold it, real light, ten-round clip."

"Any night's good?"

"I'd say so. There's always five, ten mil. It varies between those numbers. I'm an early bird, usually there when he opens the place. Every time I walked in with him, the vault was open. I asked why he don't lock it up at night. He said it's a pain in the ass, he's got alarms and insurance anyhow."

"Whatta you want?"

"Whatever you give me is fine."

This was odd. Nino owed us nothing. If he was kissing Juney's ass to get close with Maria, he was in for a surprise. I knew Maria's MO; Nino's days were numbered.

Nino wrote the address to the place on a paper napkin. I folded it up and stuffed it in my pocket.

"Gimme a week or two to check it out, Juney'll get back to you."

That night, I couldn't sleep, couldn't get the job off my mind. I drove to Brooklyn. I needed to see the place.

When I got there, I unfolded Nino's napkin and matched the address with the address on the building I was parked in front of.

Atlas Armored Services was where Nino said it would be, directly across the street from an old eight-story apartment building with crumbling brick and rusty fire escapes. Occasionally, a person passed inside a lit room, or looked out the window.

I saw the joint. I liked it. I drove home and went to sleep.

Late the following afternoon, I went back with Juney to scope it out. We talked about Nino before getting in the car.

Most tip guys aren't too bright, usually why they're jammed up, looking for an easy way out. They speak fast, anxious to get out of whatever mess they're in. Nino was different. He spoke slowly, gave details, he even drew a sketch, first time I saw this.

"He's got no bad habits," said Juney. "He don't gamble, don't do drugs."

"Then why's he doin' this?" I asked.

"Not for money," said Juney. "His family's loaded, pops gives 'im whatever he wants."

"Then why work a schlep job?"

"He's gung-ho, almos' came in his pants when you asked about the owner's pistol. How long can a fuckin' gun nut stare into 'is mirror, wit' a hand on 'is holster, askin', 'What are you lookin' at?' He wants real action, a reason to carry a gun."

"I dunno. Maybe."

Maybe Nino was sucking up to Juney because of Maria. Maybe he really was a gun nut, and needed a little excitement in his life.

"Who cares how his insides work," said Juney. "Everythin' that comes outta his mouth adds up."

Juney was driving his father's drab blue four-door Olds when we turned down Flatbush Avenue on our way to Atlas. Two young drug dealers whistled and yelled, "Five-O," pointing at our car. They thought the shitbox we were driving was an unmarked. This was good.

Daylight was fading. The blocks leading up to Atlas were busy with shoppers. Women ran in and out of grocery stores. Commuters rushed home.

We approached Atlas just as an armored truck was inching up to the entrance. My heart nearly gave out, and Juney veered over the yellow line toward oncoming traffic.

"Make the nex' left an' pull over," I told him. "I'll take the wheel. All we need is an accident report in fronta the joint."

On our next pass, the truck had vanished into the garage, and the door was closed. Bob Hannaford's brown Buick was parked in front of the apartment building, just like Nino said.

I parked on the next block, and told Juney, "Wait in the car."

I walked back and looked into Hannaford's car, pressed my nose against the glass. A mound of butts in an ashtray, crumpled napkins, and coffee cups. The Club was lying on his passenger seat. He didn't take the time to lock it over the steering wheel. I hoped this was a sign that Nino was right about Hannaford's careless habit of leaving the vault open.

I walked into the apartment building and pulled on the inside door. Locked. I usually got past the foyer by ringing every bell on the panel until someone buzzed me in without asking who I was. This time, I didn't want the attention.

I went back outside, leaned against a parked car, and waited to slip in behind a tenant.

"Thanks," I said as one held the door.

My childhood home was near Colden Housing Projects and Pomonok Projects. Playing in these buildings as a kid, I knew rooftop doors were seldom locked. I made my way to the roof.

It was suppertime. I smelled chili on one floor, fried chicken on another.

After eight flights of stairs, I was puffing, half dead. My legs were numb and my ass was all cramped up. Stuffing my face in restaurants three times a day. Late nights slouched over card tables, picking at cannolis. I was twenty-one years old, and the Mob thing was already wearing me out.

The top landing smelled like urine. I swung open the steel door and walked out onto the rooftop. I stepped around Colt 45 bottles and rusted Miller cans before noticing a makeshift tent. No one was home. To be sure, I lifted the damp, dirty blanket hanging over a broken antenna. Some poor bastard had propped it over a smokestack for heat.

I walked to the ledge overlooking the street and poked my head over.

From here, I watched every company on the block close for the night. Most men pulled out of garages and let their cars idle in front while locking the doors. One businessman was parked directly beneath me, two spots behind Hannaford's car. When I saw Hannaford was last to leave, just as Nino said, I knew this job was meant to be.

Hannaford locked the door behind him, then stood under a lamppost at the curb, facing the apartments. He reached into his pocket and pulled out a cigarette, cupped his hands, burned it, and took a drag. He exhaled a day's worth of stress.

I imagined a man who touched so much money would be wearing a hand-tailored suit. Bob dressed like a dirtbag, faded leather jacket and worn jeans. His hair needed to be combed and cut.

Bob was alone. No security. No off-duty cops. No hired henchmen.

He turned up his collar for the short walk across the windy street. He opened his car door without a key, slid into the driver's seat, started the engine, and pulled away. His engine knocked and the tailpipe rattled.

"It's freezing, don't you warm it up?" I spoke as if I was talking to him. I thought about how the job should go down. If Bob had spent a minute warming up his car, I might've considered taking him in the driver's seat. Because he sped away so quickly, I knew we had to take him on the street, between his building and his car.

I considered flattening a tire then offering Bob help, shoving him into his trunk as he reached for the spare. I ruled this out, though my reasoning was ridiculous.

Ever since I started driving, I helped people on the road.

I was once stuck in a traffic jam on the Southern State Parkway. I finally drove up alongside the cause: everybody was rubbernecking, staring at an old man with one fucking arm trying to fix a flat. The parkway was backed up a mile. Not one selfish bastard pulled over to help—except me, a criminal.

The old man was struggling with a tire iron, trying to loosen a lug nut with one hand, when I walked up behind him. After I fixed his flat, he fumbled with his wallet, tried to give me money.

"Put that away." I patted him on the back.

No one would even let me merge onto the parkway as I pulled away. I finally cut in front of someone, who honked and gave me the finger.

Another time, I passed an elderly black couple on the Van Wyck Expressway, staring at a flat. I was sure their color had something to do with nobody stopping; how many men would pull over for a couple of blondes? I pulled off the road to help. It was winter. I made them wait in my car with the heat on while I changed their flat. I may have said "nigger" a million times, but I proved then that I never meant it.

Anyway, I'm trespassing on a rooftop, planning to stuff some overworked mamaluke into his trunk so I can clean out his joint, but I couldn't use a flat tire as a ploy, thinking it would wipe out all the good I'd done helping stranded drivers. Certified fucking lunatic, the only way to explain this.

I thought about shoving Hannaford back into his place as he closed up, but if spotted from an apartment window, we'd be trapped inside, surrounded by a SWAT team.

I needed to snatch him fast, hold him somewhere, and come back to see if anyone had seen us and called the cops.

I suddenly thought of the cigarette. Nino didn't tell me Hannaford smoked. The flick of a BiC would spark the operation of a lifetime.

I walked back to the car. Juney drove us home.

Over the next month, whenever I couldn't sleep, I drove to Atlas, and tried different routes to the parkway. One wrong turn could blow everything.

Nino wasn't looking for money. Why include him? I shut him out, for his good as well as ours. I told Juney to tell him, "We'll pass, job's too risky."

I planned to wait awhile before we struck, so when Nino shows up for work one morning and hears the joint was hit, he couldn't be sure it was us. That way he wasn't an accomplice, and if his ass ended up against the wall he should pass a lie detector.

I needed two men to snatch Hannaford off the street and hand him over to me and Juney. I picked Botz and Funzi as payback for fucking me the year before.

Botz and Funzi pulled off a little score on their own and didn't give me a cut. They hit a drug dealer for thirty grand, a perfect crime since the kid couldn't go to the cops. But the kid cried to his wiseguy uncle, told him he was robbed by two guys in my crew. Wiseguys can't be involved with drugs, so the uncle came looking for me and claimed his nephew was holding his shylock money. "Lou," he beefed, "I want my money back."

I stepped to Botz. "I got a wiseguy up my ass. Why didn't you tell me about this?"

"'Cause you ain't allowed near drugs."

"You stole money, not drugs. Don't bullshit me. I got your back but youse owe me."

I met with the uncle. He settled for ten grand.

"It's worth it," I told him, "to bury this."

He agreed, with a wink.

I made Botz and Funzi repay the ten at the table. On our way home, I took ten out of the remaining twenty, and kicked five upstairs.

With this in mind, I told Botz and Funzi to meet me in the rear parking lot of Whitestone Lanes.

"Youse gotta swipe a guy off the street an' hand 'im over to me. He owes somebody big money."

"No problem," said Funzi, "where an' when?"

"I'll be in touch, be on call."

After I left them, I stopped at a friend's junkyard in Jamaica, Queens, asked if I could use his place one night. A street guy knows not to ask questions; Benny the Bug handed me an extra set of keys to his yard. "Do what ya gotta do, an' don't tell me about it."

No need for a bumper car. Everything would happen too quickly.

A friend rented me an economy car. I screwed a set of stolen plates on it.

The night of the heist, I parked the rent-a-car on Ninetieth Street, a block past Atlas. I shut off the car, killing the smoke from my exhaust, then rubbed my hands together, from the cold, or excitement, probably both.

I watched the block through my rearview mirror. Occasionally people strolled in and out of the apartment building. A police car passed, which meant nothing, so long as cops didn't roll by at the wrong time. I watched the other owners lock their doors and drive off.

I turned around in my seat to see Bob Hannaford walk out his door. He wore a denim jacket and blue jeans. As he locked the door, a van started its engine a block behind me.

A moment later, Botz turned the corner and walked along the opposite sidewalk, in Hannaford's direction. He wore a brown leather bomber and a plaid newsboy cap pulled low to his eyes. His hands were inside his pockets.

Hannaford held his jacket closed, waiting for a car to pass as Botz leaned against Hannaford's car facing the apartment building. Hannaford reached for a cigarette as Botz lifted his collar.

The headlights on the van suddenly shone as the driver angled his wheels into the street. This was Botz's cue that Hannaford was approaching him from behind.

I tightened my fingers around the key in the ignition.

Botz took a cigarette out of his pocket, and hung it off his bottom lip.

It was chilly inside my car.

Papers rustled in the wind. Christmas lights flashed along windows and fire escapes. Dead bulbs outnumbered live. Poverty sucks.

I waited for Hannaford to cross the street. I waited for Botz to spring into action. I waited to turn my key. I waited for what seemed an eternity until Botz stepped off the curb and circled the car just as Hannaford reached for his door handle. I could almost hear his rehearsed line.

"Aye, buddy, gotta light?"

The van pulled into the street as Hannaford cupped his hands around his lighter—and a gun was pressed into his chest.

It happened fast. Botz lifted Hannaford's jacket with his free hand and slipped Hannaford's automatic pistol out of its leather holster. Two seconds later, I heard the sharp screech of brakes and Hannaford was pinned between a 9-millimeter in his ribs and a van against his back. Botz pushed him into the open side door and climbed in behind him. The door slid shut as the three sped away.

I started my car. Hannaford was mine.

HELLO, MR. HANNAFORD

Funzi flashed me a thumbs-up from behind the wheel of the van as I took the lead on the Belt Parkway. He was calm, collected. Things were going well.

I tuned into a police scanner. Reports crackled over the radio: a husband beat the shit out of his wife, a bar fight, a deranged man waved a knife in front of McDonald's, and a car accident on Coney Island Avenue, but nothing about an abduction. Only we knew Hannaford was bound in the back of a stolen Dodge Ram heading east on the parkway.

Funzi followed me off the Kennedy Airport exit. I tapped my brakes and signaled for him to park on the first side street behind Juney, who was waiting in his car. I parked a block up, and walked back to the van.

I climbed into the front passenger seat, and glanced back at Botz sitting in a rear captain's chair. He smiled, a handgun on each thigh.

Hannaford sat on the floor between the two rear seats, blindfolded and gagged. He held it together, like he'd been through this before.

Juney slid behind the wheel after Funzi and Botz got out. I climbed into the back and sat beside Hannaford.

I felt the FBI knew everything about me when they called me by name in California. I wanted Hannaford to feel the same way, that I knew everything about him.

"Hello, Mr. Hannaford." I pulled off the gag.

"Yeah," he answered quietly.

"I want what's in your safe. I won't hurt you as long as you make sure we get away wit' this, understan'?"

"I gotcha. I'm insured. I don't give a hoot about the money, I'll tell ya whatever ya need to know."

"I'm gonna leave you somewhere for a while. I need the alarm code to your place an' the combination to the vault. If I don't make it back, my friends are gonna put you in a meat grinder, so everythin' you tell me better be right."

"I gotta do it myself," he said quickly, "if you wanna get away with this."

"Go on."

"When my door opens, the phone's gonna ring. All the girls who call from the alarm company know me. If they don't hear my voice on the other end, they'll report a break-in. Can I have a cigarette? They're in my top pocket. I think I lost my lighter in the street."

Juney opened the ashtray up front and pushed in the lighter. I lit Hannaford a cigarette and held it to his lips, letting him take a pull every few seconds.

"Thanks," he said.

I'd planned to leave him tied up at my friend's junkyard and free him when we finished. Now, I needed him with me to answer the phone when it rang.

I crushed the cigarette out, then pressed the muzzle of my .45 into his temple.

"I just did ten years"—this lie would haunt me—"I ain't goin' back. You fuck this up, an' I'll blow your fuckin' brains out."

When Juney grabbed hold of my arm from behind, I knew my act was good. I pointed to the hollow handle to show Juney there was no clip in the gun.

"Why fuck around?" Hannaford said. "It's not my money."

"Anybody expectin' you home, anybody gonna call the cops if they don't hear from you by a certain time?"

"No, I work late every night."

We drove back to Brooklyn.

I stayed in the back, steadying Hannaford over the bumps as Juney drove. We left the scanner on in case something new came over the wire.

I usually made small talk with the guy I was robbing so he'd know I wouldn't hurt him. This time, I kept quiet. I wanted Hannaford scared. Not too scared. Traumatized men are useless.

Like this smart-ass who ran a floating crap game in Ozone Park. He refused to pay protection. Big Paulie sent me and Angelo to rob his bankroll. We ordered him to open his safe. He was spinning the dial when Angelo decided to stick a pistol in his mouth. He was paralyzed. All he could manage were long, shrill squeals, and sucking breaths. We were so worried he'd have a heart attack, we split without the cash. He started paying every week, so it wasn't a total loss.

When a blue-and-white passed us on Eightieth Street, I knew everything was cool. There was no commotion around Hannaford's car, no cop combing the interior for clues.

Juney eased the front bumper up to the doors of Atlas Armored Services.

With one clean swipe, I pulled the tape from Hannaford's eyes, giving him a look at my boyish face for the first time. In his right mind, he'd have known I never served ten years in prison. I was twenty-one and looked eighteen.

A month earlier, I went to shake down a casino run by local hoods. The tough guy at the door asked me for ID, then told me it was fake. Who would believe the Gambino family sent me?

"The keys are in my top left pocket and the phone's gonna ring soon as we're inside," said Hannaford. "I gotta give my code."

I tucked my gun away and helped Hannaford down from the van. I'd faced enough men to know he wasn't the type to wrestle or run. He knew a couple of hours in the precinct and a phone call to Lloyd's of London was better than a wake and a funeral.

My heart pounded as I unlocked the door and followed Hannaford inside the garage. Armored trucks everywhere. A dream come true. I opened a truck door to peek inside and finally see what I'd been dreaming about for so long: a freezer without meat. Big deal. The spell was broken.

Bob and I walked into his office and stood next to his desk. I wrapped a napkin around the phone, and waited for it to ring. When it did, I put the phone to his ear.

"Hi," he said, as though greeting his wife, "it's me, Bob. I left my cigarettes in the office, just ran in to pick them up." He ran off a code. Someone spoke on the other end.

"No problems here." He smiled, like he was on a videophone. "I'm headin' out in a few. You have a good night."

I placed the phone back in the cradle.

He couldn't have done better.

Juney walked in with duffel bags. The vault was open, just like Nino said. Juney and I emptied it together, ready to leave in minutes.

I pointed to a clock on the wall, told Bob to sit still for an hour.

We left.

Juney dropped me off at the rent-a-car. I followed him to the junkyard, where we left the van to be crushed the next day.

I drove Juney home. There was a dim light in the front window. His parents were awake, watching television. They came to the door as my car idled in the street. I lowered my window to wave, "Hi, Mr. and Mrs. Trumonti."

Juney's mom held a steaming mug in her hand. "You wanna come in for some hot cocoa?"

"No, thanks, I'm dead tired, an' chocolate keeps me up."

Juney shook my hand and got out of the car. "Call me when you get up."

I waved once more as I pulled away.

At home, I took my clothes off and threw them in the bathroom hamper. I put on my father's bathrobe. My house was drafty in December since "heat's not free," as I'd been told all my life. My father was taller than me so the robe draped across my ankles, the belt hung to my knees.

When I passed my father's room, I heard him snoring. It was now over a year since my mother had died, but he hadn't recovered. He hardly left his room, not even to eat, so I'd bring home food: Chinks, pizza, burgers. I'd leave the bags on his bureau. Most times, the food would sit there and rot until I threw it out.

I peeked in; his arm was around a pillow, like he was still holding my mom. The air was stale. I crept over and gave him a soft kiss on the head, careful not to wake him.

I walked downstairs into the kitchen. The linoleum floor was sticky from spills we never sponged up.

My father kept his cigars in the refrigerator, the poor man's humidor. Sometimes I'd swing open the door expecting to see Mom's leftovers—slapped awake by a sour smell. The fridge light shone on empty shelves stained with milk, sauce, and soda. I reached into the bottom bin and took out a cigar. I peeled off the wrapper, removed the band, and bit the tip off, spitting it into the garbage pail. I rolled the cigar under my nose, sharp, bitter, not like the sweet aroma of Artie the Hair-Do's Cubans. I sat down in an armchair my mother bought when she redid the living room shortly before she died, because she knew two men would never redecorate.

As I puffed, I thought of my mother and how we never listened to her.

She didn't like my father smoking in the house. "We gotta paint every two years." "The kids' clothes stink." "I'm embarrassed to have company." He smoked anyway.

Her voice was so alive now that she was dead. Her jokes and laughter. Her kind, encouraging remarks. Sometimes I heard her yelling, venting, the petty arguments of family life.

It would take years before all her wisdom, the countless lessons she'd taught, veiled in domestic grievances, would at last sink in, and I'd realize that her nagging was only to have me, my father, and my sister do what was right.

Right now, I was young, wild, and shortsighted, smoking my father's cigar, wearing my father's robe, and living under my father's roof. But as midnight approached, I was a twenty-one-year-old self-made millionaire, if you're counting stolen bonds.

A SCREECHING HALT

I couldn't get cash," I groaned while carrying the duffel bags into my garage.

"It was a slow week," Hannaford had said during the robbery. "If you got me last week, you'd have made off with ten mil in cash, not notes."

I had to contact Uncle Jimmy.

Sneaker Pete always did right by me. I felt it wrong to contact Jimmy without going through Pete. I called him up. "We gotta meet for lunch."

I filled Pete in at the Palace Diner. His jaw dropped.

We finished eating and headed for the city.

"Me and Louie are comin' in," Pete told his uncle, "we're near the tunnel."

Jimmy knew a visit from me meant money.

We parked at a meter.

The concierge raised his head from a magazine when we walked into Jimmy's building. He jumped up to greet us. He was a real yenta, told us what every tenant was up to, who was fucking who, who lost his job, whose kid was no good. "I wonder what he says about us," I once said to Pete. "He mus' think we're a pair."

He dialed Jimmy to say we were on our way up, then ran ahead to hit the elevator button. I handed him a twenty.

Jimmy stood in his doorway holding a cup of coffee when Pete and

I got off the elevator. He looked like he'd just climbed out of bed, in a robe but no slippers. I noticed his feet and said, "Cut your toenails."

I didn't mean to embarrass him, but my mouth sometimes worked on its own. Jimmy put slippers on as Pete and I sat down on the living room couch. I told Jimmy what I had.

He was too cool to show emotion. "Bring everything in tomorrow, I'll get you top dollar."

That night, I slept well. I awoke early on Christmas Eve.

I had a busy day ahead of me. I was invited to a Christmas party at a social club on Linden Boulevard. I had to shoot into the city, drop off the bags at Jimmy's apartment, and I had plans to take my father and my girlfriend Cindy to dinner.

I had reservations for a cozy Italian restaurant with no Mob ties, otherwise I'd have to get up and kiss every wiseguy who walks through the door. By the time I'm done kissing every hood and his wife, my food is cold, and I feel like Richard Dawson from the old *Family Feud*.

I showered and ate breakfast. I put on a sweat suit, zipped up the collar, and loaded the duffel bags into my trunk for the second time in two days.

At the club, I hugged and kissed everyone, then gave an envelope to each of my closest friends. "A little somethin' for Christmas. I took down a nice score."

No one asked me anything. Cops ask questions, not us. We only spoke about a heist when we could get a joke out of it, either the nervous reaction of a victim or our own stupidity.

Once, on a heist, the Catalano brothers pushed a heavy vault onto a freight elevator. Chucky was about to step on when the cable snapped. The vault plunged ten floors and crashed into the basement. His brother told us the story. "Chucky's leg hovered over the empty shaft." Over the next few weeks, we all lifted a leg in the air whenever we saw Chucky.

I had one drink "for luck" then drove into the city. I used the Queensborough Bridge because it had no toll. A tollbooth officer seeing a young kid in a sleek ride might search my car just so he could feel like a cop.

Sneaker Pete wasn't missing a fart. He met me for a sandwich at the corner deli before we lugged the bags up to Jimmy's apartment. I didn't know how much the stuff I had was worth, but I knew Jimmy would be fair.

The three of us bullshitted a while before I told Jimmy, "I'm in a rush, I'm takin' my father an' my girl out to dinner."

Jimmy lived a stone's throw from the carriage rides along Central Park South. I drove past them on my way out of Manhattan, the only chance a city boy gets to see horses without going to Aqueduct or Belmont.

I crossed town. With my car unloaded, I sped through the tunnel into Queens, now driving like a maniac with nothing to lose but two points off my license. Halfway home, I remembered Cindy's present was at a jewelry store in Whitestone.

I made my way over to the shopping center, double-parked on the curb in front of the jewelry store, and ran in.

"I'm here for my necklace."

The guy behind the counter took out a tray of necklaces. He thought I was a new customer. "No," I said, "I already picked one, but it needed extra diamonds."

"Huh?" he asked.

I was about to say, "Gimme any fuckin' necklace," and forget about my deposit, when an older woman walked out of the back with a box in her hand.

"I remember you," she said.

"Oh, thank you." I folded my hands in prayer.

"Would you like me to wrap it?"

"I got no time!"

I didn't open the box to check it. I threw the money on the counter, jumped in my car, and was gone.

I made the ten-minute drive home in five. It was a long day but I got everything done. I saw my friends, gave out gifts, dropped off the bags in the city, and was now looking forward to dinner with Cindy and my father. And I was rich!

Driving up to my house, I slowed, about to whip a left into my driveway, from the opposite side of the street. I was cutting my front wheels over the double yellow line when my world, so fast and out of control, came to a screeching halt.

To this day, I'm sure I was dead. I came back to life lying in the street, spitting blood and teeth. I was ten or fifteen feet from my car, which was now a smoking heap of twisted steel. There were scraps of metal, broken plastic, and antifreeze puddles. Glass sparkled in the street, and was stuck in my clothes.

I never saw what hit me, so I couldn't make sense of anything. For a moment, I thought an airplane landed on my head.

I couldn't even stand, but I wanted to fight. Who? What for? I didn't know. It was my instinct to hit back.

My neighbor, Mrs. Whelan, appeared. She covered me with a blanket. Her mouth moved but I couldn't hear her, I was in a bubble.

I suddenly heard a scream. It was my father standing on the porch. He held his cheeks as he stumbled down the steps. He couldn't walk straight, like he was struggling with a heart attack.

I tried to say I was okay, but I couldn't speak. My jaw hung limp. Blood filled my nose and mouth, ran over my chin and down my neck.

My father and Mrs. Whelan lifted me up and steadied me as I wobbled like a battered heavyweight holding on in the last.

I don't know how long it was before the first ambulance arrived. Police never showed while I was there. I couldn't knock their horrible response time, it was why I got away with so many robberies.

I sat up in the ambulance to avoid drowning in my own blood. The EMT stuffed my mouth with gauze but it blocked my breathing, so he pulled it out and held a basin under my mouth. "The hospital's a few minutes away. I saw your car, people die from a lot less. There's an angel watching over you, kid."

At Booth Memorial Emergency Center, I was put in a wheelchair and pushed through electric doors over the exact spot where my mother was pronounced dead a year before.

"Mommy," I mumbled, reaching out a hand.

I was still awake when they shoved a long tube up my nose and down my throat. I was wheeled into the OR for emergency surgery.

This was the first hard smack I got for all the bad I'd done.

I was too dumb to feel it.

LIFE SUCKS THROUGH A STRAW

It was Christmas Day. The doctor who performed emergency surgery told my family, "I've worked on gunshot wounds to the jaw that weren't as bad."

I was in ICU, then rolled into a room. My head was the size of a basketball, and wrapped like a mummy. My mouth was wired shut, my jaw broken in two places.

I was shot with Dilaudid, which dulled the pain and sent me to la-la land. They hit me every four hours but the fix always wore off early. When I could stand, I'd chase the nurses up and down the hallways for my shot, pushing my IV pole, my ass hanging out of my smock.

I couldn't put thoughts in order, so I sang to myself. Family and friends talked about visiting me but I only remember wanting my shot, getting it, then singing.

When my head was unbandaged, I looked into a mirror for the first time. My face was fucked up. My lower jaw had shifted to the right.

I ran a hand over my face in disbelief. The left side was dead numb. Doc told me this had something to do with my main jaw nerve being torn or severed.

Within a week, I was released from the hospital.

My father found reason to leave his bed. He ran to the store, filled my prescriptions, and picked up cases of nutritional shakes. All my meals came through a straw.

Cindy was my live-in nurse. She sat beside my bed day and night, fixed blankets, fluffed up pillows, anything to make me comfortable. If I woke her from a dead sleep at three a.m. and asked her to run out for a Slurpee, she'd answer, eyes half closed, "Okay, what flavor?" I didn't deserve her.

Everyone stopped by to visit. When friends came over to the house, I'd ask Cindy to leave so we could discuss business. Men still needed protection, juice had to be collected, and truckloads of swag had to be moved.

Soon, the sidewalk in front of my house became a Mob meeting ground. Friends parked across neighbors' driveways. They walk-talked, hands over their mouths, in case of lip-reading surveillance.

My father kept poking his head through the shutters. He finally got an idea I was in the Mob.

One day, a friend and I went down into my basement to talk.

"What's wit' all this whisperin'?" my father asked when my friend left. "Why so many secrets? I don't understand."

To make matters worse, he got it in his head to shuffle through my mother's Mass cards. He was too frigged up to read them when she died. He came across names he saw in the newspapers, and confronted me.

"Common Italian names," I said.

"When does it end?" he muttered to himself, walking away.

The poor man was just starting to shake off the last blow when he was hit with this one.

It felt good to know people cared. I didn't realize how many friends I'd made.

On the day of the accident, Philly Fongool saw my wrecked car get hooked onto a flatbed in front of my house. I heard he cried like a baby, sure I was dead. When he saw me at home, he crushed me in his arms.

"Ba va fongool, I tawt you was dead." "Ba va fongool, I'll kill whoever done dis." "Ba va fongool, you gimme a heart attack like dis again, I'll kill ya."

A few days after I was home, I found out I'd been blindsided by a giant four-door sedan.

There's a slight hill just before my house. The driver was going so fast that when I checked my mirrors, I didn't see him behind me. He flew over the hill as I was slowing to make the left turn. He couldn't pass me on the right since cars were parked along the curb. Instead of braking and slamming me in the ass, he gunned it, and tried to make it around the nose of my car.

He blasted my driver's door at over seventy miles an hour. The impact flung me across the car, out the passenger door, and into the street. The driver's side of my car no longer existed. The driver's door was crumpled and smashed into the center console. Being unlawful saved my life; if I wore a seatbelt, I'd have been crushed instantly.

The driver was a neighborhood kid who ran home, a few blocks away. I sort of remembered him from grammar school. What I remembered of him I liked; quiet kid, his mother was a crossing guard.

My friends weren't happy with his minor injuries. They wanted to break him apart.

"It was an accident," I told them.

"At least lemme break his jaw," said Tony-Boy, "so he knows what you're goin' through." I wouldn't allow it. Since the kid had a shit policy, my lawyer suggested I sue his parents. I wouldn't do that either.

This was my first time-out from the fast life. I wasn't smart enough to use it wisely and think over my life. Instead, I watched TV. I had no attention span. I'd flip through the channels until I'd fling the remote. "Nothin's on."

A friend brought over a stack of magazines but I didn't read, couldn't get through a sentence without getting bored, or distracted. I looked at the pictures.

I couldn't fuck, too embarrassed with a fence in my mouth, missing teeth, and dragon breath. Cindy understood.

I carried an electric pump around the house to suck mucus from my mouth so I could breathe. Nights were rough. During brief periods of fitful sleep, the knots in the wires holding my jaw together would pierce my dry lips. In the morning, I'd stand in front of the mirror and pry my lips free, my fingers covered with blood.

Friends came by with ice cream shakes. Vinny the Hump brought manicotti in red sauce. He blended it into liquid, but my eyes bulged when I tried to suck it through a straw. I loved him for trying.

Nunzi the Gardener, a real tough guy, brought me a baby blue blanket his mother-in-law knitted.

And Sneaker Pete dropped off two brown shopping bags, each filled with banded stacks of crisp new bills.

MOB MED

Toward the end of January '92, gusting winds and driving rains slammed into the coast of Long Island. Roads flooded, trees snapped, and power lines fell.

I lay on the couch in my living room listening to old windows rattle when someone knocked at the door. I threw off my quilt and struggled to my feet to answer it. Tony the Twitch held on to the porch railing, his long leather coat flapping in the wind.

"C'mon, I'll getcha outta that house. The waves at the beach are twenty feet high. Get dressed, I got hot chocolates in the car."

I'd been cooped up in my house for a month. I was anxious to go. I dressed in layers, and we left.

The ride brought back memories.

As kids, me and my friends hung out on Rockaway Beach. We'd steal a car, hitch a ride, or chip in a buck apiece for gas and ask one of the older guys to drop us off. We'd pick a spot on the sand, set up a boom box, and break out the beers.

The girls at Rockaway had big hairdos and long nails. Some had tattoos, before they were common on every girl's ass and ankle. They were gum-chewing, bubble-blowing, foulmouthed, chain-smoking broads—just the way we liked them. We picked them up left and right.

The smart ones weren't as easy. I still tried.

I once asked a girl, "Whatchu readin'?"

She looked up from her book and said, "It's a textbook. I'm studying to be a financial consultant."

I had no idea what this meant.

"Good move." I nodded approval. "I thought about it myself."

We didn't know we were buffoons.

Back then, cops at the beach never gave a shit about alcohol. When we brawled with other guys, they broke it up and sent us off in different directions. No summonses, no arrests, just a warning to "cut the crap or go home."

Rockaway sand was littered with bags, bottles, even syringes after the Mob dumped hospital waste in the waters off Jamaica Bay.

Not one of us had a job. We laughed all day. When the sun went down, someone would say, "How the fuck we gettin' home?" Nothing like a clear head.

As I got older, I'd go to the beach when few or no people were there, summer nights or winter days. I'd walk off bad news, or plan a score in my head. Sometimes I went after a heist, to mull over loose ends.

I don't know what it was about the beach but ideas came to me, and answers to problems. I'd often say to myself, "Holy shit, I thought of that?"

Tony slid a Harry Chapin cassette into his tape player. He played "Cat's in the Cradle." Whenever he listened to this song, he'd go silent, stare at the road until it was over, then talk about his dad.

Tony had a rocky relationship with his father; they were close when Tony was a boy, distant in Tony's teens, and completely at odds by the time Tony turned twenty, only months before his old man died of a heart attack at the track.

"Probably dropped dead 'cause his horse won," Tony joked.

After the song, Tony would snap out of his daze. He'd swing his arms and slap the dash, give us both a laugh telling funny stories about his dad. Today, Tony blended memories of his father with the beach.

"My pop tole me about Robert Moses, some nutty Jew millionaire who built New York. Said he made the bridges out here low"—Tony looked up as we sped beneath one—"so Long Islanders wouldn't have to worry about titsoons gettin' bussed over to their beaches."

"Who the fuck are Long Islanders to keep blacks off their beaches?" I said. "Charge 'em a vig to walk on the sand is one thing, fuck 'em altogether is another."

The Robert Moses Causeway runs along the water's edge. The ocean view from passenger cars is blocked by dunes.

Tony pulled over and we got out to see the water. He helped me up the dunes.

Waves crashed into the shore. Wind whipped at my clothes, spraying my face with salt water. For the first time since my accident, I was wide awake.

"There's a glob of snot hangin' from your nose," Tony said. He went to the car and came back. "Here's some tissues an' a hat, it's a ski mask folded over into a hat."

I blew my nose then took the ski mask. "You forgot to dump this afta the las' job?"

"No, I buy in bulk. They're hard to find. Kids don't wear 'em no more, not like when we was young."

Tony filled me in on some action. "I collected a few grand for us off the street, an' I got a good tip on a massage parlor in Great Neck. The Korean Mafia threw the old madam out. She cried to me, said she rented the joint, brought the girls over, an' now they fucked her, jus' like that. Put her out on her ass."

"You screwin' her?" I asked.

"How'd you know? Juney tole ya?"

"No, you get all your tips in bed."

"Forty Gs. Friday nights. They collect from five or six joints, an' count it in hers, her old joint."

"Take Botz an' Juney. Make sure youse don't hurt the girls. Fuck the Koreans. Wear masks but yell a lot, let 'em know they got knocked off by Italians."

We stayed a good ten minutes before the wind drove us back to the car. I wiped my face dry, then looked at Tony in his wet, long black leather coat. "You look like the Gorton's fisherman's crooked brother who runs the waterfront."

We drove to the end of the causeway, where Tony said, "Wanna look for some deer?"

"Out here, on Long Island?"

"Yeah, they're all over. There's so many on Fire Island"—Tony pointed in the distance—"that people who live there don't let you feed 'em. My father took my mom for lunch on Fire Island before they was married. He bought a bag of apples in a grocery store, an' fed the deer. He got a fine."

"What's wit' these people? They don't like niggers. They don't like deers. If they make the bridges higher they can bus the deers out, but then they're stuck wit' the niggers. Bet if they could, they'd get ridda us, too."

Tony stretched his fingers and looked down at his olive-colored hand. "We jus' make the cut."

"Know what, let's feed the deer," I said, "if for nothin' else, jus' to break the law."

"Good idea. An' maybe we'll drive out here nex' week an' drop off a coupla niggers, give 'em some money to buy apples, tell 'em to feed the deers."

We laughed.

"Got anythin' they eat in here?" I shuffled through his glove box.

"Candy canes." He opened his center console. "I got some left over from Christmas. They might like the sugar."

We got out of the car and spotted three beautiful does, who looked at us as if to ask, "What are you doing, don't you know the law?"

We tossed the canes in front of them, then backed away. They were stiff, afraid, until we got back in the car. Then one approached, and the others followed. I watched them eat. I felt fulfilled, a creature-to-creature thing I liked but didn't quite understand: Tony was looking out for me, we were looking out for them, that's what life is about.

That day, Tony and I weren't gangsters, thieves, shylocks, or enforcers, just friends. We loved our families, we loved the idea of loyalty, we even loved each other. The streets, the whole Mob thing, gave us a sense of honor and camaraderie we both needed. An eighteen-year-old in the Midwest, searching for these same feelings, might join the army or marines. In our neighborhood, we threw in with the Mafia.

In late February, the oral surgeon told me my face would stay crooked if I didn't undergo a second operation. I dreaded a repeat of the pain and suffering, more months of wires, and lugging my mucus sucker around the house. In the end, I went ahead with it. They cut me open under my chin and screwed a titanium plate into my jaw.

After the surgery, my jaw was still crooked. Doc told me it would straighten out, like he was talking about a wheel alignment. His tune changed as March turned into April and my jaw was the same. He went from "this plate will definitely fix the problem" before the operation, to "sure hope it does" afterward.

I was conned. I didn't need the operation.

I told the doctor, "I shoulda known you was a crook when I saw you in a mask an' gloves. How much you make on an operation like this?"

He dodged the question.

"If he suckers one schmuck like me a month," I told Tony, "it's an extra two hundred grand a year in 'is pocket, a little seaside condo in the Caymans. They live in big mansions an' drive fancy cars, bums like us, out for a buck."

Eventually, my wires came off, and I got a new front tooth.

I had plenty of reason to smile. My name was put on the new list to get straightened out.

My friend Sal just got straightened out, and now he was getting married. For his bachelor party, me and ten friends flew to Florida and boarded a cruise ship to the Bahamas—Mob Med.

Our first night on ship, Patty Irish got drunk. He and I took a walk on deck. We were walking past some geek in a suit when Pat burped and said, "Excuse me."

The geek called Pat a pig.

Pat told him, "Go fuck yourself."

"No, you go fuck yourself," the guy said in a tit-for-tat tone.

"Don't be an asshole!" warned Pat.

"I'm not an asshole, you're an asshole." The little weasel pushed his luck.

Pat hit him. The guy fell backward into the pool, which, lucky for him, was drained at night with a safety net slung across it. He lay there rocking, asleep like a baby.

"Whatta you think, you're on Wall Street," Pat yelled down at him, "where you can go back an' fort' wit' words all day, an' nobody does shit about it? Fuck you. No, fuck you . . . ," Pat mimicked him, as we walked away from our first assault.

Pat went inside for more drinks.

I met up with Tony-Boy on deck. He was hitting on two women. He introduced me. They were a few years older than us. Heavily made up. Low-cut dresses. Fake tits. Players.

"What's with the cast?" one asked me.

The week before, I broke my knuckles on someone's head.

"I broke my wrist skiing."

"Which mountain?"

"Mount Rushmore." I couldn't think of a ski slope.

They laughed, knew we were hoods. Just as they agreed to come back to our room for a bottle of wine, this kid out past his bedtime ran over and tugged at my shirt. "Y'all from New Yahk?"

"What's the problem, son, los' ya mother?" I asked, as I'm thinking, Sonofabitch, what's this little runt want with us as we're about to get lucky?

"Ya buddy's gittin' an ass whuppin' inside." The kid pointed to the lounge.

Tony and I took off. I knew it was Patty Irish, figured the geek rounded up his Ivy League friends. But when I passed the pool, he was still in the net, sound asleep.

In the lounge, a group of ship's officers were huddled around a couch. I looked over someone's shoulder and saw Patty Irish's freckled face pressed into a cushion.

He rolled an eye toward me, then said out of the side of his mouth, "Hit 'em, Louie!"

I slammed my cast into a sailor's face. I clocked another one as Tony-Boy threw himself into the mix.

Pat got up swinging. He was tall, the sailors were short; they ran around in circles trying to get away from him.

As they ran out of the lounge, me, Tony, and Pat were yelling, "You know who the fuck we are?" as if these world travelers might have any idea who in the hell we were, a drunken Irishman and a bunch of guidos from Queens.

Pat said, "Let's take over the ship." He insisted it would be no different from sailing his fifty-foot Sport Fisherman. We let him carry on drunk, while some cute broad told me what happened.

"They wanted to close the bar. He hopped over the counter and started mixing drinks for everybody. The bartender ran away and came back with those sailors you beat up. They tackled your buddy when he wasn't looking."

Word spread quickly. Our guys came running from all over the ship. We crammed into Vinny Milano's room.

"We're gettin' pinched when we dock in the Bahamas," I yelled from the bathroom, where I was washing blood off my cast.

Franky Stitches agreed. "They didn't do it yet 'cause the brig can't hold all of us."

"Besides," said Tony-Boy, "we jus' knocked the shit outta them. I'd board a lifeboat if I was them."

We talked about Caribbean prisons. Some swore they were great. "Forget the guards, even the wardens are for sale," said Franky. Others spoke as though the jails were like Devil's Island. Nobody knew shit.

Chucky told Vinny Milano to get ahold of Bruce Cutler. A minute later, the captain called Vinny's room, and invited him to his quarters.

"They're not pinchin' us," Vinny said when he got back. "The captain poured me a scotch, an' asked if I could control youse."

"Get outta here!" I said. "The hull mus' be filled wit' dope. Why else would they give us a pass? Crooked bastards!"

When we went ashore, the captain kept his word. No cops.

We had a calm day on dry land.

When we got back to the ship, the crew, bruised and bandaged, stood at attention as guests boarded. I draped a jacket over my cast, not to flaunt my weapon.

Cruise lines hide incidents to keep a good record, probably why the captain buried the brawl. In our minds, they found out who we were and got scared.

Back in Queens, I waited for the new list with my name on it to get passed around to the five families. I had a dozen good men under me, even more through them. I was already equal to a made man, since I answered directly to the heads of my family.

The ceremony was formality.

PART II

THE INVESTIGATION

A FIST AT THE DOOR,
A KNIFE IN MY BACK

O ne April morning, I was awakened by a knock at the door.

"Go away." I pulled the sheet over my head.

The knocking got louder and harder. I threw off the covers and climbed out of bed.

"If that's the meter reader, he's dead."

My bedroom window was above the front porch. I lifted the blinds and saw two men in trench coats. "Shit! DTs."

I sat on the edge of my bed.

"Who's to say I'm home? I got enough boxes of pasta to las' me a year. I'll wait 'em out."

I thought about pulling a switcheroo.

A couple of years back, cops surrounded Botz's apartment. Botz called his brother, Tommy, who looked just like him.

"Swing by my place," he said to Tommy. "Wear bright clothes an' a baseball cap."

Ten minutes later, Tommy parked in Botz's driveway. Botz opened the door, hustled him in, and closed it behind him.

"The bulls are sittin' on the corner," said Tommy. "For you?"

"Yeah, gimme your clothes."

Neither brother had shaved that morning, adding to their resemblance and disguise.

Botz put on Tommy's red Windbreaker and Yankees cap, left the house, and drove away in Tommy's car. Seconds later, Tommy left in Botz's car and drove the opposite way.

The cops hit the siren, cut in front of Tommy, and jumped out with guns drawn.

Tommy took the key out of the ignition and tossed it into the street. He raised his hands. "I give up."

Botz was long gone by the time Tommy was torn from the car and thrown to the pavement. Tommy told the cops who he was. They grabbed his wallet to check his license as he snickered. They roughed him up, a couple of kicks, then let him go.

Botz found out he'd been fingered in a robbery. He turned himself in six months later when the case was weak, and beat the rap.

I couldn't think of anyone who looked like me. Besides, could cops be that stupid twice?

I picked up the phone and called Juney. If my line was bugged, the cops on my porch weren't tapped in.

"Pick me up in the alleyway behind my house." I hung up, got dressed, and ran into my basement. I undid four locks and two dead bolts, opened the back door, and ran out into my yard.

I climbed over neighbors' fences and waved to Mr. Sabatini, who was crouched over his vegetable garden.

"Nice day for a walk," I said, smiling. He was more concerned about me stepping near his plants than seeing me hurdle fences at seven a.m.

Juney was waiting in the alley as I swung my leg over the last fence and got in his car.

"Bulls?" he asked.

"Yeah, go to Sneaker Pete's."

"Whatchu do?"

"What didn't I do?"

Every morning, small-time thieves who boosted merchandise from department stores showed up at Pete's store. Pete was bringing stolen goods in through his back door when me and Juney got there.

"Close shop," I told him, "I might have to go on the lam."

Pete paid the thieves and locked the door behind them. I was telling

Pete about the trench coats on my porch when Limpy, Pete's salesman, limped into the back room. "Hey, Pete, FBI's out front, they wanna talk to the boss."

"You tole 'em I'm here, you idiot? I got stolen shit all over the place."

I poked an eye out. "Same two from my house."

One of them spotted me. "Hello, Mr. Ferrante."

I walked out.

"FBI," said the agent. He flashed his badge.

"We'd like a word with you, outside."

"I don't talk to agents."

Since my car accident, I spoke out of the side of my mouth. They must've thought I was doing my best Cagney impression.

"Then take this!"

He waved a subpoena in front of me.

I heard somewhere that if the paper doesn't touch you, it's not officially served. So I backed away.

"It's yours." He slammed it on the counter.

"Give it to my lawyer."

"Who's your lawyer?"

"Anthony Castanza." I gave him the name of my accident lawyer.

"Do you have his number?"

"Not on me."

"Where's he located?"

"Northern Boulevard."

"Do you have his address?"

I shrugged my shoulders. "Queens."

He grinned, and they left.

Pete walked out of the back room smoking two cigarettes. One hung from his lip, the other was in his hand. "FBI," he said, "we're fucked."

"I never saw 'em behind us," said Juney.

"We had no tail. They musta known Pete's store was one of our haunts. We stop here every day."

I walked to a pay phone and called some friends, curious to know if

I was in the middle of something big. I knew feds liked to round people up at the same time. Maybe they hand out subpoenas the same way. No one heard anything.

I called Anthony Castanza. His card was in my wallet the whole time. I didn't want to open it in front of the agents, worried scraps of paper with loan shark figures would fall out.

"FBI? Get a real lawyer," Anthony whined.

"But you are a real lawyer."

"I'm not really real. I'm an ambulance chaser, no match for the FBI."

"Well, I tole 'em to call you. Jus' find out what they want, then I'll get somebody real."

The following day, the same agents returned to Pete's store and gave Pete a subpoena.

Pete lived on cigarettes and coffee. When I stopped by his store that night, the bathroom door was open. There was a coffeepot on the toilet tank and cigarette butts in the bowl.

"You been shittin' all day?" I asked.

"No, no, I go in there to think."

Next morning, Botz called me. "I got one too."

He sounded excited, like it was a ticket to the Super Bowl. I think he felt left out until now. He was the opposite of Pete. I told him I'd meet him later at the sanitation yard where he worked.

Before Botz ran with me, he got drunk in a bar and decided to stick up the liquor store on his corner "for kicks."

Botz got nabbed walking home. I never let him live this down. "You were robbin' liquor stores for beer money when I met you."

Botz pled out and served a couple of years up north. He came home and hooked up with me. He was still on parole when the FBI served him. His parole officer could've revoked his parole, but didn't. We figured the FBI told his parole officer to back off so they could watch him.

A capo from our family put Botz to work at a sanitation yard where another parolee worked. The two, knowing their POs dropped in regularly, washed out the shell of a broken-down box truck and hooked up a construction light inside. They set up a card table with folding chairs and played gin rummy for a buck a point. If either of their POs showed up to check on them, the yard foreman tapped on the side of the truck and yelled for the guy who needed to appear before his PO.

When I dropped in on Botz to bullshit about the subpoenas, the foreman knocked on the side of the truck. Botz came out with a wrench in his hand. "Oh, shit, it's you." He dropped the wrench.

"Play solitaire," he yelled inside. "I'll be right back."

We walked the yard, talking over the noise of bulldozers pushing trash. We couldn't figure out who was talking and how much the FBI knew.

"Who else got served besides me, you, an' Pete?" asked Botz.

"Uncle Jimmy got one too; they came to his house. I'm bangin' my brains out tryin' to figure out how they put us all together. I'm goin' into the city tonight, see what Jimmy thinks."

"Whatever we gotta do," Botz said before I left. I didn't know what he meant. Either he was ready to do time or wanted to off the snitch when we found out who he was.

That day, the FBI spoke with Sneaker Pete's lawyer. They read off a list of heists and hijackings I did, some I didn't even remember. They said that I was the target of the investigation.

Pete was relieved to hear this. So was I; I couldn't take watching him crumble another day. He was never too clean to begin with. After his subpoena, he stopped brushing his teeth and combing his hair altogether. His normal dandruff level rose from a light dusting to a blizzard.

"Go home later an' take a bath," I told Pete on our way to see Uncle Jimmy. I stuck my head halfway out his car window.

"I'm starvin'." He rubbed his belly. "Let's get somethin' to eat."

"Go to Butino's," I said.

Butino's was an Italian buffet near the junkyards in Maspeth, only a couple of miles off the expressway. It was easy for us to grab a bite there before driving through the tunnel. We knew the owner; his mother did the cooking. He'd usually seat us, then bring over our favorite dishes.

"Why the puss?" Butino asked as he put plates in front of us. Neither of us answered. He sensed tension and left us alone.

I poked at the food, trying to eat, when I suddenly blurted, "We're not goin' into the city."

"Why not? Maybe my uncle knows somethin'."

"Your uncle's the rat."

"You're crazy!"

"Wish I was."

We spent a few seconds staring at each other before I broke the silence. "You said the feds mentioned an electronics truck to your lawyer?"

"Yeah, so?"

"We never stole one."

"I know, they're confused, that's good."

"They ain't confused, you are. An' so was I, 'til now."

"I don't get it."

I reminded Pete about the time he thought Jimmy was taking advantage of us. He wanted Jimmy to think we had a better fence so he came up with the idea of promising Jimmy a load, then telling him later that we sold it to a higher bidder.

"I ain't in on it," I told Pete. "Jimmy's been fair. You're jus' lookin' to squeeze your uncle for more money."

I wouldn't give in, until the perfect situation presented itself and Pete insisted. "Jus' to keep Unc honest."

I knew some poor bastard who married a spendthrift. His wife shopped all day while he broke his ass. He couldn't keep up with her spending, couldn't cut it with two jobs, so he took on a third at Busy Body Electronics. A few days into his new job, he called me on his break.

"There's a trailer full of electronics on one of the loading docks. Who knows how long it'll be here. You gotta move quick. You'll need a rig, it's on blocks."

I made some phone calls, got ahold of Mario. He borrowed a rig while I met up with Jimmy, who scribbled off an address in Yonkers where I was to deliver the load.

Mario drove. Funzi came. We went that night.

We bounced around, the three of us cramped across the front seat. Mario dropped his cigarette; Funzi hit the shifter with his knee, trying to pick it up. The windshield was cracked. The horn didn't work, nor the speedometer.

I asked Mario, "How fast we goin'?"

"We're good," he said, "I'm ridin' wit' traffic."

He was keeping pace with a Maserati I swore was clocking ninety.

Mario and Funzi started fighting over the radio station until the knob broke off. The truck swerved in and out of lanes as we moved from one blunder to the next.

At the store, Mario pulled our bumper up to the rear gates. The lot was deserted except for one trailer, its ass against the dock.

I clipped the padlock, removed the chain, and swung open the gates. Funzi directed Mario through the entranceway.

I opened the side door of the trailer and took a peek inside. A wall of boxes. I shone my flashlight on the writing: TVs, VCRs, and stereos.

"We're good to go," I said to Funzi. "Hook it up."

Mario backed the tractor into the trailer, creating an eighteen-wheeler. Funzi connected the lights and brake lines, and we were speeding down the expressway five minutes later.

We drove less than two exits when Mario said, "We got shit, may as well dump it now."

I looked at him, waiting to see him smile, even though it wasn't funny. He exhaled smoke, then tossed the butt out the window, shaking his head.

"Whatchu talkin' 'bout? I seen it myself, we're loaded."

"Louie," said Mario, "I'm drivin' trucks thirty years, it's fuckin' empty, I can feel it when I gas an' brake."

"You'll see." I was sure of myself. "It's that new lightweight shit, not that big bulky crap you grew up wit'."

We pulled into Sergio's shop to take a quick inventory before delivering the truck. I jumped down and broke open the rear door.

"Full." I pointed at the boxes.

"Don't make sense," said Mario. "Get up there an' throw one down."

Funzi hoisted himself up onto the ledge. He lifted a box like one of those fake boulders they use in Hollywood. "Muthafucka!" He threw it across the shop. He picked up another and threw it even farther.

We'd stolen a storage unit packed with the empty boxes for the store's display models.

When I told Pete, "We got shit," he called Jimmy and lied. "We came off bigger than expected, but dumped the load to a higher bidder."

This lie made Jimmy the only man in the world who believed our phantom load was real. If the feds mentioned it, Jimmy was talking.

"I need a cigarette," Pete said. He lit me a Newport, then lit one for himself.

I took a pull and exhaled. "Jimmy was a fraud."

"That filthy sonofabitchin' bastard!"

"Your uncle musta spit out everythin', even shit he heard."

"How long ya think he's been a stoolie?"

"Not long, or they'da bagged us years ago. Call your cousin, find out if Jimmy jus' took a pinch, an' for what. I bet it was somethin' big for him to turn."

Before we left Butino's, Jimmy called Pete's cell phone.

"Answer it," I told Pete, "but tell 'im we can't make it, maybe another day."

When Pete hung up with Jimmy, he said to me, "He sounded real nervous when he heard we wasn't comin'."

"Sure. He mus' be wired. Better yet, agents are probably in his bedroom. I can picture the scene: me an' you, two chooches sittin' in his livin' room, askin' Jimmy who he thinks the rat is, wit' the feds behine the door, fallin' over themselves, laughin' at us. Jimmy woulda walked us through every crime. I can hear 'im now, talkin' into the mic buried in his chest hairs, 'Ya think they know 'bout this . . . , an' how 'bout that?' 'No way,' I'd've said, 'no one knows 'bout that but us' . . . an' the entire FBI."

"If we didn't stop for a bite, we'd be dead already," Pete said.

Pete called his cousin George, Jimmy's son. I put my ear to the phone.

"I'm not supposed to tell you anything," George said, "but I will."

"He broke in three seconds," I whispered to Pete, "jus' like his ole man."

"My father got pinched for dope," George went on, "but he's out on bail. He's givin' everyone up, even I got a subpoena, but he tole me not to worry about it, 'cause I'm in on the deal he cut for himself."

George made sense. A few months back, Jimmy had approached me and Pete with a drug deal.

"China White," he said, "straight from Hong Kong. It goes for one seventy-five a key, after it's hit once. I'll give it to you for one twenty-five, uncut. You two can move a key a week, and split two hundred grand a month."

Drugs weren't Jimmy's game. That kind of talk sounded strange coming out of his mouth. Why dabble in babania so late in life? That day, I doubted Jimmy for the first time.

"Let's do it, it's a no-brainer," Pete said on our way home.

"You're a no-brainer."

Pete was sharp. It was greed talking.

I shied away for several reasons.

First, the family had a strict rule against drugs. Certain guys still handled powder, but at their own risk.

My friend Nicky No Luck was with a crew in Canarsie. His brother-in-law gave him a good coke connection in Colombia. Nicky asked his skipper to release him so he could rake in some drug dough.

His skipper let him go, with conditions: Nicky had to cut all ties with the crew, and move out of the area, so there'd be no mistaking that Nicky was on his own and not secretly operating under Mafia council.

Nicky agreed and his skipper gave him a kiss and his blessing, "Good luck."

But Nicky No Luck lived up to his name. He was swept up in a drug sting and handed a life sentence by a hanging judge. I didn't want to end up like Nicky.

The other reason I chose to stay away from drugs had to do with my immediate family.

My mother's only brother was a heroin addict for thirty years. When I was a kid, my mother and grandmother paced the floors all night, wondering where he was and if he was alive. Methadone programs. Trips to prison. He put everyone through hell. I refused to bring this curse down on another family.

Lastly, I loved heists and hijackings, and saw no need for a career change.

It was a good thing I talked Greedy Pete out of it, or we would've been facing more charges, plus a death sentence from the family.

George told us his father was a "dry snitch"; Jimmy agreed to squeal but refused to testify in open court.

The bureau was at a dead end. They had no evidence, and their snitch wouldn't take the stand.

I cleaned out my house.

My first run, I left with more weapons than Rambo used in four movies.

Next, I got rid of a pile of bullet-riddled telephone books lying around the basement. The Mob doesn't operate a shooting range. After we bought guns, we'd go down to the cellar, stack phone books up against the wall, and fire rounds into them, testing the guns to make sure they worked. A small-caliber handgun would drive a round deep into the Queens Pages. The blast from a big gun would send its bullet straight through the Queens Pages, and more than halfway through the Yellow Pages, the bullet lodged somewhere between Plumbing and Real Estate.

Guns hot, powder burning, ears ringing, we'd air out the room, and leave.

There were scraps of paper all over my bedroom, the same room where I pushed Tonka trucks and played with G.I. Joes. Some scraps had tips:

"Tues Thurs safe sixty grand."

"Teller #4 Mon Fri 10–6."

"Fogarty Trucking JFK loading dock 8."

Other scraps had shylock figures:

"Johnny Ravioli 2500."

"Billy Brains 8000."

"Tootsie Roll Teddy two weeks behind."

Sneaker Pete said, "Don't throw away papers, burn 'em. I heard feds go through your garbage."

I stuffed all my papers into a shopping bag and drove underneath the Van Wyck Expressway, where it rises over Flushing Meadow–Corona Park.

I chose this spot because it was dark and deserted, same reason I picked it years before, first time I burned a car.

I was sixteen when my mailman handed me his keys. "Can you get ridda this?" He pointed to a red, late-model Monte Carlo parked behind him. "It's mine, I want the insurance money."

"Sure." I took the keys.

"Five hundred," I told him. "An' gimme a day or two to zip aroun', have some fun before you report it."

My friends and I took turns driving. We had a ball.

When the joyride was over, we went to a gas station and filled up an olive oil can. Gas swished around in the can as we drove.

Juney lit a cigarette and hung his arm out the window.

"Put that out!" I smacked his hand.

We parked under the Van Wyck. I doused the interior, stepped back, tossed a match, and nearly fried myself. I had no idea the car would blow that fast.

Today, I got out of my car and took a big shopping bag out of my trunk. Trucks rumbled above. I dumped a pile of small papers into a dented hubcap, lit it, and watched them burn. I remembered the night when flames from the car touched the overpass, a big blaze for such a small crime. This time, I was burying a thousand felonies in a small fire.

Insurance jobs, tag jobs, stolen cars, chop shops, trucks, vaults, banks, credit cards, gambling, extortion, loan-sharking, I wondered how much the feds knew, and how far they went back.

To avoid being picked up on a bug, Pete and I started to walk-talk in St. John's Cemetery, a few blocks from Pete's store.

During our strolls we came across the headstones of Lucky Luciano, Vito Genovese, Carlo Gambino, and other infamous gangsters.

"Saint John mus' be the patron saint of the Mafia," I joked to Pete. He believed me and started praying to him.

Jimmy's betrayal hurt me.

How could Jimmy snitch me out after so many years on the street? He built such a strong name, and sold it so cheap.

Jimmy ate and laughed with me, hugged and kissed me, taught me so much, then roasted my ass to get his own off the fire. There had to be more, something to make me say, "Oh, so that's why." I wouldn't agree, but maybe I'd understand.

I racked my brain. Was there anything I'd done to Jimmy to deserve this?

I thought of small things like telling him to cut his ugly toenails, and big things like going with George, Jimmy's son, to Florida, where the kid met his mother for the first time.

Twenty years earlier, Jimmy divorced George's mom. He kept George and set his ex up down south, twelve hundred miles away. The woman never sought custody or even tried to visit. When George got older and asked about his mom, Jimmy said she was a "crackpot" and forbade him to see her.

Sneaker Pete's mom and George's mom were sisters. Jimmy was Pete's uncle through marriage, not blood. Pete never mentioned this when Jimmy was king shit. He said it a thousand times after Jimmy ratted.

Like George, Pete was raised by his father. Every few years, Pete drove down the coast to see his mom, a token visit to keep himself in the will; if she had ten bucks and a lava lamp, he wanted it.

Whenever Pete visited, he saw George's mom. She worked in the same factory as his own mother.

One summer night, Pete pulled up in front of my house. "Wanna come to Florida?" he asked. "My wife an' George are in the camper. I rented it, ya gotta see the inside."

I needed a break from the action. I called Juney. "Hold down the fort while I'm away."

We joked along the ride. George sometimes grew silent and stared out the window as we laughed.

"What's on ya mind?" I asked. "Wanna talk?"

"I'm takin' him to see his mother for the first time," Pete answered for George.

"Wit' your uncle's blessin'?" I asked Pete, knowing Jimmy didn't want George to see his mother.

"No," answered Pete, "George is a grown man."

"So's your uncle."

I felt like shit, dishonoring Jimmy's wishes.

"It's got nothin' to do wit' us," said Pete.

"Bullshit! We're drivin' 'im."

George's silence while we talked about him was proof he'd never make this trip alone. George may have wanted to go for a walk, but Pete was holding his leash.

We drove nonstop. Near Florida, George started to talk and convinced me this was what he wanted, to see his mom just once.

After a night's sleep in Daytona, Pete and I took George for lunch, then drove him to the factory where his mom worked. We got there early, before work let out.

Pete and George chain-smoked. They flicked butts out the window for over an hour, until two of the palest women I'd ever seen under a Florida sun stepped out of the factory, squinting. They both lit cigarettes; one crumpled the empty pack and dropped it to the ground. Their pocketbooks were old thrift-shop specials. They wore tube tops, their tits squished out the sides.

"There's your mother." Pete pointed the butt of his cigarette toward the two women.

I cringed in my seat, feeling sorry for George. His face blossomed with a big smile. Did he see what I saw?

He pulled at the door handle, almost fell out of the camper. He ran toward his mom, melted into her chest and cried, "Mommy, Mommy, I love you."

My eyes watered up. Pete snickered as ashes from his cigarette broke off and fell into his lap.

"You're heartless," I said. "How can you laugh at that?"

"That moron jus' hugged my mother. His mother's behine her."

Pete's mom pushed George away.

George's mother stepped up, but it was too late, George was spent.

"Hi." He reached out a hand.

Poor bastard, I thought, even this couldn't go right for him.

George dragged himself back to the camper and slumped into the seat.

The women gave Pete a quick hello, got into an old clunker, and sped away.

I patted George on the shoulder. He'd waited so long for nothing. He dropped the visor and looked into the vanity mirror, searching for a resemblance.

As we pulled away, Pete laughed, George was about to cry, and I knew why Jimmy forbade George to see his mother. I felt I'd betrayed Jimmy just being there.

Lying in bed, remembering this wretched scene, my subpoena crumpled up in my hand, I considered Jimmy's actions as payback.

I was naïve, and didn't yet know the power of self-preservation.

SAMMY THE BULL(SHITTER)

I was at Little Paulie's house watching TV and eating pizza when the front door opened and Big Paulie drifted in with a vacant look on his face.

"Who's dead?" I expected to hear a friend got whacked.

"My brother," he slurred, "I jus' lef' the lawyer's office. Sammy went bad." He dragged himself up the steps.

Less than a year before, federal agents pulled John Gotti and our underboss, Sammy "the Bull" Gravano, off the street. Since then, the two were housed in a high-rise federal lockup in downtown Manhattan.

Sammy was a tough guy, hard as steel. I couldn't believe he was begging prosecutors to let him off the hook, blowing them for leniency.

"No way," I said to Little Paulie, "Sammy's gonna do the 'Frankie Five Angels,' guaranteed!"

When we played cards in social clubs, we'd often mimic scenes from *The Godfather*.

In the movie *The Godfather II*, Frankie Five Angels is about to testify against Mafia boss Michael Corleone, when he recants his earlier testimony. He plays dumb, claims the government made him lie. Because of this, Corleone is free to go.

I mixed movie reels with reality, thought Sammy planned to snitch then double-cross the government so John could walk.

"Sammy knows he's finished, why not save John?" I said to Little Paulie. "He'll go out like a champ. I'd do it."

My mind was so mobbed up, I couldn't accept that the number-two man in our family went sour. What's it all for, if our underboss is a punk? We were tough guys, more honorable than everyone else. So we thought.

That night marked the beginning of the end for the Mafia. After Sammy flipped, other big-shot mobsters thought it was okay.

I gaped at the wound opened by Jimmy the Jeweler, tried to find something he said or did that might've given me a clue. Nothing. Had he been acting all along? Was Sammy an actor, too?

I don't think so. I came to the conclusion that many mobsters would never have imagined their own treachery had they never been arrested.

THEY'RE EVERYWHERE

I grew up in an attached row house.

For as long as I can remember, my mother planted flowers and mowed our small square of front yard. After she died, the flowers wilted, the grass burned, and the bare hedges trapped garbage that blew in the wind.

I was embarrassed whenever I brought home a date, so I called Nunzi the Gardener.

I was backing out of my driveway one morning when Nunzi tapped on my window.

"You bein' watched," he said in his thick Sicilian accent as he rolled his eyes across the street. "Two guys. If I'ma right, they gonna follow you whena you leave. Checka you mirra."

"Thanks."

I circled my block, then shot down a one-way street the wrong way. They followed me. I got onto the expressway, punched the pedal, and lost them.

The following day, I heard an engine humming in my driveway. I looked out the front window and saw a tow truck.

A lanky bearded man hustled up the steps. I opened the door before he knocked. "What's up?"

"I jus' wanna give you a heads-up, cops been watchin' you all week. They sit in fronta my house." He looked down the block. "Keep your eyes open."

"Thanks, they're agents. Anythin' I can do for ya?"

"No, I'm good."

Starting that week, I saw agents everywhere, real and imagined.

I was driving with Sergio when I pulled into a gas station on Wood-haven Boulevard to see if the car I thought was tailing me would pull in behind.

When it did, I laughed to Sergio. "See, I tole ya."

The car stopped alongside a pump but waved the attendant away.

I paid for my gas, then peeled off a bill. "Fill up their tank, too." I pointed to their car. "Tell 'em we're headin' out to Montauk, it's a long ride."

After the attendant relayed my message, the passenger waved. "Thanks."

I drove off while the nozzle was stuck in their tank, and lost them.

One afternoon, Juney and I stopped in Roy Rogers on Union Turnpike. We ordered burgers and fries. Two suits were standing behind us. I turned around with my tray as they stepped up to the counter and ordered "one small french fries."

"See if they watch us," I told Juney.

The place was nearly empty, and they sat at a table next to us.

As they picked at their fries, I leaned over and said, "No expense account? Splurge, the roast beef's delicious."

They smirked, and followed me the rest of the day.

Another time, me and Sneaker Pete were chowing down in a diner in Ridgewood. A guy in a neat cheap suit sat in the booth behind me and ordered a coffee.

By now, I was a complete nut; everyone was an agent. I even thought the hot dog man who parked his cart by Sergio's shop was undercover until I watched him steal a set of hubcaps from an old Chrysler and put them on his own car.

Even then, I doubted him. "It's all parta his con," I told my crew. "Let's not talk by the hot dog stand anymore."

So the guy inside the diner really got me thinking when he held a newspaper up in front of his face.

I turned to look at him twice before I whispered across the table to Pete, "Who the fuck reads the paper in the air? He's an agent."

"Las' week you thought the cook was an agent." Pete laughed, looking at the toothless black man wearing a tall chef's hat, flipping burgers on the grill. "You even made me ask the owner when he hired 'im."

"All right, I was wrong about 'im, but this guy behine me's no good."

As we got up to leave, I said to Pete, "Watch this." I poked my head around his paper. "Have a nice day, Mr. Agent."

"And a good day to you, Mr. Ferrante."

He threw me off balance, since I barely believed my own bullshit.

THE ITALIAN CHINCESS

I was used to seeing agents watching us at all the known hangouts. They even showed up at wakes and funerals. When John Gotti's father was laid out at Romanelli's in June '92, an agent aimed a zoom lens at me from across the street as I walked into the funeral home. But they were photographing everyone. Now I landed the starring role, and I loved it. It puffed up my ego, fed my hunger for excitement; I got high without robbing.

I was driving home from Howard Beach one night when I picked up a tail but lost it on the Van Wyck Expressway. As I pulled into my driveway, I heard a helicopter. I opened my door and looked up, blinded by a spotlight. I could hear the pilot in my head, "Up here, stupid!"

Botz told me later, "I threw out my garbage unda a spotlight. I was in my boxers, I shook my nuts at 'em."

"They were by me too," I said. "That's good news, means they got shit, they're tryin' to shake us up."

After seeing agents in the sky, I thought they were behind every cloud. Now how do I lose them?

I gave a young kid from my neighborhood a hundred bucks to follow me into the Midtown Tunnel. We stopped traffic in the middle and switched cars. I drove out in a noisy Firebird with big red dice dangling from the mirror. I could barely see through the tint. I circled Second Avenue and drove back to Queens.

I thought I was slick, but I tip my hat to the feds. No matter how many times I lost them, they never went away.

Agents started to question everyone around me, even girls I dated.

Cindy lived with her mom in a garden apartment in Rosedale. One day, she got home from school and found her mom crying. "You're wanted for questioning by the FBI," said her mom.

Cindy knew it had something to do with me. She called.

"They left their number," she said. "What should I do?"

"Call 'em back."

"What should I tell them?"

"Whatever they wanna know."

I never spoke in front of her. She knew nothing.

The agents paid her a visit at her home. They showed her mug shots of felons old enough to be her father. "Can you identify any?" She couldn't.

When the agents told her the men were snitching on me, she boldly pointed to one of the photos. "You believe a man with a black eye?"

The agent shrugged.

Cindy walked them to the door, insisting I was a great guy, kind, caring, and compassionate. If I was, this wasn't the side of me they were particularly interested in.

Agents visited another girl. She'd given me her number in a diner on Northern Boulevard. We spoke on the phone then hooked up. I screwed her in the backseat of my car, and dropped her off.

I forgot about her until she called, a year later, during the investigation. She reminded me who she was, then said, "My dad was away on business when the FBI came by and told us he faced twenty years in prison. They left their card. When my dad called them, they mentioned you, said something about a heist, and that he should come clean. Apparently, they traced your phone number to mine. Did you commit a crime, because my father works for an alarm company paid to secure a warehouse they say you robbed. They swear you and my dad are in cahoots."

I now knew the FBI was going through my phone records. Mobsters could be linked to me, big deal. Girlfriends, so what. Only one phone number concerned me. It belonged to a woman I'd often sneak off to meet. If the FBI paid her family a visit, it could cost me my life.

Growing up, I lived around the corner from Dr. Robert Siena and family. My mother was close with Mrs. Siena; her two children were the same ages as me and my sister.

When Dr. Siena became a big to-do, he and his family moved to a wealthy Jersey suburb. Our families stayed close because of my mother; dinner once a year, family functions, shit like that.

At nineteen, I went to a twenty-first birthday party in Jersey for the doctor's daughter. I hit it off with a girl at the party and we made plans to see each other again.

Dr. Siena heard about it, and phoned me. "Be careful, her dad is the Mafia boss who wanders Manhattan in a bathrobe, talking to parking meters."

Siena still saw me as a kid, had no idea I was in the Mafia.

Vincent "Chin" Gigante was the most powerful Mafia boss in the country. What are the odds I'd meet his daughter? And that she'd become one of my closest friends?

At the time, Chin Gigante and John Gotti were archenemies.

Five bosses sit on the New York Mafia Commission. Although all are equal, Gigante was more equal, a legend in his own time.

John Gotti killed Paul Castellano and took over the Gambino family without consent from the Commission. Because of this, Gigante ordered a hit on Gotti.

FBI agents had planted a bug that happened to pick up a conversation between members of Gigante's hit team. The agents visited John to warn him of the hit. I heard John played it cool, pretended he had no idea why anyone would want to kill him, but cursed his ass off after they left.

Aware of the tension between John and the Chin, I kept Rita a secret.

But Gigante found out about me; he had better intelligence than the CIA.

He ordered his daughter to Greenwich Village, where he lived in a run-down apartment with his ninety-year-old mother. When Rita walked in, he threw a fit, but she had her father's balls. "Go shit in your hat," she told him. "You pick your friends, I'll pick mine."

We stayed friends. I still went to her house, but I watched my back.

Betraying Gigante's wishes was dangerous. Bringing the law to his house was suicide.

I had a hunch the FBI would poke his ass a little, pay him a visit and say things like, "Your daughter's hanging out with a hood from the Gambino family."

I went to Rita's house to warn her that the FBI might drop by.

"Big deal, I'm used to them," she said.

"They must think I'm the big middle man between two families, the missing Mafia link." I made Rita laugh. "Meanwhile, your father wants to kill me, an' half the time, so does John."

CLOSING IN

The FBI was looking for a witness.

Who'd flip first?

Guys like Barry the Brokester came to mind, working men who moonlight in crime. The Mob has plenty of these characters.

I made a few bucks with a thug from Bensonhurst named Bruno the Butcher. I bumped into him in social clubs and other Mob hangouts, restaurants, cafés, and a pool hall. Since Bruno was with a tough crew, I thought he was named "the Butcher" because he cut people into pieces.

Once, I sold Bruno a load of fox coats. When it came time to pay, he wanted to meet me in the parking lot of a shopping center on Long Island.

"No problem," I said, but I was a little leery on the way there. I slid a gun out from under my seat and tucked it between my legs as I pulled into the lot. I looked around for anything suspicious, then backed my bumper up against a brick wall.

Right on time, Bruno strolled out of a supermarket wearing a white, bloodstained smock. I laughed as he walked over to my car and handed me a bankroll, dried blood on his knuckles. He smelled like beef.

"You're a real butcher?" I asked.

"Yeah, I'm union. Their pension's great."

He lit a cigarette and looked at his watch. "I'm on break, fifteen minutes."

My image of Bruno as a ruthless killer instantly changed to a nice guy who recommended the best cuts.

Would Bruno stand up if he was about to lose his pension?

Would Barry stand up if his books were subpoenaed?

Besides the Barrys and the Brunos, there are men who turn to crime when they can't find a job.

Lenny was a skilled carpenter who could build just about anything with his hands. As long as Lenny had a paycheck coming in, he was afraid to park illegally; a ticket might cost him a day's pay.

But when Lenny was out of work, he was ready for a score. He'd look for me and ask, "Got anythin' goin' on?"

I didn't think Lenny would squeal if he was unemployed when the agents paid him a visit. He'd be better off in jail; no rent, no car insurance, and three squares.

But if agents dropped in on Lenny while he was working, I pictured him saying, "I'll tell ya whatever you wanna know, jus' don't tell my boss."

What about my tipsters? Most were average hardworking guys. Would they stand up?

When I was eleven or twelve years old, me and my friends stole car batteries. We'd walk the streets looking for a parked car on a dark deserted block, break the door glass, pop the hood, yank the battery, and run.

I'd walk up to just about anybody. "Wanna buy a hundred-dollar battery for ten bucks?" No one turned me down. Did they think I worked for Sears? They didn't care. They lived paycheck to paycheck.

Grown men scraped through their pockets and dug into old taped-up wallets. Some asked, "Can I square away with you when I get paid?"

When I hijacked, most tips came from these same guys, in need of a little scratch to pay off credit cards or catch up with the mortgage. Some owed shylocks and bookies. When they heard or saw something at work, they'd call me with a tip.

What if the feds leaned on them?

With all this on my mind, I went looking for any of my old tipsters who might fold. I told them the FBI might drop by, and promised to pick up their lawyer fees. I hoped this would give them less reason to cooperate.

Since the feds were playing connect the dots with my phone records, they often beat me to the punch, dropped in on guys I didn't even remember.

Some guys called me when the feds left.

One day, I got a phone call from a guy who routed trucks. "Can we meet, somewhere outta the way?"

"Sure," I said.

We met in the indoor parking garage at Queens Center Mall.

"They scooped me up off the street," he said. "They dragged me down to FBI headquarters, said I gave you a few tips."

"What else did they say?"

" 'We don't want another punk willing to spill his guts behind closed doors. We need somebody to take the stand.' They offered me the Witness Protection Program. 'Don't worry about Big Lou,' they said, 'we'll protect you and your family.' "

I left that garage with a knot in my stomach.

My jig was up.

MY DEFENSE

The Witness Protection Program is the VIP club for rats. No two-bit snitches allowed, all members approved by the attorney general in Washington. Before trial, the witness is protected like the president; no one in the program has ever been whacked. After testifying, the witness gets a new life in the boonies.

"I can't believe they're gonna support some street bum for the resta his life to put me away," I said to Sneaker Pete as we sat in a café.

"Maybe it'll blow over," he said, sweating over a cup of coffee.

"They'll never put this much money inta me an' jus' walk away. I wouldn't, would you?"

Pete dropped his head. "Anythin' you ever wanted to do, do it now."

A day later, I walked into a bar to pick up money and bumped into a friend.

"Hey, Lou," he said, "I asked the whole bar, nobody's got balls. Wanna go skydivin' wit' me in the mornin'?"

"Sure, what time?"

"Pick ya up at five."

It was close to midnight. I went home to get some sleep.

My friend beeped his horn in front of my house before sunrise. I got in his car and we drove out east.

I always wanted to skydive, but would never have gone if I knew I had to listen to a safety instructor for three hours. I really thought we'd pull onto the runway, pay the pilot, and jump. I was falling asleep when the instructor clapped and said, "Let's gear up."

Finally, a parachute.

We walked onto the runway. A woman was under the hood of a small plane with a wrench in one hand, an oil rag in the other. The propeller was spinning and the motor coughed.

"A real jalopy, 'bout ready for the junkyard," I said to some guy next to me.

I was looking around for our plane when she slammed the hood down, looked at us, and said, "Let's go."

We piled in.

As the plane gained altitude, I looked out into the open sky and made a deal with God, in case there was a God. "If I'm gonna die in jail, then do me in now. Get it over wit'. Keep the chute closed."

When I was a kid, my mother taught me to pray every night.

I got older. Life got tougher. My mother, who stood for everything true, suffered and died a slow horrible death. I prayed to God, asked Him to help her. Her illness seemed to get worse with every prayer. What good was praying? Now I needed help, and had nowhere else to turn.

At five thousand feet, the jumpmaster threw open the side door. "You're first," he said. "Ready?"

I jumped. My chute filled with air and I began to drift to earth with a terrific sense of peace in my crazy head; I somehow knew that one day things would work out and I'd be okay.

Two weeks later, me, Angelo, and Funzi flew to Florida to meet a land developer. We wanted to invest some dirty money.

While we were in Florida, Funzi wanted to stop by his uncle's house to say hello. His uncle was happy to see us. After a few martinis by the pool, he said to Funzi, "C'mon, I wanna introduce you to my neighbor. I'm always tellin' him about you." We all went next door.

We were in the neighbor's living room a few minutes when the front door opened and an attractive older woman walked in and waved. We all said hello, but her eyes fell on me, like she knew me. I didn't recognize her.

She went into the kitchen and called to her husband. He got up and excused himself. When he came out, he looked confused.

"My wife is a psychic," he said to me. "We're married over thirty years. When she feels this strongly about something, she's never wrong. My wife saw a vision when she looked at you. You have a destiny."

"What's that mean?" I elbowed Angelo.

"Means you're gonna be the boss someday."

"Then youse better start listenin' to me now," I joked.

I never asked what she'd seen, didn't care.

Years later, when I began to read, after I learned to write, as I pushed through Manhattan crowds trying to nudge my way into a publisher's office, I remembered that day, and what that woman had said.

When I got back to New York, I heard that Mickey Rourke had flown in from LA and went to dinner with Big Paulie. At dinner, Rourke told Paulie that some kids he knew out west wanted to make a rap song about John.

When Paulie mentioned this to me, my wheels turned. If I made a song that said John was railroaded by the feds, and it got some attention, I'd have a defense when the feds finally pinched me: I stuck up for John, and the government came after me.

I talked to Big Paulie, told him what I wanted to do.

"They might yank me off the street tomorrow. I'm facin' life in prison, an' I ain't got a defense."

"Good luck, Louie."

I got on top of things fast.

I needed to write a song. Where to begin?

Fat George was a friend of mine. He looked like an Italian sumo wrestler, covered in tattoos. He worked behind the bar in John's social club in Queens. On the spot, he'd make up a funny song about every wiseguy who walked through the door.

He was also a prankster. One time, he pranked the FBI.

Every day, the same two agents assigned to John's club sat in a parked car across the street. One day, George was alone in the club, bored. He left the club and waved to the agents as he walked past their car. He bought a pack of cigarettes on the corner, then picked up the pay phone and dialed 911.

"There's two guys sittin' in a blue car, looks like they're screwin' somethin' on, maybe a silencer. They're on 101st Avenue, by John Gotti's club. Please send help, looks like a hit."

Minutes later, four marked cars and two undercovers sped onto the scene. They came to a screeching halt around the agents' car, and jumped out with guns drawn. When the agents identified themselves, a cop asked, "Then who the fuck called us?"

The agent pointed to George, who was leaning against the phone booth, laughing. "That fat fuck over there."

I asked George to write a rap song about John.

Two days later, I had lyrics. Now I needed music.

I reached out to a friend in Middle Village who knew Pete Nice, the lead singer of the rap group 3rd Base. I invited Pete to dinner.

He listened to my story and said, "I'll cut a track and teach you how to rap."

Later that week, we met at a recording studio in Manhattan. I sucked. I practiced. I still sucked.

We recorded the song. My close friends called me "Big Lou." I used this as my stage name. I made albums and cassettes with John's picture on the covers. Then I reached out to our guys in the music business.

"You'll ruin me."

"You crazy?"

"May as well drive me to jail."

"Tell John I love 'im, but I'll be sittin' nex' to 'im if I touch this."

I picked up the Yellow Pages and found a music distributor in Queens. I barged into his office. He called security.

"Put the phone down." I tossed my tape on his desk. He stared down at John's mug on the cover of my cassette. It scared him more than a fish wrapped in newspaper. He hung up the phone.

"Play it," I said, "you'll like it."

He played it, and liked it. He distributed it worldwide.

I made kids hang posters all over the city.

The reporter Joe Queen from *Newsday* called me. He interviewed me over the phone, asked why I wrote the song, and how I felt about John Gotti's conviction. I spoke with the deepest intellect and utmost profundity—"Gotti Got Screwed!" appeared across the top of page six. The entire page was devoted to my song.

After that, other stories followed.

"New Rap on Gotti. Relax, This Time It's a Hit Record."

The Buffalo News ran a story in their "Lifestyles" section.

The *Houston Chronicle* said, "His hit is all the rage in Queens."

The *Chicago Sun-Times* said my song "has a lock on New York."

And the *Times-Picayune* printed my lyrics.

Even *Time* magazine squeezed my name on their last page.

I made a statement for the AP wire, which carried my voice across the nation.

News television crews tracked me down in Manhattan after I filmed my music video on the courthouse steps. I was interviewed sitting in a director's chair, wearing a baseball cap. The clip was aired on the six o'clock news. "Gotti didn't get a fair trial," I told a million viewers.

Reporters came to the club on 101st Avenue and found old-timers in sweat suits, smoking cigars. "I don't know nuttin', never hearda the kid, or the song."

Other reporters interviewed kids not bound by omerta. "I love the song," said one, "you can buy it anywhere."

Local stores couldn't stock the tapes fast enough. Downtown Manhattan's Tower Records sold out two weeks in a row.

I was standing on a corner with Sneaker Pete when a couple of Spanish kids in a Datsun hatchback stopped at a light, blasting my song from their boom box. They were bopping their heads.

Me and Pete laughed. The kids thought we laughed at them, and stared us down.

"That's me," I yelled as I jabbed my thumb into my chest, "I'm rappin'."

"Loco." They gave me the finger and drove off.

Girls asked for my autograph. More local fame meant more cheap sex.

I was invited to a luncheon with the head of Rhyming Records. He offered me a hundred grand for the rights. I turned him down. I should've taken it and run.

Two weeks later, the law struck back.

The same newspapers carried a different theme.

"Feds Rap Back at Gotti Pal," said the *Daily News*. "Lou Takes a Rap," said another edition.

"From Rap to Rap Sheet for Gotti Song Producer," said *Newsday*.

One paper said I was "best friends with John Gotti Jr."

My singing career was over before it started, but my courtroom defense was in place.

IT'S ALL FUN AND GAMES
UNTIL YOU GO TO JAIL

Tony Varro got busted.

Agents paid him a visit at his house, told him he faced a few years in the can, but said they'd forgive him if he talked. He didn't. They pressed him, showed up at his car wash, made his life difficult. He held up. When they cuffed his wrists, reality set in, and he squealed.

Using Tony, they put together a case against me.

Not long after they broke Tony, agents banged on my door. I looked out the window. The block was surrounded. Cars, guns, vests. I couldn't escape.

It was early morning. I got dressed and walked into my father's room. He was asleep. I kissed him good-bye. He opened his eyes.

"Dad, I'm goin' to jail."

"What? Whatta you mean?"

"I love you. I'll call you later."

I walked out with my hands up.

"U.S. Secret Service," said the agent who cuffed me on my porch.

"I threatened the president?"

I didn't know the Secret Service took over credit card fraud, the crime I was pinched for.

The judge set bail at $200,000. My father put his house up and I was released that day.

A few weeks later, I pulled into my driveway. Just as I turned off my car, both doors swung open and guns were pointed at my head. I thought it was a hit, but nobody fired.

"You had to come home now?" one of the gunmen said. "We jus' ordered Chinese."

I knew then they were detectives.

They cuffed me, read me my rights, and stuffed me into the backseat of their car.

During the ride, they told me I'd been nabbed for an old armed robbery related to a credit card scheme—the crappy tip from Tony.

At the precinct, the arresting detective called the newspapers as I sat next to him, chained to a wall. "We got Big Lou," he said, then paused and looked at me. "Yeah, he was very quiet, very passive, when we arrested him. He even told us he owns his own recording studio on Northern Boulevard." The newspapers quoted him.

When the cops marched me out of the precinct to bring me over to the local jail, reporters rushed me, snapping photos. The morning papers ran a shot of me with a smirk on my face.

Detectives pinched Ricky too, my new codefendant. The chief organized crime prosecutor took the case.

I pleaded not guilty. I was already out on $200,000 with the Secret Service. I posted another $50,000 and walked out.

I needed a good attorney.

I went to see famed trial lawyer Larry Robinson. He had a good gab. I retained him for twenty grand in cash. He looked around and slid the wad into the top drawer of his desk. The way he did this gave me a sudden urge to reach across his desk and slap him, a feeling lawyers would stir in me for the next ten years, until I finally tried to strangle Andy Pellegrino with his own necktie in a prison visiting room.

Andy had such a crappy way about him that the guards who pulled me off him shook my hand in the strip room.

"Good job," they said. "We gave you as much time as we could." They sent me back to my cell instead of the hole.

A week after I retained Robinson, he called to say, "I can't take your case, it's a conflict of interest. I interviewed Tony Varro a month ago."

"You didn't realize that before you took my money?"

"No."

He never returned it. I didn't even threaten him. I was out on two bails, didn't need a third.

I went to William Kunstler's office, told him who I was. He hugged me at the door. "Any friend of John Gotti is a friend of mine."

I told him all about my rap song. "Great defense, I love it," he said. "I'll beat the case, no problem."

He took a hundred grand off me, then broke the news. "Tough case, there isn't much I can do."

At trial, Kunstler sat at the defense table editing his own book while witnesses testified.

I got pinched with two other codefendants besides Ricky. I never met either of them until we stood together in a courtroom. Apparently, we all committed crimes with Tony Varro, who kept his stolen money and ducked a prison stint for telling on us. Ask Tony if crime doesn't pay.

Me and Ricky wore two-thousand-dollar suits. Neither of us had a job. The prosecutor could've subpoenaed our suits and asked, "How did you pay for them?"

The judge didn't want to hear my innocent rapper defense.

"He can take the witness stand and testify that he wrote this tape," he said, knowing I wouldn't take the stand. I was guilty; I'd probably trip up. Besides, they'd grill me about organized crime, a million questions I wouldn't answer.

During a recess, I went to take a leak with Kunstler. We stood next to each other at the urinals.

"So whatta ya think, Bill?"

"I think, as we get older, we should have more sex, it cleans the prostate, prevents cancer." He shook his pishadeel and put it away.

I'm fucked, I said to myself.

At the defense table, Ricky and his lawyer sat to my left, his lawyer right next to me. Ricky constantly whispered to his lawyer during the trial. I couldn't take the suspense. I finally leaned over to his lawyer and said, "Lemme in on this."

He looked up, deep in thought, rubbed the tip of his nose with his fingers, and said, "Ricky just told me to buy a Norelco nose-hair trimmer with some of the money he gave me."

We were doomed.

When the jury went out I turned to Kunstler. "How'd we do?"

"Hung at the worst."

"Me or the verdict?"

"The verdict. They don't hang anymore."

We blew trial.

Kunstler tried to keep me out on bail, pending appeal. The judge just smiled.

Marshals closed in and took me away.

My car was left on the street, outside the courthouse. I never saw it again.

My wallet was taken. I wouldn't need money or ID anymore.

From that day on, I was known as prisoner number 42365053.

PART III

PRISON

Chapter titles end here. In prison, there are only numbers and barbed wire.

CHAPTER 1

Two guards led me into the federal lockup in Brooklyn's Metropolitan Detention Center. They handed me a bedroll and left. Imagine the police escorting you into the heart of a riot and leaving.

Men screamed and cursed, pushed and fought. The dorm was built fucked up from the get. The ventilation sucked. I could barely breathe. All day and night, fluorescent lights flickered, and there were no windows. I quickly lost track of time.

The dorm was designed for 50 single beds. It had 125 bunks. Men shit in the showers because there weren't enough stalls to handle the rush after chow. Toilets were never added to accommodate the overcrowding.

The bunks were so close that when someone next to me sneezed, I got hit with the spray. And nobody covered his mouth. Most farted all day; they just leaned to one side. A pig who slept next to me would open his legs and wave a hand to bring a whiff to his nose, like a chef smelling a good dish.

The shitters were next to the chow tables. I forgot what the smell of food was like. I only knew the smell of shit. Some men wouldn't flush, just got up and walked away from the bowl.

Gambling and prostitution went on all night. Bottom bunks were turned into poker tables with a pile of cigarettes in front of each player. Punks sashayed through the aisles wearing red Kool-Aid lipstick, out for a trick. A blow job cost a book of stamps.

Shitting, gambling, fucking, and sucking, all crammed into a big steel box the size of a high school gymnasium. This would be my home until I was sentenced and sent to a permanent prison.

My codefendant Ricky was with me in this detention center. He lost his mind. Every morning, he whined:

"Someone shit in the showers, I can't go in there."

"Rhino told me to do his laundry."

"I can't take my bunk, Flacco bends over and farts in my face."

At chow, Ricky showed me the worm in his potato.

"Looks delicious." I tried to make light of it. "Let's split it."

He didn't find it funny.

One day, he walked up to me in bare feet. "Someone stole my sneakers."

I got his sneakers back.

Another day, I put a shiv to some guy's throat who wanted to fuck him.

If it wasn't one thing, it was another. He fell apart, and signed up for sick call. He wanted pills to knock him out.

A week later, he walked over to my bunk, the night before he disappeared forever. "Now, T-Bone wants to fuck me."

"I'll take care of it." I put my sneakers on and grabbed my shiv.

"Don't bother," he said. "I'm gettin' outta here, I can't take it anymore. I swear, I won't hurt you. I'll make up some shit about a few junkies from the neighborhood. Maybe I'll throw in a coupla assholes I never liked."

"Don't do that, you gotta live wit' yaself."

"I don't belong here. I don't even have a tattoo."

He walked away, mumbling to himself.

That was the last time I saw Ricky.

The next day, his bunk was stripped and his locker empty.

A few days later, Kunstler came to visit me. "Your codefendant cut a deal. He's going to assist the prosecution. Can he hurt you?"

"Yeah, I'm fucked."

I faced five years for the trial I lost with Ricky. I was coming to terms with this when Ricky decided to sing.

I knew his promise to spare me was bullshit; I was his get-out-of-jail-free card. I waited for a new indictment.

CHAPTER 2

I was pretty sure the feds needed another witness to back up the new case they were preparing with Ricky. Jimmy the Jeweler was a dry snitch so they couldn't use him. Besides, he never met anyone in my crew.

I rarely hung out with my crew, we were strictly business. I'd choose who I needed for a score. We'd hook up, usually in a diner. I'd tell them the plan. We'd split up, and wouldn't see each other again until the robbery.

Before a heist, we'd meet by Sergio's shop and go over the plan once more. Sergio would roll his door open and we'd drive out in a stolen van. After the robbery, we'd go back to Sergio's shop, check the load or split the loot, then go our own ways.

Tony Varro didn't know my crew, and neither did Ricky. So how did the agents put us together?

California.

Our trip there and our visit to the SFPD was on file. When Jimmy gave me up, the feds pulled the file and found Jackie, Botz, and Slippy's names together with mine. They busted balls, anyone who knew us.

Cheech Battaglia was a tough guy, a lot older than me. The crooks in my neighborhood were taking orders from him while I was still home watching *Sesame Street*. Cheech took a pinch for manslaughter, and went off to serve hard time.

I grew up and made a name for myself while Cheech was away.

Botz was tight with Cheech, practically grew up in his house.

Cheech came home from prison flat broke. He needed a good score to set him straight, but all the guys he ran with were dead or in jail, except Botz. He asked Botz for some work.

Botz came to me. "We can use 'im," he said, "he's good."

I gave Cheech a shot, sent him on a couple of jobs. No problems.

Then one day, I heard a rumor.

"Cheech got a blow job in jail," said Juney. "Two parolees tole me."

"Bring 'em to me," I said, "maybe they got somethin' against 'im."

Juney brought them by the club while I was playing cards.

"I never hadda beef wit' 'im," said one, "got no reason to lie."

"Cheech used to be a solid guy," said the other, "but he cracked up inside, lost his mind. That's my word."

I believed them.

I told my crew, "Stay away from Cheech, he's no good."

"I don't believe 'em," said Botz.

"You can still drink wit' 'im," I said, "but keep 'im outta our business."

Botz was tight-lipped but I didn't know he couldn't keep his mouth shut when he was drunk. I only found out when a bartender told me, "After a few shots, he rambles on about scores youse pulled. He bullshits so much that two cops stopped drinkin' at my bar, afraid IAD would yank their badges for failin' to apprehend a criminal."

Cheech was also taking in everything Botz said at the bar.

After we shut him out, Cheech started pulling petty crimes by himself.

Before long, Botz told me, "Cheech took a pinch. I heard from his brother he's facin' life wit'out parole."

"Why life, he kill somebody?"

"No, but he's got a million priors."

A few weeks passed before Botz brought up Cheech again.

"Agents went to see 'im on Riker's Island," he said. "They know Cheech was close wit' me, an' wanna give 'im a break if he talks."

"Will he?" I asked.

"I doubt it."

Botz was wrong. Cheech talked. The feds listened.

Now Cheech and Ricky would perform a duet on the witness stand.

Kunstler came to see me. "Bad news, Lou, the feds are indicting you tomorrow."

"Already? You're shittin' me? I'm not even sentenced on this case yet, an' the stickup charges from the state are hangin' over my head."

"I'm sorry, Lou."

The next day I was dragged to court. The FBI charged me with "Heading a crew of Gambino family associates."

Some of my crew were indicted with me. A statement of the facts in a motion prepared by the government read:

> The indictment resulted from an investigation by the Federal
> Bureau of Investigation into the activities of a crew of individuals
> headed by Louis Ferrante. The investigation demonstrated that
> the Ferrante crew was responsible for a series of armed robberies
> and hijackings in Queens and Long Island.
>
> Information obtained from confidential informants demon-
> strated that Ferrante formulated the operational plans for the
> robberies and hijackings.

Before I entered the courtroom, I made a statement for the press: "They're still afta me for singin' that song about John Gotti."

The next day, an article headline read, "Gotti Pranksta Held as Gangsta."

One article said I faced 60 years in prison. Another said 125 if convicted on all counts.

My life was over.

CHAPTER 3

The law was trying to flip me by way of multiple indictments. I watched people break under the pressure of one indictment, very few held up under the pressure of two. I now had three indictments: two federal and one state. I was constantly back and forth between the jail and the courthouse, spending endless days in a bullpen.

Bullpen therapy starts with an early-morning kick to my bunk. "Get up! You're on the court list."

I was shoved into an underground cage with dozens of other men, all half asleep.

When I was called, I'd step out of the cage and into a strip room.

Searched. Hands and feet chained. An iron box clamped over my wrists to keep my hands from moving.

We're all led into a dark garage and crammed into vans.

After a twenty-minute ride, we roll down a driveway. The driver flashes his badge at a guard in a security booth. "Eighteen packages."

We're "packages," with tracking numbers, like UPS.

The van door slides open. We struggle down. Men moan as limbs untwist. We're herded into a dungeon beneath the courthouse; it's damp, filthy, and barren, except for a steel toilet jutting out of the wall.

In the beginning, I'd double over from stomach pains before I'd drop my pants and bare my ass. Once I became hardened, I'd plop down on the toilet seat, like I was reading the morning paper. You don't feel humiliation when you don't feel human.

One at a time, we're called to stand before the judge. Men return talking to themselves, or whoever will listen.

Every so often, a public defender descends into the dungeon, presses his beak through the bars, and calls out a list of clients. He'd advise each to "accept the plea offer."

"But I'm innocent," they'd say.

"It's still a good deal. I don't care if you didn't do it, look at what you're facing."

I've seen lawyers confuse clients, give one man advice intended for another. A lawyer may tell one client, "You've got two priors, they're offering you fifteen years, I'd take it and run."

In the next breath, he tells another, "Twenty years isn't so bad for all those drugs. You'll be home by the time you're forty. Look at me, I'm forty-five and still look great."

The lawyers shoot this shit out so fast, then run upstairs.

The defendants try to straighten out the mix-up among themselves, switch the scripts to fit the correct tragedies.

I wondered how many defendants these lawyers represented at once. I asked one. He pretended not to hear me, probably thought I was counting his money.

Years later, I read an article in the *New York Times*, titled "For the Poor, a Lawyer with 1,600 Clients."

When my name is called, I'm taken from the cage by three marshals and led onto a freight elevator.

"Put your face in the corner."

In the courtroom, I'd stand next to my lawyer—I'd go through seven shysters in all—who chitchats with the judge and prosecutor. They crack jokes and chuckle as I stare down at my blue wrists.

The judge shows the courtroom he's ready to begin by glaring down at me.

The docket is read.

My prosecutor steps up like a horse out of the gate.

Events unfold before me—and without me.

When my response was required, my lawyer told me how to answer. When I whispered a question to him, he'd say, "I'll explain everything to you later."

When I believed I had something important to say aloud, I was told by the court that I couldn't speak.

When all was said and done, and my fate was sealed, I was asked if I had anything to say.

Back then, I didn't understand anything that went on. I only remember being anxious to return downstairs to eat my cheese sandwich and sip my six-ounce fruit punch.

By noon, the bullpen has beaten us down. Men lay on the cold, concrete floor.

One man always claims the toilet paper roll as a pillow. When he leaves he gives it to a friend, or sells it for a stamp, which he collects back at the jail.

Whoever is using the toilet paper roll as a pillow must give it up if someone needs to shit, but it must be returned.

One afternoon, a guy borrowed the roll, shit, farted, and flushed in front of us all. When done, he didn't give the roll back. He lay down, wedged the roll under his head, and closed his eyes. I could tell by the shameless way he used the toilet that he'd been around and knew the rules. He must've thought the guy he robbed was a newjack.

I saw it coming.

The guy who lost his pillow walked over to the guy lying on the floor, punted his head like a football, took back the toilet paper, and lay down a few feet away.

Another fight over this rare jewel the rest of the world wipes its ass with started the same way. Only the man who'd been robbed waited for his thief to snore, then walked over to the toilet and pissed into an empty juice container. He poured the piss between the thief's cracked lips. Straight down the pipe; he coughed and gasped.

Both men had codefendants in the cage, and a brawl broke out. We were packed so tight that everyone swung and kicked, including me, a hyena among the pack.

Are we animals because we're caged, or caged because we're animals? I think it's both.

All of us "packages" are eventually shipped back to the jailhouse, where we stand around for hours until each of us is screened by a psych.

I walk into a room and sit across from a shrink who doesn't lift his head to look at me.

"What happened in court today?"

"Nothin'."

"Do you feel okay?"

"Yeah."

"Do you feel like hurting yourself?"

"No."

"How about hurting someone else?"

"No."

"All right, send in the next man."

He scribbles something and closes a folder.

I've been jailed with men who've committed suicide . . . I can't imagine how they were able to fool these doctors.

CHAPTER 4

I talians sometimes call prison "college."

Inside, older mobsters instruct the young about the Life. They talk about the old days and praise "stand-up guys" who died loyal to the Code. Most of these stand-up guys died in jail. Some were whacked and buried in a swamp, like Sonny Black, the mobster played by Michael Madsen in the movie *Donnie Brasco*.

"Sonny was a man's man," a mobster who knew Sonny told me. "He knew the rules. He fucked up an' knew he had to go. He left his jewelry to a friend, got in a car, an' drove himself to his own execution. Now, that's a real man."

The Code is passed on over a game of pinochle or gin rummy. Old done-in fucks bullshit about ancient sit-downs, and how the decisions went.

Jail is Mafia school at its finest, and no tuition.

I was happy to be enrolled, proud to do time. A badge of honor, a chance to prove I had what it takes.

Guys who do long bids and come home are idolized. And if I never get home, given a life sentence, then "Fuck the gov'ment, I'll die a man of honor."

This was my attitude.

CHAPTER 5

The detention center had religious services. Every Sunday was a chance for Italians from different dorms to meet in church. We went to bullshit, not pray. We'd sit in the back whispering louder and louder until the priest stopped the Mass and yelled at us, like we were a bunch of chatty kids in school.

Meanwhile, Rocco cut up six people and dumped them in the East River. Guido clubbed two men to death with a five iron. And we're all going, "Sorry, Father, sorry, it won't happen again."

The priest never threw us out. He was happy as long as we received, figured the wafer might affect us one day.

Tutti took action in church, passed out betting slips. He'd move the line, change the spread a point or two in his favor.

If someone bitched, he'd say, "Then go bet wit' somebody else."

He was the only bookie in the jail.

Small bets, like stamps or cigarettes, were paid inside the jail. Bigger bets were settled in the visiting room between friends or family.

Iggy was a Gambino soldier, one of the last gangsters to wear a toupee on the street. It was taken from him at the door, along with everything else, when Sammy the Bull gave him life for being at the scene of a murder.

Me and Iggy partnered up in gin against two Russian mobsters.

They played like shit and soon owed us a few grand. Two or three visits went by and they didn't pay.

Iggy got aggravated. "When you gonna straighten out wit' us?"

"You like Lincoln Town Car? We deliver where you want."

"No," said Iggy. "We want cash."

"Moon roof. Leather seats. Tilt wheel—"

"We don't want it. I know what kinda car it is, big enough to fit three Russians in the trunk."

The Russian nodded. "Or six Italians."

Iggy didn't want the car, and the Russians didn't like being threatened. We understood each other.

A week later, a guy with a Rasputin beard flew in from Odessa and paid the debt to our guys in the prison parking lot.

When Italians aren't playing cards, they're making trouble with each other.

Some bored-to-death mobster will start a rumor about a kid so he can stick up for the poor bastard after it gets out of hand. He might float the idea that the kid is a rat. The rumor spreads until no one knows who started it. Then, the troublemaker steps in and says, "This kid's a good kid. He's wit' me. Anythin' you heard is bullshit."

Meanwhile, the kid lived with a knife under his pillow for a month.

I slept near this quiet kid named Juan. Juan was a mule. He swallowed a kilo in Guatemala, and got caught in Newark.

One day, Juan crept over to my bunk and dropped his pants. A pound of raw macaroni fell out. "I steal from kitchen. Two stamps."

I gave him twenty stamps. "Bring me ten more times." I held up all my fingers. "Comprende?"

"Si, señor."

The next day, the jerk who slept next to me grabbed Juan by the collar. "I wanna pound too." He must've seen Juan come over to me.

Juan could only fit one pound of macaroni in his pants at a time, and didn't know who to give it to. He got nervous and told me what happened.

The jerk who shook him up was Italian. I talked to him that day. "Back off, he's my guy, don't fuck it up. I'll send you a dish when I cook."

"I need at least two dishes. Frankie the Fish eats wit' me."

I knew where he was going with this. Frankie the Fish was a Lucchese capo, and the jerk wanted me to know that a capo was involved, and I'm fucking a capo out of a dish of macaroni.

Inside, Mob families stick together. If I don't have a capo from my own family to go to bat for me, I'm fucked out of the macaroni. But I did.

That day, Frankie the Fish came over to me on the Rec Deck. "Louie, I heard you gotta hook for pasta."

"Yeah, Frankie, a little spic I know sneaks up a pound of ziti unda his balls twice a week."

"Twice a week," he says, "one for you, one for me."

"No, Frankie, two for me. But I'll send you a dish, 'less you don't like my cookin'."

"It's not that. If it's too oily, I get agita. If it's too hot, it burns my ass. I rather cook it myself. You understan'."

"I really don't follow you. Maybe you should talk to Tommy Cigars. He eats wit' me."

Tommy was a capo in my family, and this was my way of letting Frankie know that I had a capo behind me.

It took Frankie and Tommy two days to arrange a sit. Two days of messages back and forth to see who would walk the thirty fucking feet to see the other. Finally, the Fish agreed to meet Cigars.

They walked arm in arm for an hour on the Rec Deck, which is twenty by twenty feet. We all watched through the glass. How they didn't fall over from dizziness is beyond me. Every now and then, one would swerve into the other. They'd hit the wall, straighten out, and keep walking.

When they left the Rec Deck, Tommy came over to me. "We're all friends here. We don't wanna look like gavones. We're gonna give 'em our pasta once a week, an' they're gonna cut us in on their broccoli rabe. This way, everybody eats macaroni wit' broccoli rabe once a week, instead of us eatin' plain agli olio twice."

After all this bullshit, Juan walked by us carrying a duffel bag.

"Where you goin'?" I asked.

He shrugged, played dumb, but picked up a step.

Later, I heard he asked for an immediate transfer, claimed the Mafia put a contract on him.

We were back to eating shit seven days a week. We blew a good thing for a fucking pound of macaroni.

And what did we accomplish?

A beef. A sit-down. Negotiations. Reminded us of the Life, brought us back to the good old days when we were somebodies.

CHAPTER 6

In the early nineties, Vito Petina was a powerful capo in the Colombo family. He was appointed acting boss when the real boss, Carlo Turso, went to jail for life.

Vito was top dog for a few years when Carlo sent orders from prison to step down so his son could take over.

Vito said no, and war broke out.

The family split into two factions, those loyal to Vito, and those loyal to Carlo. The shooting started, and Brooklyn turned into the OK Corral. Ten men were gunned down on the street, even innocent civilians.

Vito lost the war when he went to jail and got five life sentences. After Vito was gone, his faction was accepted back into the fold, and once again the Colombos were one big happy family.

Vito Petina Jr. and I became close in prison. He was serving a few years. Before Vito Jr. was transferred to another jail, he said to me, "Keep an eye out for my father, he's due back on appeal an' might end up here."

A few weeks later, Vito Sr. walked through the door. Vito was in his late sixties and beat up from the long bus ride. His eyes looked like two bruises, but I recognized him right away because he looked just like Vito Jr.

After everyone greeted Vito, I introduced myself. We hit it off. We ate together, we partnered up in pinochle, and I had the hack assign him a bunk next to mine.

One day, after we threw in the cards, Vito and I walked over to our bunks and sat down.

"Wanna peel garlic or crush tomatoes?" I asked. We started to make sauce.

It's tough to get near a boss on the street. In jail, you can bullshit with a boss all day because he's got nothing else to do.

"Vito," I said, "I heard so much shit on the street, never knew what went down. How'd the war really start?"

He took a deep breath, exhaled, and leaned back on his bunk.

"I was drivin' home from a nightclub," he began, "when I pulled up to a light. Two guys in a Benz pulled up nex' to me, wearin' baseball caps. I was a little tipsy, but I'm thinkin', Sonofabitch, the driver looks jus' like my underboss.

"I tapped my horn, an' waved. The passenger looks over at me, I could swear it was Little Donnie, one of my fuckin' skippers. What the fuck are they doin' nex' to me at a light, in the middle of the night, wearin' baseball caps? Then it dawned on me, they're lookin' to clip me. An' I'm fuckin' wavin' like a schmuck. I punched the gas. They chased me a few blocks, but I lost 'em.

"I drove to my son's house, an' called a meetin' for all my skippers, my underboss, an' my consigliere. I woke everybody up, but my underboss an' one skipper who was nowhere to be found . . . the two hit men in the car. I knew Carlo sent 'em. We went to war. Some guys went wit' Carlo. Some stayed wit' me. That's how it started."

Vito left out the reason they wanted to kill him, but it was still a good story, more than I got outside.

"You got five life sentences, what're you appealin'?"

"The gov'ment was tryin' to kill me."

Here we go, I said to myself, another loony. Every mobster swears he's caught up in a government vendetta against Italians. Shit, I even tried it, but I knew when to quit.

"I ain't shittin' ya, Louie." He wagged a finger. "The same bum who whacked my men durin' the war, an' tried to kill me, killed Martin Loot'a King."

"Really?" I had to hear more, just to see how nutty a boss can get in jail.

"Greg Scarpa was a capo in my borgata. He sided wit' Carlo when the war broke out. He was a fuckin' killin' machine, an' a snitch for t'irty years. Ever see the *Mississippi Burnin'*?"

"No."

"Good flick. Anyway, a coupla nigga lovers got killed down South. Hoover couldn't find the bodies, an' he needed to crack the case. Half the country was pissed, an' the president was up Hoover's ass. Hoover had his agents fly Scarpa down South. They tole Scarpa they had a lead, some redneck who owned a TV store. They drove Scarpa to the store, gave 'im a gun, an' sent 'im inside to do their dirty work. Scarpa went in an' stuck the gun in the guy's mout'. The guy spilt his guts. Next day, Scarpa was back in Brooklyn, tellin' us about his beeyootiful vacation to Florida, while agents were diggin' up bodies in Mississippi. Hoover cracked the case, real fuckin' hero. At the same time, he was claimin' the Mafia didn't exist."

"Wow."

"Wow what? It gets better. Scarpa shot Paulie Carbone wit' a rifle from across the parkway. Who the fuck uses a huntin' rifle in a Mob war? Not 'less you're an expert shot. An' who trained 'im, the Academy of Fine Hit Men, located unda the Brooklyn Bridge? My lawyer got aholda all the classified shit on Scarpa. The gov'ment admitted he was in Mississippi but no one knows where the fuck he was when King got whacked. Outta town? Anutter one a his vacations? I bet my ass he was in Memphis."

"Is that where King bought it?"

"Yeah, wit' a high-powered rifle, jus' like the one that got Paulie. What better way for Hoover to get back at the blacks for runnin' him aroun' in Mississippi than to have the same guy who cracked that case clip the head jigaboo in Tennessee. James Earl Ray was nothin' more than a pansy."

"He was gay?"

"What I say, pansy? I meant patsy."

"What's this all gotta do wit' you?"

"Durin' the war, we was hidin' in safe houses. Frank Wagner was Scarpa's handla, the agent he reported to. That dirty bastard gave Scarpa our addresses, tole 'im where we was hidin', so Scarpa could kill us. Ya see, if Scarpa won the war, an' became actin' boss, Wagner woulda been the greatest agent that ever lived, imagine havin' a boss as your personal snitch?"

Every night, I fell asleep listening to Vito. "Louie, a fuckin' marksman. He killed that poor moolie who won the Noble Prize. It'll come out when I'm dead."

Vito lost his appeal, and went back to the pen.

Years later, I'd find out that Vito wasn't so crazy. It's now known that Hoover used Scarpa to solve the Mississippi murders of Goodman, Schwerner, and Chaney.

Vito was also right about Agent Wagner conspiring with Scarpa to kill him and his men. Ten years after Vito and I parted, the government put Wagner on trial for murder.

By then, Scarpa got shot in the face by a hood, and died in jail.

James Earl Ray also died in jail, swearing his innocence.

And Vito, the crackpot, broken-record Mob boss, is still in jail. But if they place Scarpa in Memphis on April 4, '68, he's three for three.

CHAPTER 7

On Super Bowl Sunday, the warden treated prisoners to pizza from the outside. The cons who hauled the food carts into the dorm gave our kitchen workers extra pies.

I bet ten books of stamps on the game, and also placed a bet with an outside bookie. I was losing my ass and cursing up a storm when Tommy Cigars leaned over to me. "We get our extra pie yet?"

I shrugged my shoulders.

The old fart looked like he was stuck in his chair; I figured he wanted me to find out.

One con from each ethnic group works behind the kitchen counter in the dorm; this way leftovers are divided equally, and there's less fighting.

We put an Italian guy in the kitchen. He was a Brooklyn gunrunner with no Mafia ties until the Colombos ran out of weapons during their war. "We were shootin' people, an' dumpin' the guns so fast," a Colombo soldier told me, "that we went anywhere for new pieces, even this tuttarru."

In jail, this tuttarru wasn't really part of our clique, but he was the only Italian willing to work the ten fucking minutes a day handing out trays.

As I walked up to the kitchen counter, the blacks and Spanish were making off with their extra pies.

"You got our pie?" I said to the Italian.

"Ancora, wit' these fuckin' demands," he said. "No pizza left!"

I laughed, wasn't sure if he was kidding.

When he didn't laugh, I knew we'd be fighting.

I walked around the counter and opened the kitchen door. He clenched his fists. I slid my hand under a hot slice and smacked him across the face with it.

The black kitchen worker was a foot over my head, the Spanish guy, same height as me. They grabbed me. I pulled away and clocked the bigger first. He crumpled against the freezer, out for the count. Every Italian tough guy swears he's Rocky, but deep down we know it's bullshit. After this knockout, I believed it.

The Spanish guy flew out the door yelling, "Policia, policia!"

I'm fucked.

I walked out of the kitchen like I was coming home from church. I sat next to Tommy Cigars, and stared up at the TV. Maybe I can get away with this?

"How's the halftime show?" I asked.

"What happened to your knuckles?"

"Tell ya later."

I put my hands in my pockets and played dumb. I was dumb; imagine how good it looked.

Goons stormed in, twenty or thirty strong.

The guy I hit rubbed his chin, then pointed at me.

The goons tackled me, cuffed me up, and put me in the hole.

I was in the hole a week when a hack knocked on my door. "You're goin' to see the DHO."

A DHO is a disciplinary hearing officer, a prison judge who conducts hearings for major violations.

I backed my ass up against the food slot so the hack could cuff my wrists, then stepped away from the door so they could open it. In the hole, you don't leave your cell unless you're cuffed.

Two hacks marched me into a room and told me to sit.

The DHO sat across from me. He was a good four hundred pounds, eating Kentucky Fried Chicken out of a bucket.

If anyone understands a fight over food, it should be him.

With his free hand, he shuffled through papers, then looked at the hack. "Where are the other three?"

"They all signed statements against Ferrante, so Counselor Gomez let them off."

"Oh, really?" he said, then turned to me. "Were you involved in a fight?"

"No, siree."

He sucked on a chicken wing, then stopped. "Did you hit anyone?"

"No, sir."

He sucked, stopped. "Anyone hit you?"

"No, sir."

He sucked, stopped. "Then you're innocent, since it takes two to fight."

He pointed his bone at one of the hacks. "Release him from Segregation immediately."

"But, sir, he hit two inmates. Their statements are in front of you."

"I don't see the men who wrote them in front of me. Next time, tell Counselor Gomez I call the shots around here. All inmates involved in a fight will remain in Segregation until I arrive. Now return this inmate to his dorm!"

The two hacks hustled me back to the hole, where I grabbed my toothbrush and waited by the door.

About an hour later, the DHO left.

By then, the whole Seg Unit was bitching about how they got shafted. A con across from me kept repeating how "that fat-ass chicken-eatin' muthafucka should drop dead."

I liked the DHO, almost wanted to stick up for him.

When the joint finally quieted, I asked a hack, "When am I goin' back to my dorm?"

"When we find your paperwork, it musta fallen behind a desk."

They weren't happy with the DHO's decision. They couldn't stick him, so they stuck me. I took off my clothes and lay down.

The hole was torture. Nothing to do. Had I known the pleasure of books, the solitude wouldn't have been as boring. But day after day, when the book cart was wheeled past my door, I only remember getting pissed that the wheels squeaked; I wanted to sleep and the cart disturbed me.

A week passed before a hack banged on my door. "Cuff up."

The DHO walked in as I was led out. He looked at me, tried to place my face. I got hungry; he reminded me of chicken.

CHAPTER 8

There were three wall phones in the dorm. Hispanics claimed one, blacks another, and we had the third, which we shared with the Chinese, for a little fried rice.

Blacks ran their phone smooth. So did we. The Hispanics had problems. Ricans, Dominicans, Cubans, Colombians, there's too many, they can't get along.

I was on our phone when a Spanish guy next to me hung up the Spanish phone. Two kids made a grab for the receiver at the same time.

"I'm nex', muthafucka."

"Fuck that shit, I was waitin'."

One kid had a fake leg; it looked like he stole it from a pirate. The other was beefed up, like a prizefighter.

I made up my mind. If Muscles takes a swing at the Gimp, I'm jumping in.

"I gotta get off," I told my friend.

Just as I hung up, the Gimp slapped Muscles. Muscles put his hand to his face.

Good, I thought, the Gimp stuck up for himself.

Muscles dropped to one knee as blood seeped through his fingers.

The Gimp spun around, tossed his razor into the garbage pail, and hobbled over to his bunk. He lay down and folded his hands behind his head.

It was over before it started, but Muscles would wear a scar across his face forever.

After seeing this, I swore I'd never sleep on anyone in jail. If a guy had no arms, I'd kick his feet out from under him. Ninety-nine years old, he won't see a hundred. If I ever left prison, I wasn't leaving with a slash across my face.

About a month after this fight, some guy named Gino put a label on this fat Italian kid from the Bronx.

"You're a fuckin' rat!" Gino told him in front of us all. "You put my cousin in jail."

"I'm no rat!" said Fatso. "You got me mixed up wit' someone else."

Gino threatened to cut Fatso. Bad move. In jail, you do what you have to do, or you don't. But you never talk about it. Gino made a mistake.

I slept directly across from Gino. Fatso slept a few rows over.

Early the next morning, I opened my eyes and saw Fatso wobble into my row. Everyone in the row was sound asleep. Fatso crept up and looked at each face.

Iggy slept next to me. "Psst, Ig, wake up."

He opened his eyes. "What's up?"

I nodded toward Fatso just as he pulled back Gino's blanket. "Take this, you fuck!" He sunk a rusty razor into the skin beneath Gino's earlobe, sliced the flesh down to his chin, then tossed the weapon near my bunk and hustled his fat ass out of my row.

I looked over the edge of my bunk.

Two razors were melted onto the end of a toothbrush, spaced a quarter of an inch apart, meant to leave a strip of flesh dangling between the double incision made with one stroke. Twice the blood. Twice the pain. Twice the scar. And twice as hard to heal.

Over the years, I'd see men react differently when cut. Most hold their face while fighting off their attacker. Some roll over and play dead. "Thanks for the scar, may I have another?" They get a dozen more.

Once in a while, a guy ignores the bloody meat hanging on his face and attacks his enemy.

Gino was one of these men, but getting caught in a dead sleep slowed him down. He stared at his bloody sheets, tried to figure out what happened, then reached into a slit in his mattress, pulled out a shank, and took off after Fatso.

Too late. Fatso turned himself in; four guards held him against the wall.

A day would come when I'd see too many scar faces to remember them all, too many to care. One man cutting another's face would become as normal to me as a butcher slicing a side of beef.

CHAPTER 9

My federal judge handed me a five-year sentence for the credit card case, the stiffest bid he could give me under the statute.

My lawyer filed an appeal. My other indictments were still pending. By this time, we'd thrown away the bullshit rapper defense. The new charges were so bad it was like Manson claiming they pinned Helter Skelter on him for singing unpopular hippie music.

Cards, coffee, and bogus sit-downs were my daily life.

Inside, Sunday dinner reminded us of home, how things used to be. Those of us who faced life in prison never knew if we'd ever see those days again. All we had was each other.

By chance, a legitimate guy who once ran a Mob catering hall was hired as the prison's food administrator.

I was locked up with a Bonanno soldier named Anthony Prado. He knew where the food administrator lived and sent a couple of guys to his house in Flatbush. They knocked on his door and told him, "Start orderin' more Italian food for the jail."

A week later, boxes of manicotti, stuffed shells, and ravioli were stacked in the freezer.

We got the fattest Italian kid a job in the main kitchen; the more rolls of fat, the more food he could hide. He smuggled everything to our dorm.

One Sunday, he stole a pound of provolone, stuffed artichokes, and portobello mushrooms. Lorenzo the Clown made linguini with clam sauce. Anthony Prado soaked tomatoes in olive oil, and Tutti pulled a loaf of Italian bread out of his underwear just before we sat down to eat.

Everything was exactly the same as home, but no loved ones.

We joked. We laughed. We hid our misery. Some hid it better than others.

After dinner, we toasted with paper cups filled with grape juice.

Tommy Cigars filled his cup. "What's tomorrow, Columbus Day? Here's to Columbus." He raised his cup. "America. We found it. We built it. Dem *Mayflower* muthafuckas came a t'ousand years later. Now look what they're doin' to us."

"Tomorrow's Labor Day," Tutti said. "I didn't wanna interrupt ya. Columbus Day's nex' month."

"How the fuck would I know? I never worked. Why don't you give a toast, smart-ass."

"Here's to the workin' stiffs, who get a break once a year," said Tutti. "Ah salute."

Anthony raised his cup. "Here's to the lawyers," he said, "that they all drop dead."

The next day, William Moses Kunstler died.

CHAPTER 10

After Ricky and Cheech had gone bad I was reindicted along with seven of my crew. Four made bail. Botz, Mario, and Slippy were denied and stuck in the detention center with me. The prosecutor said they were "dangers to the community." This was the understatement of the year; the national crime rate should've dropped a few points.

It took us some time to get assigned to the same dorm. Finally, we were together.

One morning, we were brought to court for an identity hearing.

We were charged with a hijacking in which the driver claimed, "The guy who stuck me up had a space between his teeth."

Botz had a space between his top front teeth. While we were still on the street, I told him, "Get it fixed!"

"I'm afraid of the dentist."

Now it was the night before the hearing and I wanted to knock his teeth out.

"C'mon," said Botz, "there's a million guys wit' spaces between their teet'. Don't mean it's me."

"You're right, maybe it's David Letterman."

In court, the judge seated us in the empty jury box; the defense table was too small for eight men and eight lawyers.

A case was called before ours and a female attorney walked past us to stand before the judge. One of my codefendants whistled. The rest laughed. The judge gave us the look of death.

After the hearing we were again separated, this time sent to different jails, payback for our antics.

Every week, our lawyers argued, "It's necessary for them to be together to fight their case."

When we were reunited two months later, I warned my codefendants, "No more horsin' aroun'. I don't wanna rot in jail 'cause we're whistlin' at broads."

They nodded along. I felt like Captain Kangaroo.

We were back together a week when Mario came to me, pissed about something.

"I'm doin' time since the sixties," he said, "did a few bids."

"I know, Mario. What's on your mind?"

"Back in the day, we didn't stand for no rape-os in jail."

"I heard. A rape-o didn't las' five minutes wit'out gettin' stuck like a pin cushion."

"Yeah, an' I did my share of stickin'."

"You don't have to tell me. What's eatin' at you? Ain't no rape-os in here."

"Yeah, there is." He clenched his teeth and pulled me aside. "I speak a little Spanish, picked it up in the joint. Yestaday, some amigos were sayin' this new guy in the dorm is a rape-o."

"Rape is a state charge. Why's he in the feds?"

"Kidnapped a little girl, took her over state lines. Feds picked 'im up. I'm killin' 'im. The muthafucka's dead!"

He flashed a shank, then slipped it back in his pocket.

"Slow down, Mario. I ain't been down long as you, but jail's like the street. We take care of our own. Let the Spics clean up their own garbage. They'll get 'im, give 'em time. Probably why they was talkin' 'bout it."

"I'll give 'em 'til tomorrow."

"Give 'em a week. I want us together for the nex' lawyer meetin'. Afta that, we'll take 'im out together, me, you, Botz, an' Slippy."

He walked away like a kid who found out Santa was fake.

Next day, I was playing three-man gin with Botz and Slippy when the alarms rang.

"*Lockdown. Lockdown. Emergency lockdown.*"

"Prob'bly a fight." I folded my cards.

"Where's Mario?" asked Slippy.

Whenever a fight breaks out, the hacks slam all doors shut to keep gang members from rushing to help each other.

Me, Botz, and Slippy looked out through the thick unbreakable glass that separated us from the Rec Deck. We saw Mario beating the rape-o with a metal folding chair. The last of Mario's blows crashed down on the rape-o's head as hacks surrounded him, their billy clubs raised in the air.

Mario dropped the chair, put his arms up, and kicked the guy one last time before they cuffed him and took him away.

A week later, a con just released from the hole walked over to me. "I got a message from your co-dee, said he beat the rap, hacks didn't see what happened. He'll be out any day."

Every morning, Lieutenant Dreyfuss made rounds, first through Seg, then through the dorms. Whenever I saw him, I'd say, "Mornin', Chief, how's Mario doin' in the hole?"

I saw Lieutenant Dreyfuss the day after I heard Mario was getting sprung. I winked at him, and said, "Thanks."

He walked by but didn't respond. Either he didn't know what I was thanking him for or couldn't admit what his hacks had done for Mario.

Before turning the corner, he looked back. "I got a little daughter at home."

CHAPTER 11

Our only contact with the outside world was in the visiting room, where we'd see family and friends. There, we'd also bump into mobsters from other dorms, and other mobsters visiting them. We'd wave and yell from across the room. We'd hug and kiss. We'd talk in sign language or whisper messages back and forth, our hands over our mouths because of the cameras. This big drama while swearing we're innocent and have no idea why in the hell we're locked up.

The visiting room is also where drugs are smuggled into the prison. Italians smuggle food.

Whenever Fat George visited me, he'd roll up slices of prosciutto or provolone and stick them in his pockets.

Once inside the visiting room, he'd buy a bag of potato chips from the vending machine, eat the chips, then stick the prosciutto in the bag and pass it to me. I'd lay the bag on my lap. When the hacks weren't looking, I'd eat the prosciutto. We got away with this for a while.

One visit, as George handed me the bag, the phone rang at the front desk.

"We're busted," I said as I shoved the prosciutto in my mouth as fast as I could.

The hack hung up the phone and rolled a finger at me. I threw the bag in the garbage before I went up to the desk. My mouth was so full I couldn't speak. I nodded my head as if to ask, "What's up?"

"Camera got ya, Ferrante, you should see yourself."

I was brought into the back room, stripped and searched.

Another hack dragged the garbage pail in behind me and went through it like he was combing the scene of a homicide.

He pulled the potato chip bag out, and stuck his nose in it.

"Inspector Clouseau," I said, "it was cold cuts."

"Quiet! I'll make that determination."

I was put in the hole.

I scratched my ass for about twenty minutes before the captain walked over to my door. He poked his head into the food slot. "I'll give you a choice, a month in my hole or we prosecute your friend for smuggling contraband into my prison."

"Prosecute, for prosciutto? Gimme a break, I'll stay."

He smiled. "I just wanted to see where you stand. I come across my snitches in the strangest ways. My hole's overcrowded, I'm sending you back to your dorm."

"You won't bus' my friend's balls?"

"No." He laughed. "I already ate the evidence."

CHAPTER 12

"H"ow'd you control 'em?"

"Wit' a gun."

This was the question Matty the Hatter asked me as we watched my codefendants drag a snitch out of the dorm, still lying on his mattress.

"Take your bed too!" they told him. "Nobody wants to sleep on it afta you."

That same day, I was called into the unit manager's office.

The unit manager ranks above the hacks and answers only to the warden. My unit manager was Luis Campos. He looked like Al Capone, short, stocky, and bald, with a round face. He wore a gaudy watch, a thick nugget bracelet, and sharp suits instead of the cheap uniforms the hacks wore.

A hack led me into his office, then left.

"Have a seat," said Campos.

Every time I went to court, the feds hounded me to snitch. They must've recruited this putz to work on me, make my bid hell, or offer me something special.

He pointed to a pile of papers on his desk. "I find complaints about your codefendants under my door every morning."

"Whatta you want from me?"

"Keep them under wraps, calm them down, make this shit stop."

I glanced at the pile, shook my head. "How do you know it's all true?"

He lifted the blinds behind his desk, revealing a two-way-mirror view of the Rec Deck. Slippy was crunching his fists into some kid's collar, right outside the window.

"I see him do this to somebody every day. I read your papers, and I know you're the boss. Talk to them, otherwise I'm putting everyone on a bus in different directions. I won't have this."

"I'll see what I can do."

I told my codefendants what happened. They were proud of themselves. Even though, they promised to cut the bullshit.

Campos wasn't the only one fed up with my codefendants. The older Italians were also getting on me about them, but we were their muscle; they liked to hear themselves complain.

Late one night, me and my codefendants were playing poker with Wild Will Cusamano, a middle-aged skipper charged with a few bodies. The overnight hack swaggered over to Will's bunk (our card table). "Last hand, then off to bed."

The hack was maybe twenty years old. I looked at my codefendants, thinking this moron has no idea what he just got himself into.

Everyone looked at the hack, then down at their cards, like he wasn't there. When we finished the hand, Will shuffled and dealt new cards.

"Game's over," said the hack. "Now go to bed!" He put his hand on his baton.

As I wondered which of my codefendants would bust first, Wild Will got up and stood in the hack's face. "Are we fuckin' children? I'm a fuckin' murderer, you imbecile. Now you go to bed!"

The hack stepped off. Will sat down and picked up his cards. We played until four in the morning.

Later that afternoon, the day hack walked over to me. "Campos wants to see you in his office." I was sure the night hack ratted us out, once he was home safe.

I got a whiff of Chinese food as soon as I walked into his office. I sat in the same chair as before.

Campos reached out a hand. "Thanks," he said. "A week without a note."

I banged my knuckles twice on his desk. "I can't shake, against the rules."

He pointed to a brown paper bag on the side of his desk. "I'm leaving in a few minutes, come back with a laundry bag. I'll leave the door unlocked."

He was giving me the Chinese food, but covering his ass by leaving the office. If I got pinched with the bag, he'd say I stole it.

What if it's a setup? Who gives a shit. I'm facing 125 years, pinch me for a fucking egg roll.

I came back, took the bag, and left.

Me and my codefendants ate like we were going to the chair.

Over the next few weeks, Campos hit us off with McDonald's, Burger King, always something different.

Mobsters from Brooklyn and Queens get arrested every day. They're led into the dorm around the clock. Whenever we saw a new guy, we hugged and kissed him, like a long-lost relative.

Mickey the Midget was an underboss who landed in our dorm.

Campos called me into his office. "What's the Midget need? Anything I can do for him?"

"I'll introduce you," I told him. "You can ask 'im yaself."

When Campos made his rounds the next day, I waved him over to Mickey. The two acted like long-lost friends. They talked about where they grew up, even knew a few of the same people. Before Campos walked away, he said to Mickey, "I'll get you anything you need, just ask."

You can't give a mobster a blank check, he'll take your wife.

At first, Mickey asked Campos for little things, like "an extra visit, so I can see my goumada," or "better soap, that don't make my balls itch."

Campos gave Mickey the extra visit, and was so excited to hand him a bar of Irish Spring that he walked away whistling the soap's famous jingle.

Next, Mickey asked, "Can you bring me a slice of pizza?"

After that, he asked, "Can you get me a slice from my favorite pizzeria?"

Within a week, every Italian was in on it.

When they found out Campos lived around the corner from a social club, they sent guys to his house with cash. He bought steak and lobster and smuggled it in for us.

I was walking with Vito Petina when he pulled Campos aside. "I love my wife's cookin'," said Vito. "Oh, how I miss her meat sauce."

Two days later, we had Mrs. Petina's meat sauce over spaghetti. After that, every guy had his wife cook his favorite food. The wives would meet Campos on the street, and he'd smuggle in the trays.

Soon, the whole dorm knew what was going on. Hacks make twenty-six grand a year. Every one of them wanted to play. Before long, each shift change meant another sack of food from a different hack.

Our orders got out of hand. One bag had ten pounds of veal, hot and sweet sausages, a tray of eggplant, and a dozen sticks of pepperoni. I ate beef pizzaiola on Tuesdays, osso buco on Thursdays. Cannolis for dessert.

When Anthony Prado said, "I'm dyin' for a Big Mac," we ordered fifty.

"I can go for some clams," said Tommy Cigars. We ate six dozen cherrystones, straight from Sheepshead Bay.

Officer Velez was six feet two, on steroids. He had biceps the size of my head. He dropped us off a bag that was so heavy, me and Tutti had to drag it together.

The poor bastards around us were trying to swallow dry kidney beans as we sucked on barbecued ribs.

We needed the back row for privacy. We gave the blacks five hundred a bunk to pack their bags and scoot. We hung blankets on the ends of the row, and set up a buffet table on an ironing board.

When the hacks made rounds, they sat down and ate with us. Velez no longer owned a white shirt without gravy stains. Burns would hang his tie over the chair, unbutton his collar, and roll up his sleeves. He wouldn't answer his walkie-talkie for ten minutes. He listened to us talk, and sounded more and more like us. He'd suck up a spaghetti and say, "You shoulda whacked that rat bastard, an' youse wouldn't be here right now."

One day, a Korean con walked into the back row with a couple of shirts hanging over his arm. He asked us for the ironing board. We all stopped eating and looked up at him like he asked for our mothers.

"Sure," said Anthony, "give us a few minutes."

When we were done eating, Anthony gave him the board.

The Korean was a scutch, started bitching about the board every day. He knew what we were up to and wanted to stir things up.

One night, Bobby Biafra excused himself from the table. He put his arm around the Korean. "C'mon, buddy, I'll show you where they keep the spare."

Bobby took him into the mop room and cracked him over the head with the iron. Blood was everywhere.

I stood next to Bobby as he wiped down the walls. "We're all fucked," I said—still shoving jumbo shrimp into my mouth.

The hack on duty covered for us. When he changed shifts, he told the next hack, "There's an Oriental with a bandage on his head. Him and another guy had to *iron* out a few things. No big deal, all under control."

From then on, when we gave the Korean the ironing board, it was to press our shirts. He was creative with an iron. He made fancy creases. I walked around with a checkerboard on my back. Anthony Prado had ruffles. Vito Petina had his initials. When we were all together, we looked like Menudo.

Campos called me into his office. I sat in my personal seat.

"You think I'd make a good wiseguy?" he asked.

I laughed. He lowered his head.

"You serious?"

"Why not? I'm a stand-up guy."

Every nut finds me.

"You gotta be Italian," I told him.

He raised his hands and crunched his fingers together. "Madunda-mie. Ooh gots in gool. Sta minchia. I know the talk."

Campos started to wear colored handkerchiefs in his breast pocket, and a pinky ring. He cracked up, even asked, "Can I come to a sit-down?"

I said no. Not because of our rules; I didn't want him to find out we were bigger morons than him.

While I consoled Campos, the orders kept coming, and guys were asking for crazier things.

Vinny Pietro had young girlfriends, one prettier than the next. He had white hair and wanted to look younger. He told the hack, "Bring me in dye combs, so I can brush some color into my hair." He started going on visits a platinum blond. The lieutenant once gave Vinny a double take, then walked away, scratching his head.

As much as we pushed, the levee wouldn't break.

Our run came to an end only after the hacks got greedy and started working with other inmates. The worst thing we ever asked for was white wine in a water bottle. The blacks and Spanish asked for drugs. One cartel boss had a cell phone brought in. He'd go into the bathroom stall and call his wife in Colombia.

After a few phone calls, everyone was on to him. Either his wife was in the toilet bowl or he was on the phone.

I woke up one morning to find Anthony in front of the TV. He pointed to the screen. "You see the news?"

"Not yet."

"Feds pinched the whole prison, Campos too. We're locked down."

I listened to the report. Newscasters on every station were talking about the jail we were in:

> Federal officials said corrupt guards let top mobsters turn a
> new federal jail in Brooklyn into a Mafia social club, where they
> dined in high style with smuggled-in meatballs and manicotti,
> and washed it down with wine.

Campos and ten other hacks were cuffed and marched into a van.

The next day, we saw the story in the newspapers.

"Campos arranged Mob sit-downs and stood chicky," read one.

"Campos wanted to know who would be whacked next?" read another.

Anthony pointed to a picture of Campos in chains. "Look, he finally got his wish."

We made jokes and laughed, but it wasn't funny. Poor Campos had lost his mind, had no idea what he'd gotten himself into. But he stood up, took six years on the chin. He'd have made a better mobster than a lot of guys I knew.

CHAPTER 13

I hired a new attorney.

Mario got out of the hole, and my crew was back together. Although it was killing them, they stayed out of trouble until our next lawyer visit.

The day we met with our attorneys, we all sat around a table in the basement of the courthouse. Slippy and Mario were cuffed together. I was cuffed to Botz.

I usually didn't understand the lawyers, so I'd ask questions. Sometimes my lawyer tried to hide a smile, amused by my stupidity.

Botz's questions were outright ridiculous, even by my standards.

Maury Bradford, an arrogant prick, represented Botz.

The lawyer visit began with Botz interrupting Bradford so he could rattle off a list of dumb questions.

Bradford finally told him, "Shut up so I can speak."

"Don't tell me to shut up," said Botz. "Talk to me again like that an' I'll strangle you wit' that fuckin' Mickey Mouse tie!"

Bradford looked down at his Disney necktie, insulted.

"For months, I've been trying to tell you in a nice way that you're an idiot," said Bradford. "Let me do the thinking if you ever want to see the streets again."

Botz got up and chased Bradford, pulling me along by the handcuff.

Bradford ran out the door. The marshals ran in.

"A small misunderstandin'," I told them.

Bradford poked his head in when things cooled down. He was willing to swallow his pride—to keep his retainer.

"Can everyone behave?" asked a marshal.

"Of course," I said, then made Botz and his lawyer shake hands in front of the marshals.

When the marshals left the room, the lawyers got around to the good news.

"We have exculpatory evidence," said Bradford.

"What's that?" I asked, before Botz could open his mouth.

"Apparently, there's a crew of armed robbers already serving time for a robbery you've all been charged with. This could be helpful at trial. It might show the jury that your informant can't be trusted."

"Of course he can't be trusted," blurted Botz. "Why ya think we're here?"

"If other men were convicted of a crime your informant claims you've committed," continued Bradford, "it will cast doubt on everything he says."

The meeting broke up on a high note.

We were brought back to the dorm.

It was a long day. Court knocks the shit out of you. Chains, bullpens, a fight in the cage, Botz chased his lawyer, I wanted to go to sleep. My bunk was next to Botz's. I lay down.

"Ganight, Botz."

He was lying on his back, staring up. "What luck."

"What's that?" I asked.

"That skulpatory shit."

"I know, we caught a break."

"I mean, what are the odds?"

"Slim an' none."

I shut my eyes and was half asleep when he started again.

"Can you believe this shit?"

I was startled awake. "Huh? What?"

"What the lawyers tole us today."

"Botz, it might help us, but we're still pretty fucked. Go to sleep."

"But, Louie." He sat up on his bunk. "I don't think you get it. What are the odds that a crew jus' like us hit the same bank as us, on the same fuckin' day?"

I sat up. "It *was* us, you moron. We did it, not them. They got fucked, the same way we're gonna get fucked if you don't shut up an' lemme sleep so I can think tomorrow."

"I don't get it," he said.

"You could be up all night wit' that one," someone said in the dark.

CHAPTER 14

After Mario got away with beating the rape-o over the head with a chair, he thought he was a vigilante. He came to me a few days after our lawyer visit.

"Look." He held up a newspaper and pointed to a story.

I took a quick look. Gerald Matthews was representing a young Vietnamese gang member who kidnapped a thirteen-year-old girl.

"Fucked up," I said, "these lawyers'll take any case."

"Can you read the story?"

I took the paper to my bunk. Mario followed me.

The bastard raped and tortured the girl, even stuck a curtain rod in her vagina.

A chiropractor slept a few bunks down. He cracked our backs every morning. In return, we made sure nobody cracked his skull.

He heard us talking and said, "It's a capital punishment case. The government is seeking the death penalty. Matthews is arguing that his client is underage. There are no birth records for the kid in this country so the judge wants to give him a medical examination to determine his age."

"I'll kill 'im," said Mario. "Fuck his age!" He snatched the paper back from me and said, "C'mon, take a walk."

I followed Mario a few rows down, where he opened a locker door and pointed to an ID tag hanging up inside. We hung our IDs inside our lockers when we didn't have to wear them. He held the newspaper article up to the ID tag and read the three-syllable name out loud.

"That's him," he said, "the Chinks ain't washin' their dirty laundry."

In prison, Asian minorities fall under Chinese protection.

"How do you know they ain't plannin' to stick 'im?"

He pointed to a table in the back. "They're playin' mah-jongg wit' the little fuck right now."

I didn't try to talk Mario out of it. Why should I?

"Let's do it right," I said, "so we don't get caught. No foldin' chairs like las' time. We'll strap up, an' stick 'im in the showers."

He smiled. "That's my Louie."

That night, we had a codefendant meeting, but not with our lawyers.

"Let's get 'im," said Slippy.

"Right away," said Botz.

"It's Tuesday," I said, "there's a good hack on Thursday night. He'll look the other way. We'll hit 'im then."

We all agreed.

"Don't bump inta the kid 'til then," I warned Mario. "You might lose it an' smash his brains in. Wait for us."

The next morning, Mario told me, "I couldn't sleep las' night. Fuckin' prick is on my mind."

"Today's Wednesday," I said, "hold on one more day. He's ours."

When the lights went out that night, Mario slid into bed fully dressed. He pulled the blanket up to his chin.

"What's up wit' you?" I asked.

"Nothin'."

"Then why you wearin' sneakers to bed?"

"Shh, count time." He put a finger to his lips.

Talking wasn't allowed during the 11:00 p.m. count.

After the hack flashed his light in Mario's face, then mine, I whispered, "Why . . . are . . . you . . . dressed?"

"Shh, still count time."

"You little fuck."

After the count, Mario threw off his covers, and pulled a wool hat down to his eyebrows. He picked up a steel mop wringer from the other side of his locker and took off.

I sprang from bed in boxers and ran after him. Whatever he was doing, I had to back him up.

I ran a few steps when I heard steel ring through the dorm like a church bell. When the lights went on, the kid was out cold, blood all over his face, the mop wringer next to him.

"C'mon." Mario tugged at my arm as he ran by me, back toward our bunks. On his bunk, Mario lay facing me, his head on his pillow. I lay facing him.

"I got 'im good." He grinned.

"Why couldn't you wait?"

"I didn't wanna involve youse, better I took care of it myself. You mad at me?"

The goon squad stomped in, screaming and hollering their tough guy bullshit.

"Take ya hat off," I said, "it's ninety degrees in here."

"Oh, I forgot."

He pulled it off and tucked it under his pillow, winked, then closed his eyes.

I closed mine.

CHAPTER 15

Before long, prison officials knew every inmate involved in the "Rigatoni Ring." No one was charged, but they shuffled us around the dorm.

All the good hacks got pinched, only assholes were left.

Officer Clark hated Italians. He thought he was Eliot Ness. He'd walk around sniffing lockers, convinced we were still smuggling in food. One day, he swung open my locker door and said, "I smell cauliflower." I let him search my entire locker before I told him, "Guy nex' to me got gas, every night aroun' this time."

He got aggravated and moved me to a bunk in the first row, right in front of the hacks' station.

Officer Polaris was known throughout the prison for babying cons. He did things by the book, even read the rules out loud. One evening, Officer Polaris walked into our dorm at the start of a shift. The men booed and cursed him, some spit on the floor as he passed. When Polaris yelled, "Count time," everyone grabbed their crotch and yelled, "Count these nuts."

Polaris took our abuse, and waited for visiting day.

The worst thing a hack can do is fuck with the visit. Our families take off from work, sit in traffic, and stand in the cold for hours, just to see us. They're treated like criminals: talked down to, directed through metal detectors, and ordered to remove belts, bracelets, and shoes.

A visit lasts two hours. The visiting room calls the dorm hack to tell him which inmates are to report to the visiting room.

The day Polaris chose to fuck with us, he answered the phone but pretended the calls weren't for visits.

The cons knew better. They circled his podium like sharks. Some made threats behind his back. When he'd spin around to see who spoke, five or six faces smiled back at him.

"The visiting room is experiencing problems." He shrugged. "It's not me."

When the visit ended, everyone "motherfucked" him, including me.

Normally, Polaris walked the dorm all night, searching for someone to scold: "You're up late." "Go to bed." "Close your locker." "Cover your balls."

That night, when the lights went out, he planted himself behind his steel podium. He was afraid to mix with us.

Our bunks were arranged in perfect rows. From my lower bunk in the front, I could see all the way to the back of the dorm by looking through the spaces between the bunks. Men moved in the dark. Something was about to go down. Polaris knew it, too.

"Quiet down and go to your bunks," he said.

A hundred men yelled back, "Fuck you!"

The Spanish yelled, "Tu culo mio!" Your ass is mine.

Someone slammed a bunk up and down on the floor. Everyone joined in until the whole dorm shook.

Polaris radioed for backup.

I bunked next to Vincenzo, an old Mafioso from Sicily.

Vincenzo reached into his locker, took out a big red apple, and beamed it at Polaris. The apple hit Polaris in the eye and broke apart. Vincenzo slid under his blanket.

Polaris hit the floor and screamed into his radio.

The dorm went berserk. Every object not tied down flew through the air, hitting Polaris: batteries, transistor radios, cans of tuna. He was crawling toward the door when a mop bucket crashed into his back. He let out a cry, curled up into a ball, and was done.

So were we.

The goon squad raced into the dorm and pounced on a few men who weren't in their bunks. They helped Polaris to his feet. He pointed toward my row before he was put into a wheelchair and wheeled out, like a real wuss.

Everyone else in my row was sixty-five and better, so the goons figured it was me. "Get the fuck up."

I was tackled before I could stand. They dragged me to Segregation. I was stripped naked and thrown into an empty cell.

I paced until I tired myself out. After a few hours, I lay on the bunk, ass down, hands over my pishadeel. I dozed, but the hacks wouldn't let me sleep. Every five minutes, someone banged on the door, and shone a light in my face.

In the morning, clothes were shoved through my food slot.

I got dressed, crouched by the door, and waited for a breakfast tray.

Instead, the captain poked his head in. "You threw an apple at one of my officers?"

"No, I didn't."

"Then who did?"

"I have no idea."

"No food."

He slammed my slot closed.

I got family and friends, I said to myself, they can't starve me.

Can they? Hunger makes you think.

That night, I tapped on the glass and signaled to an orderly who picked up the trays. He looked in at me.

"I need food." I motioned a hand toward my mouth. "Hungry."

"Uno momento," he whispered through the crack along the door frame.

I waited, but gave up on him.

I was reading prison graffiti when I heard a broom brush against the floor just outside my door. The sound stopped, and a piece of sliced bread slid under the door. I dusted it off, and tore into it.

About ten minutes later, I heard a mop swish by. A grape jelly packet slid under the door. I licked it clean, even turned it inside out to get the last drop.

Next morning, the captain crouched down and opened my slot. I was tough, now that I'd eaten.

"I didn't throw the fuckin' apple, an' I dunno who did. Bring me a mattress."

As he laughed, I reached through the slot and grabbed his necktie. I wrapped it once around my knuckles before it snapped.

I stared at the tie in my hand. "A clip-on?"

He unbuttoned his collar. "You think we'd wear real ties with you fuckin' animals."

I threw it back at him.

He slammed the slot closed and walked away.

He called me an animal. Am I an animal?

That day, I beat my knuckles against the walls until I fell to the floor. I lay there, staring up at the caged bulb all night.

Who am I?

What is it that makes me this way?

Do I have a purpose?

These were the gist of my thoughts, although I wasn't yet able to phrase them this way.

With this, my journey had begun.

CHAPTER 16

I wasn't charged with assaulting an officer, never saw a DHO, but still spent two months in the hole before I was sent back to my dorm.

When you're released from a concrete box after so long, you feel free, even though you're still in prison. You've also been changed forever.

In solitary, you talk to yourself. I always had all the answers. For the first time, I had a million questions, and no answers.

Polaris was gone, transferred to Control, an isolated monitoring room with no human contact, where he belonged.

Vincenzo greeted me at the door.

"Don't throw no more apples while I'm aroun'," I joked.

"Me?" He pointed to himself. "I no throwa the apple."

Greaseballs from the other side won't admit that their left nut knocks into their right when they walk, it's just how they are. I didn't take it personal.

I got a hero's welcome. Everyone knew I took the rap for Vincenzo.

I'd always been proud to prove myself. This time, I didn't care what anyone thought. Something strange had come over me in the hole.

Vito Petina called me over to the card table. "Hey, Louie, we held your spot." He pulled out a chair.

"I'll pass, Vito. I jus' wanna take a shower."

You shower two or three times a week in solitary, and it's a pain in the ass. You're cuffed, taken out of your cell, and locked inside a stall just big enough to stand up in. Sometimes the guards return for you right away, while you're still soaped up. Other times they leave you there for hours, shivering under the showerhead.

In the dorm, I took a long hot shower, then jumped on the phone.

I had the urge to read.

I don't know why I wanted to read, maybe books had answers to all those questions I'd begun asking myself, maybe I had plenty of time to kill and that seemed like the best way to kill it. I was sick of cards and coffee, and I needed something to do; I couldn't plan a score.

When I was growing up, there were no books in my house. My father read the racing form and my mother picked bundled magazines from the trash in front of a doctor's office on her way home from work. I cheated my way through high school, and never read a book; I was busy with my chop shop at night.

I didn't know anyone who read. So, where do I begin?

Fat George had half the Bible tattooed on his body; he must've read it.

I called him up. "Hey, Fatso, got any books to send me?"

"Where you been? Haven't heard from you."

"In the hole. Tell you all about it on the visit. Any books?"

"*Playboy, Penthouse*, big tits, fat asses, whaddya into?"

"I'm lookin' for real books, stuff you read."

"I read 'em."

"Can ya send me some books or what?"

"There's a bookstore by Anthony Bellagio's club. What kinda books?"

"I dunno. Ask someone who works there. Tell 'em about me, maybe they'll have some ideas."

"I'll get some out to you right away. What else you need?"

"That's it. Ciao, paesan."

"Ciao."

In prison, men break from the Mob only when they snitch. They slowly distance themselves from friends and codefendants, knowing that soon they'll be burying these same people.

Stoolies change when it suits them, they turn on the Mob in exchange for freedom. No mobster I ever met changed for the sake of truth. Mobsters take the stand and claim they suddenly see the light. If they really saw the light, they'd realize they deserve their lumps. They're full of shit.

I wanted to break away from the Mob without snitching them out. It wasn't in me to squeal. And as tough as it was to admit it, I deserved to be punished. How could I pretend otherwise?

As I waited for my books, I went through the motions. I played cards with the guys. I cursed. I laughed at jokes. But I could feel myself pulling away.

CHAPTER 17

When Campos's gravy train derailed, and our lawyers weren't exactly pulling miracles out of their asses, my codefendants acted up again.

In return for drugs, Slippy protected a cross-dresser from gang rape.

Leopold looked and acted like a woman. He'd posed in a few European magazines done up as a girl. He had his family send in copies and he passed them out. Either he had no idea he was in prison or enjoyed lowlifes fawning over him. Cons jerked off to his photos, and fought over who got them next. When the photos were worn out, one guy stood over Leo's bunk, dropped his pants, and jerked off, staring at him.

Leo knew he was getting locked up, and swallowed balloons before agents came to arrest him. He foolishly told everyone in the dorm, "My stomach's loaded with dope."

Every time Leo went to the bathroom, gangs waited outside the stall, demanding to poke through his shit, and search him on his way out. Every gang put a claim on him.

With big balls, and a big knife, Slippy stepped in to defend Leo; he wanted the drugs.

I went looking for Slippy when I found out he dug his claws into Leo. "Back off, you're embarrassin' us. Not bad enough you got his drugs, the ole-timers think you're pimpin' 'im out. They're bitchin' to me."

Leo had murder charges. He had no hope of beating the rap, and floated around the dorm gossiping about the murder.

He was involved in a love triangle that turned deadly. Leo and lover number one got rid of lover number two.

"We ran a warm bath," said Leo. "When he sank into the tub, I bopped him over the head with the claw of a hammer. He stared at us, paralyzed, before he slid under. We made love on the floor, then cut him into pieces. We washed his blood down the drain, stuffed his arms and legs into trash bags, and dumped him all over the city."

Cops found the victim's head connected to the torso. This led to Leo's arrest. Feds picked up the case because all three lovers sold drugs together, a federal crime.

One day, Leo was sitting on Anthony Prado's bunk, blabbing about his murder. I was two bunks down, twiddling my thumbs.

"So, you cut off his arms an' legs," said Anthony, "but they found his body, still connected to his head. Why didn't you cut his head off, an' get ridda it?"

"Ugh!" Leo squirmed. "You're disgusting. Cut someone's head off? I could never." He stomped away.

With that, my name was called for a package. My books couldn't have come at a better time.

I opened the package and spread three books out on my bunk:

Napoleon, by Vincent Cronin.

Mein Kampf, by Adolf Hitler.

Caesar's Gallic Wars.

"Wow. Heavy shit."

I sat there staring at them, fanned the pages, and ran my hand over the covers. When I got up, I called George.

"Get them books yet?" he asked.

"Yeah, who picked 'em?"

"The broad at the store."

"Whaddyu tell 'er?"

"That you were short and bossy. With that, she started pullin' shit off the shelves. Any good?"

"I dunno, they look good."

That night, I tried to read *Napoleon*. I'd get through a sentence or two then see a jumble of words on the page. My mind would drift and land on thoughts I could handle, like steak or sex.

I kept turning to the pictures in the middle of the book. I saw Napoleon through the years. Young, handsome, on fire. A little older, a few more pounds, less hair. Old, fat, and miserable, with a scowl—like every mobster around me. Was I on that road? Was it too late?

The next day, I was back at the card table. I was running from the books and I knew it. I couldn't lie to myself. After a few hands, I got up and walked away. I never returned.

Vito found me on my bunk, reading the back covers of my new books for the millionth time.

"What happened? I thought you was back. I can't win wit'out ya."

"Vito, I might get stuck here for the resta my life." I held a book up. "I wanna make use of the time."

"Smart move. I won't bother you no more."

At first, I was easily distracted. I couldn't read during the day, too much noise.

At night, men snore, cry, or moan in their sleep like they're being stretched on the rack, but it's quieter, so I read all night under the red glare of an EXIT sign.

I constantly came across words I didn't know. I looked every one of them up, except words beginning with Y and Z; the last pages were missing from my first dictionary; I bought it for a stamp. On lined paper, I'd write each word next to its meaning, and study the sheet each night before going to sleep. In my sleep, I'd turn the words over in my mind, imagining new ways to use them.

Eventually I got through all three books, understanding almost nothing of what I'd read. Hitler used a lot of big words. I knew he was full of shit because my lawyers used big words, and they were full of shit.

I asked George to send more books, and I began reading all day and night. Noise no longer distracted me.

One day, someone told me the prison had a library. I asked the hack for a library pass and went to look around. All those crowded bookshelves made me feel like shit. The few books I'd read took me so long, and such effort, yet all of them could be put into one shopping bag. I was intimidated. My spirits sank.

But I psyched myself up. If Caesar conquered Gaul, and Napoleon conquered Europe, I could conquer the library.

I devoured the shelves. Most of the books were old and musty, some had no covers, others were missing pages; it didn't matter. If someone took the time to write it, I read it.

One night, I came across what Dryden said of Ben Jonson, "Other men read books, he read libraries."

I smiled myself to sleep. I was like Ben Jonson, whoever he was.

I gave myself impossible deadlines; if only I can read one more chapter before I conk out, if only I can finish two more books before the end of the month. I lost sleep and missed meals.

I was so anxious to finish one book and begin another that I'd drop each after the last word.

One day, I read beyond the last page and came across a bibliography; every book led to the next. I now had a teacher.

I loved histories and biographies.

From my bunk, I traveled through time and space. I camped with Spartacus and his army of dispossessed, crossed the Urals with Pugachev and his fed-up Cossacks, and marched across the opulent lawns of the capital with the black saint of the South. I tasted victory when I drove the Persians into the sea at Marathon, and more recently when I stormed the beaches of Normandy. I learned dignity in defeat at Appomattox when Lee bowed his head and said, "Our valor and devotion could accomplish nothing more."

I loved Shakespeare and read him over and over, like one who reads a love letter that warms the heart.

I sometimes talked to myself in Old English, like Chaucer might've spoken.

No sooner did I crave a book than it appeared. I was still reeling from Tolstoy's *War and Peace* when I found *Anna Karenina* in a broken urinal, washed it off, let it dry, and read it.

I'd read until the muscles in my eyes ached, and the letters blurred.

Each morning, moments before dawn, I'd wedge two pinches of toilet tissue into my ears to stop roaches from crawling in—they don't crawl out—then crash onto my books, and so to sleep.

But I never slept long. Before realizing the beauty of books, sleep was an escape. I would've rather been unconscious than awake and face-to-face with life. Now sleep was a pit stop, a time to rest my eyes and give my brain a chance to file everything away.

Prison is a lonely place. The more books I read, the more knowledge I gained, the less I had in common with those around me, and the lonelier I felt. I'm still not too good in math, but I knew loneliness squared.

CHAPTER 18

I'd been reading about a year when something strange came over me while I was asleep. I awoke from a dream but couldn't remember it. I scratched my head. A minute later, I picked up a pen and began to write. I wrote until the pen fell from my hand.

The next day, I read what I'd written.

It was the opening pages of what would become a novel about human relationships, and rewards and punishments for good and evil, the way I was starting to view life. The book was set in the antebellum South.

From that moment on, I held a pen as often as a book. I made notes all day, even while eating. Between bites, I'd stop and jot something down on a napkin. I trained myself to scribble in the dark.

I read the masters of nineteenth-century fiction: Thomas Hardy, Victor Hugo, Dumas, Flaubert, and the Brontë sisters. I studied the style of each, how a character is introduced, how a chapter begins and ends, and how a plot progresses.

One night, a gang fight broke out. Men tumbled against my locker and over my bunk, fists flying. The pages of my book were scattered everywhere. I crawled on the floor, gathering them up as everyone fought around me.

Goons stormed in. They cuffed up and dragged out anyone with bruises, blood, or scratches.

Early the next morning, they came back and shook down the dorm. They searched for knives, but as payback for the brawl, they took away our property. I lost everything I'd written. I watched as all my hard work was thrown into a garbage bin—probably where it belonged. It sucked. I had a lot to learn.

I started again, determined to write better.

CHAPTER 19

Shakedown.

Goons rush in at dawn, twenty or thirty deep. They're gassed up, high on power. "Rise and shine, muthafuckers!"

They're after contraband: a knife, a pipe, a lighter, a joint, a needle, a hit of dope, tattoo ink, anything unauthorized.

We're lined up and ordered to strip. "Hold out your hands. Raise your arms. Lift your nuts. Turn around, bend over, and spread your cheeks."

My asshole is on display.

We're marched out into the corridor. Everything we have is taken. Letters from loved ones are mistaken for inside gang mail. Pictures, books, magazines, everything goes.

We return to find bunks stripped, sheets thrown in sloppy balls all over the dorm. No one knows whose linens belong to whom. I end up with someone else's. If the sheets belonged to a pig who hadn't washed in months, maybe years, I'm fucked. That night I sleep beneath semen stains and the smell of ass and balls in my face.

Cons rake through anything left behind. They make a grab for stuff that doesn't belong to them. This leads to fistfights.

Time and again, people taking away years of my life for the crime of robbery, robbed me of everything I had. I felt bitterness, rage, and hate. In the end, I blamed myself. Taking away what is mine gave me an idea of how my victims felt. Most cons don't get this, it makes them worse.

After losing my pages during one of these shakedowns, I began to send home each chapter for safekeeping, but I also wanted my father to see that I was trying to make good on a bad life, that I wasn't a total loss. Maybe this would help him get over losing his son, not long after losing his wife.

"Dad, take a look at what I'm writin'," I'd say. "Tell me if you like it."

It was a way for us to interact, gave us something to talk about over the phone. We developed a relationship we hadn't had since I was a boy.

Prison is designed to break the individual. It outright destroyed me, the old me. I was building someone better.

CHAPTER 20

For a long time, the best plea federal prosecutors offered me was twenty years; I'd be home in my forties.

One day in court, the government dropped the numbers for everyone on my case and we pled out.

At sentencing, the federal judge gave me 87 months on top of my 60-month sentence. He slammed the gavel.

As the marshals dragged me out of the courtroom, I figured out that I'd gotten a total of 147 months. But I couldn't figure out what that equaled in years. I used to sell illegal fireworks on the Fourth of July. I knew a gross of bottle rockets was 144, and there were twelve packages in a gross. I got around twelve years.

I felt like shit, but I saw the bright side, twelve years to read. Was this enough time to read every book in the world? I kicked myself in the ass for such a ridiculous thought; I could read at home.

My family wasn't in the courtroom. I never told them my court dates. I knew without family present the judge would see me as a lost cause, and have less reason to be lenient. But I couldn't let my family hear the horrible things the government said about me, much of it true.

That night, when I got back to the dorm, I called home and spoke to my stepmother. "Hide the newspapers tomorrow. I got sentenced this mornin' an' reporters were there."

"No problem," she said.

I tossed and turned all night, trying to figure out how to break the sentence to my father. If you say to my father, "We'll get together next week," he'll say, "I should live that long." How do I tell him, "I'll be home in twelve years?"

The next morning, I called the house to speak to my stepmom, to see if she hid the papers. My father picked up the phone, crying.

"What's the matter, Dad? Why you cryin'?"

"Uncle Anthony just called, says he read in the newspaper you got seventeen years."

My uncle fucked up the math. He added the twelve to the five I already had.

"No, Dad," I said, "I got twelve, total."

All of a sudden he stopped crying. "Oh, that's not so bad."

And that's how the blow was softened.

My next appearance was in state court. I pled guilty to the charges, and the state judge ran that sentence concurrent with the fed time.

Give or take, with good time, I'd spend about a decade in prison. This wasn't a life sentence. Or was it? Guido once said, "Every day in jail is a life sentence, 'cause you never know how long you'll live, or what can happen in here."

He was right.

Butchy was serving three years. Ten months into his bid, he fell, hit his head, and died. Chickie was serving six years. He got cancer in the fifth, dropped dead a skeleton, weeks before his scheduled release.

I was reading in the dark when the hack came over to my bunk. "Get dressed, you're outta here."

A couple of old-timers woke up to see me off. They kissed and hugged me at the door.

"Keep readin'," said one, "go make somethin' of yaself."

All along, I thought they'd held a grudge after I walked away from their card games. But I stood up. I was no snitch. That was the bottom line.

I hugged my codefendants before we were separated forever.

I was taken downstairs, chained, black-boxed, and put on a bus. We left Brooklyn faster than the Dodgers.

I was on my way to the max, Lewisburg Penitentiary.

CHAPTER 21

Two weeks before I was arrested and put in jail, in June '94, I visited the Brooklyn Animal Shelter with a friend of mine who'd lost his pup.

We looked up and down aisles lined with steel cages; it was a walk down death row. Animals followed us with hopeless eyes. Some barked, some spun in their cages as we passed.

In the summer of '97, I was walked into the solitary confinement unit in Lewisburg maximum security penitentiary. Inmates wait here until they're cleared by security to enter the general population. Dirty, unshaven men stared at me through thick glass in their doors as I passed.

I was locked in a cell. I remembered the animal shelter, the constant barking, banging and echoing off the walls. I remembered the hopeless animals. Here, hopeless men barked at each other all day and night.

My cell had dried shit and urine on the walls. Prison poetry, like "Fuck Your Mother" and "Suck My Dick" was scrawled across the cement blocks.

At night, roaches covered the floor, crunching under my feet as I paced. The hack had to bang them off the glass to count me with a flashlight—four times a night. They crawled over my head, and across my chest. One day I stopped swatting them from my body, only my face.

I rolled up a blanket and stuffed it in the space under my door to keep the rats out. When the lights were dimmed, they'd stampede down the corridor, turning into cells that weren't barricaded.

The noise never stopped; it was torture.

As days went by, I was able to tell one loudmouth from the next as I stared into the concrete wall.

There was a Puerto Rican who'd go on and on about how he loves to suck a woman's pussy, work himself up, then announce that he's about to jerk off. He'd shut up for a minute, then start again. He did this several times a day. I named him Bram Stroker.

There was a radical reverend, forever reciting verses from the Bible he swore condemned the white man's treatment of blacks. I named him Archbishop Desmond Cuckoo.

I referred to another black con, who always hassled the white guards for a pen, a pencil, toilet paper, anything, as "the White Man's Burden."

And then there was the "Pure-Blooded American" (whatever this means), who tirelessly dragged on about the Jewish conspiracy that is, for some reason he couldn't explain, behind all of our incarcerations. I called him Reichsmarschall Hermann Boring.

I'd fall asleep from sheer exhaustion, and wake again and again from the rantings of some tireless madman going on and on about the fights he had, the girls he fucked, and the money he made.

One pig smeared his own shit on himself. Another gargled his own urine, then spit it at the hack for not giving him an extra slice of bread.

Almost every day, some ballbuster would stuff sheets into his toilet and flush over and over, flooding his cell. The water would run under his door and along the tier until the goons suited up, rushed in, and beat his brains in.

I exited this cell like a long-held breath being released from the lungs, and entered the general population. It was August 1997.

I needed fresh air. I hadn't been outdoors in exactly three years, over a thousand days without sun. Patches of skin on my cheeks had peeled off, probably from years of artificial lighting.

I made my way through steel doors and metal detectors, out into the yard.

My vision was blurred, and light hurt my eyes.

The first few steps were dizzying. I felt like I was floating in space. I remember wondering if the sky could suck me up, or fall on my head. I headed for the awning that covered the weight pile. I stayed under there a few minutes, until I figured out the root of my phobia; I'd been stuffed in a small box too long.

I walked out with hesitant steps.

After a lap around the track, I bumped into some Mob friends from the streets, all serving life. They hugged and kissed me. A strange welcome, too warm for such a cold place, like welcoming me to a leper colony. They craved fresh company. They outyelled each other, eager to hear about the outside world, news from the old neighborhoods. I told them, "My news is three years old." They said, "That's news to us."

I was introduced to Jimmy Doyle, the Irish boss of the Westies. We talked awhile, then broke off from the rest. Jimmy was a nice guy; I couldn't picture him cutting someone's head off.

Jimmy introduced me to Michael Merrifield, a tall, Nordic-looking con, about forty. When Doyle mentioned, "Michael is the leader of the Aryan Nation," Merrifield grinned with pride, the kind of pride one might expect from a working man introduced as the CEO of Dell or Microsoft.

Merrifield is a career convict who measures his achievements by how much time he's spent behind the wall, and how much of his life has been wasted in solitary. When cons like Merrifield bump into each other, they brag about how many men they've stabbed, or how many murders each has gotten away with in prison.

Institutional living is all they know; most have been shoved through countless prisons since childhood.

Imagine a boy who grows up in a trailer park in the Midwest. His mother is a whore waitress who pulls the swing shift at the truck-stop diner. The whole family is beaten silly by a drunken father until split up by the state, brothers and sisters sent to different foster homes. In and out of prison since youth, they serve life on the installment plan until many, by adulthood, have at last been condemned to die behind bars.

Michael Merrifield was one of these cons. Not a hint of the outside world was apparent in anything he did or said. He wouldn't even speak to anyone serving fewer than six or seven years.

Outside, men like Merrifield pump gas to survive, harassed day in and day out by the Arab owner of the station. Inside, they get respect, and rule over men who've fallen into their world.

Outside, they don't own TVs, and can't pay their phone bills. Inside, they control the televisions and run the phones.

A loser outside, Merrifield governs within these walls. He is sought after for advice and holds meetings of diplomacy. He is a shot caller, who makes life-and-death decisions.

Because a con serving one or more life sentences can only give the system one life, he can kill whoever he pleases. The law, having exacted its ultimate penalty, has lost its power.

The guards in the gun towers announced lock up. *"Recall. Recall. Clear the yard."*

I kissed Jimmy, banged knuckles with Michael, and walked back to my block.

I took off my shirt and lay down on my bunk, boots still on. You never take your boots off until you're locked in for the night, in case you have to fight.

I had my first taste of fresh air in years. My legs hurt and my head was spinning from all the laps around the track, but it felt good to have been outdoors.

Suddenly, sirens went off.

I sprang up and ran outside my tier block to see what was up. The prison was a madhouse, men screamed and jumped all over the place.

A hack flew by me carrying a bloody machete. More hacks ran out of A Block carrying homemade weapons.

Whites shouted:

"That's nigga blood. I seen 'nough to know. Nigga blood's dark red."

"Two dead, maybe three. Shit jumped off in A Block, dey took out some niggas."

"Dem niggas had it comin'."

Merrifield had planned a mass slaughter. He'd been with me minutes earlier. He wasn't nervous, or preoccupied. In a million years, I'd have never guessed what he was about to do. Like a gladiator, he returned from his last walk under the sun, strapped up, and entered the coliseum.

He and his Aryans moved from cell to cell, targeting senior Black Muslims. With lightning speed they entered the first cell, ran their victim through more times than a training dummy for a bayonet charge. They entered the next cell and hacked to death the umpire for the summer sports in the yard. Someone later joked that he'd made a bad call earlier in the day.

In the pen, I'd learn to joke of death. It's too real, too close, to be taken seriously.

Blood was everywhere, splattered on the walls, trailing from one cell to the next, even leaking over the tier.

Later, when the captain inspected the murder scenes, he dry-heaved, sickened from the sight.

The cons yelled, "What's a matter, coppa, never seen a little blood b'fore?" and "You sissy muthafucka, go home an' bake cookies."

The captain fled the tier, blood on his shoes. He left the prison in shame. In Lewisburg, once respect is lost, it's gone.

Following the murders, the prison was locked down. We were kept in our blocks.

No phones. No visits. No commissary. No mail. No yard. No nothing. We ate shiny green bologna on moldy bread three times a day.

Whites were on high alert for revenge.

I was one of only three whites on my tier block. I carried a machete wherever I went. It cost me a carton of smokes. It was made from a metal shutter removed from one of the air ducts on H Block, a tier block under construction. I strapped it to my waist, beneath my robe, when I went to the showers. I tucked it into a slit in my mattress when I slept.

After two weeks, we got mail.

A week later, an army of storm troopers filed into the tier block, ready for combat. They wore black riot gear, boots, vests, shields, and Darth Vader helmets. They came to flaunt their strength, to keep us in check.

A hack later told me why the glass was tinted on their helmets. "To hide our identities in case we 'accidentally' kill one of you."

I wondered what sort of violence people might enjoy when they can hide behind a mask, or their actions are legal, like the KKK or the Gestapo. Both were on a crusade to rid the world of subhumans. These gorillas were hostage to the same concept. I had every reason to distrust them.

They marched in eager for confrontation. A first row knelt, forming a wall with shields and nightsticks. A second row stood behind them, holding what looked like machine guns across their chests. Guns aren't allowed in prisons for fear of inmates taking them in a riot. They must've been loaded with gas canisters, beanbags, or rubber bullets.

The new captain swaggered in behind his men. He was dressed in a sport jacket. Cocky, he ran a hand through his slicked-back hair. A manicure, university ring, first time I smelled cologne in years. He cracked his gum, blew a couple of bubbles.

"The National Guard is outside the prison. I'm sure you've heard the helicopters. I have direct authority from Washington to use maximum force. Does anyone know what this means?"

Who would answer?

"It means we can kill you and get away with it. Does everyone understand this?"

He nodded his head with an "I thought so" look, then commanded his robots to back out of the tier block.

Later in the week, five-man goon squads took each of us to the phones.

When my turn came, I was stripped down and walked into the alcove just outside the block, where the phones hung.

Two goons stood on either side of me. Another jammed his baton into my neck, and told me to dial. He spoke through a mic in his helmet that distorted his voice.

I called my father; he hadn't heard from me in over a month.

"What kind of prison are you in, any fights in there?" he asked.

"No, none." I put his mind at ease.

I didn't lie; there were no fights in Lewisburg, only murders.

Here, I learned that a cut was kids' stuff. Adolescents cut faces. Cowards cut faces. In Lewisburg, men chopped, hacked, and gutted.

CHAPTER 22

I stood with him in my cell.

He pressed his nicotine-stained finger into his chest, then into his throat. "The heart or the neck, two kill switches, shuts 'em down dead in their tracks. Always remember if someone's comin' at ya, the heart or the neck. An' drive the steel deep inta 'im. Don't freeze up an' leave it inside the muthafucka. Pull it out an' wave it aroun'. Let the blood drip, the rest'll take off. Then get ridda it. Drop it, throw it, get it outta ya hands. Don't get caught wit' it."

I nodded along. The old lifer was teaching me how to murder a man with a machete.

"Always keep your eyes open," he went on, "there ain't a square incha this fuckin' joint where somebody ain't been slaughtered, I seen plenty fall. When we're off lockdown, I'll show you where we stash the knives in the yard. We got three or four by the bocce courts, another two buried by the tomato plants."

"Anythin' else?"

"Yeah. Welcome to Lewisburg."

CHAPTER 23

The Aryan Brotherhood is the most violent and feared gang in the prison system. They hate blacks, Jews, everybody, including themselves.

Most cover their bodies with tattoos: swastikas, lightning bolts, black men hanging from trees, skulls, crossbones, bloody daggers, and barbed wire.

Because they run tight, five or six Aryans in one joint can keep a thousand disorganized blacks in check.

But the Black Muslims are just as organized. They're a very religious group—that swears the white man is the devil. They see no contradiction between religion and hate.

In the pen, Aryans and Muslims carry "bone crushers." A bone crusher is a prison machete strong enough to penetrate a man's skull. Lewisburg has an industrial shop where inmates work, and make bone crushers in their spare time. They cleverly smuggle them from the shop to the housing blocks.

In the days following the murders I heard bits and pieces of how the race war began. A lifer named Gruff, one of three whites on my tier block, sat down and told me this story:

"This Aryan Brother named Horse went to the hole. The Seg Unit was packed so the hack doubled 'im up wit' an Arab muthafucka from the '93 Trade Center bombin'. The hacks wanted the AB to kill the muthafucka, figured it wouldn't take long. We all wanted the Arab dead when we heard he was here. We was all sharpening our knives but they never let 'im outta the hole.

"Anyway, when Horse got sprung, he was wearin' a kouffi an' carryin' a prayer rug. The fuckin' Arab converted 'im. Horse was droppin' to the floor five times a day toward Mecca.

"The ABs got fuckin' twisted. They stepped to Horse in the yard, told 'im to get the fuck off the compound, check in, cut yaself, jus' get transferred. Horse told 'em to go fuck themselves, said he loved Mohammed. They walked away, but started talkin' 'bout bangin' 'im out."

"Where'd Horse live?"

"Right across from me, in B Block. I had a front-row seat for the hit. He was hunched over 'is desk, writin' a letter when I heard footsteps, fast, hard, knew right away somethin' was goin' down. I sat up an' reached for my banger as two ABs stopped in fronta Horse's cell, drew bone crushers, an' went in. They planted 'em in his chest. Horse let out a death scream. Blood shot outta him like a garden hose. Somehow he pushed through 'em, I don't know where he got the strength, musta been shock. He didn't get far, slipped in 'is own blood, an' slid on 'is chest.

"They jumped on top of 'im an' hacked at his neck. I ain't never seen so much blood. They walked away proud, like they made their point.

"I threw my banger out the window, turned up my radio, an' laid down on my rack, like nuttin' happened.

"When they picked Horse up an' put 'im on a stretcher, his head almos' fell off.

"After a few days, the blacks looked weak, 'cause they wasn't doin' shit about it. So they picked this kid named Knoxville. Poor fuck wasn't even an AB, but he fit the bill, blond hair, blue eyes. Knox was young, had no hate in 'im. I knew 'im. He trusted the coons, drank wit' 'em, smoked wit' 'em. That's why they picked 'im, he was easy."

"How'd they get 'im?"

"He was drinkin' hooch, laughin' wit' 'em when one jigged 'im. The rest jumped in. Knox got stabbed in the face so many times the chaplain tole us his coffin was closed.

"The ABs went fuckin' nuts, they swore revenge for Knox. The coons said, 'We even, one Muslim's dead, one white.'

"But the ABs weren't buyin' it, they said, 'Fuck no, two whites are dead, an' three niggers are goin' down.' They was goin' back an' fort' wit' this shit when you landed."

CHAPTER 24

Lockdown ended slowly. After a couple of months, the warden began to give each tier block fifteen minutes of "freedom" a day.

My block was led into a small courtyard between two housing blocks. Hacks hung out the windows above, watching us walk in circles, like leashed dogs circling a parking meter.

We walked alone, until the warden felt it was safe to let us mingle with another block.

Security was beefed up all over the prison. Extra cameras were mounted everywhere, more metal detectors, and barbells were tied down with cables with just enough slack to bench-press.

When the warden believed we weren't about to kill each other, he allowed the whole prison to roam the main yard together.

During lockdown, cons had cut up plastic chairs and made knives to bypass the metal detectors.

Nothing changed. Everyone was armed.

The hacks knew this, but as long as metal detectors didn't buzz, they didn't care. They don't earn enough to risk their lives. Unlike police or firefighters, there's no glory in their heroism.

Whites were proud, they had one up on the blacks.

Some blacks talked shit. "We gonna chop up some white boys." Stuff like that. But most blacks were a bed of clams. They lost their swaggers, and lowered their heads at the sight of blond hair. A few cons from each race checked into protective custody, afraid of getting hacked up. Some weasels purposely got pinched with shanks in order to be removed from the mainline on a disciplinary, instead of a cowardly check-in. This made me laugh. Am I supposed to believe a man can walk through a metal detector forgetting he's strapped with a twelve-inch strip of sharpened steel?

The sight of heartless murderers terribly frightened of being killed is natural justice.

The law had spoken in Lewisburg.

CHAPTER 25

After lockdown, all inmates were ordered to work full-time. I was measured for a kitchen uniform.

I agonized over being separated from my novel. Writing was my escape from all the madness. I'd fallen in love with Aleesa, the heroine. A slave, she saved me from getting sucked into all the racial hatred swarming around me; how could I love her and hate them?

The characters I created became the friends I didn't have. I guess I was like a child who makes up imaginary friends to escape a harsh reality. I didn't want to give them up for ten hours a day.

In the end, reality ruled; I got my uniform and reported to the kitchen.

Lewisburg's kitchen had rats bigger than cats, and they weren't afraid of us. They walked around like, "Fuck you, this is my joint."

Sometimes, when I dumped large bags of rice or pasta into a vat, mice slid out, jerked in the boiling water, then floated to the top.

In the pen, cons are served enormous amounts of food to help swallow the harsh sentences. After every meal, we threw away pails of untouched meat, rice, and potatoes. Once, I was throwing out a dozen roast beefs, still in their nettings, when I asked the food administrator, "These get sent somewhere, a farm, a school, help feed the hungry?"

"Nothin' leaves these walls," he said. "Not even you!" He must've thought I was a lifer.

At the end of my shift, I'd mop the chow hall. When I'd finally get back to my bunk, I'd fall flat, read a page or two, then doze off with the book on my chest.

With little time to read, I became super-depressed. And life without Aleesa left me like a brokenhearted lover.

To combat my depression, I began to smuggle books to the kitchen. I looked for places to read. I hid in the vegetable cage, and behind piles of garbage, under counters infested with roaches, and behind ovens crawling with rats. I finally got caught in the freezer behind a stack of crates; my steamy breath gave me up.

"Don't bring a book to work again, or you'll go to the hole."

And that was that.

I was in the kitchen a few months when Jimmy Doyle pulled some strings.

"I got you a job at Education," he said. "Now you can read all you want."

CHAPTER 26

In the pen, sex is an extension of violence—the strong fuck the weak.

Any con afraid for his life will get bullied into giving up his ass. And rape is rampant. Once a con is raped, he becomes a "bitch," or sex slave. A bitch does laundry, cleans his master's cell, and gives blow jobs on demand.

One con on my block would bend his bitch over his bunk and spread a "girlie" magazine out on his bitch's back. He'd look at pictures of naked women as he fucked his bitch from behind.

One day he bragged about sticking pencils in his bitch's ears while getting a blow job. "Vroom, I rev the engine on ma bike, an' he go fasta."

A punk, unlike a bitch, wants to be a woman. These "women" choose their men.

Punks also fuck each other. They "marry," and have a "wedding," usually in the yard on a sunny day.

They're wed by a preacher, a bullshit, Bible-carrying con, who moonlights as a dick sucker himself. This preacher might scrape up a white robe, or a plastic cross, and give them their vows in front of a gang of punks.

We see this in the yard and laugh, but among ourselves. Punks are vicious; the emotions of women and the brute strength of men, a lethal mix.

Like gossip on the street, word of the wedding spreads.

I was reading on my bunk when a punk poked his head in. "Y'all hear who tied the knot?"

I ignored him.

He announced the wedding in every cell, knowing nobody gave a fuck, but it made him as happy as if he were gossiping under a hair dryer.

So what did I do for pleasure while all this craziness went on?

I jerked off. I was in my prime and it was the only way to release my aggression.

I thought about good sex I'd had while I was free, mostly cheap flings: the backseat of my car, a hotel room, on a staircase, in an elevator.

Sometimes, the women were familiar; I had dated them.

Sometimes, it was a one-night stand; I remembered the face, the moment, but not the name.

When these images became stale or blurred by time, I turned to magazines, "short eyes," "fuck books," and "paper pussy."

I'd been in jail a few years, when one day I was about to jerk off, and I got nauseous thinking about the magazine in my hand, and how gross it was to shoot a load into a filthy toilet.

When I pushed away thoughts of sex, I started to crave women in a different way. I longed to touch a woman, to run my fingers through her hair and listen to her soft voice.

Neat or disheveled, even asleep, snoring from a stuffed nose and drooling from the corner of her mouth, a woman is beautiful.

I had to be deprived of women to realize just how precious they are.

CHAPTER 27

The prison made high school dropouts get a GED. My job at Education was to tutor them.

One day, I was in the Education Department looking for textbooks when I found a locker filled with videos: *Gandhi, Lawrence of Arabia, A Man for All Seasons. . . .*

Fred Latham headed the Education Department. A small balding man with a fast walk, like a white George Jefferson. I spotted Latham in the hall. "What's up wit' all them tapes upstairs? Can I watch 'em?"

"You can't, they're for classes."

"What classes? I'll sign up."

"There are none."

"Can I start one?"

"Sure, write a curriculum and drop it in my mailbox."

"What the fuck is a curriculum?"

"Find out."

I found out fast, thanks to the dictionary. I put together a curriculum and paid a con to type it for me. Theatrical History was the title of my class. We'd watch a film, then I'd compare its accuracy to books I'd read on the subject.

I saw Latham a few days later and handed him my curriculum. He didn't get back to me, so I hounded him until he gave me a room and told me to start. "Tuesday nights," he said. "But it has to be open to everyone. With all this nonsense going on in here, I can't risk one color bitching that another has special privileges."

I posted an announcement for the class on every tier block. Only Italians and Irishmen showed; the rest didn't care or thought it was a trap, that they'd never make it out of the classroom alive.

Every Tuesday night, I'd roll an old TV to the front of the room and start a film.

When the door closed, everyone dropped their guard. We joked, laughed, and forgot where we were for a couple of hours.

On our way out of the room we'd tense up, back into the hell of maximum security. Our scheduled night was only canceled twice, for stabbings earlier in the day.

Latham saw that it worked, and allowed us two nights a week.

CHAPTER 28

I was walking with Jimmy Doyle in the yard when he stopped in the shadow of a gun tower. He looked up at the guard, who was holding a rifle, and said, "This is all I know. I spent my whole childhood in juvenile homes, my adult life in prison. I ain't got but a few years on the street in between. Hell, I got outta this place a thousand times, I'll get out again."

Jimmy was serving life with no parole. Unless the earth shook and the walls fell, he wasn't going anywhere. But Jimmy had that age-old Irish spirit that knows no surrender. He fought as a kid on the streets of Hell's Kitchen. He fought in prison, and in between stints, he fought his way to the top of the Westies. The fight was still in him. Even a life sentence couldn't shake it out.

Most lifers shared Jimmy's fantasy of being free. The system gives dead men hope by always allowing for another appeal. A con can lose ten appeals, but swear the eleventh is "the best one yet."

"New case law."

"This time they can't deny me."

"It's a lock."

"I'll be home for Christmas."

When the appeal is denied, the lifer mopes around depressed, violent, or suicidal, then files another appeal, and starts the same bullshit over again.

Aldo Cheesecake was different.

"I'm dyin' in jail, an' I know it," Aldo said to me. "Jimmy an' the rest of 'em fight like bastards, give all their money to scumbag lawyers who know better than to take it. When they're broke, they go to the law library. Look at Frankie, he reads law all day. He's got five lives, plus forty. He's jumpin' all over the fuckin' place 'cause he thinks he's gonna overturn his case this month."

"I heard he's got a good shot."

"Louie, he's appealin' the forty. Big fuckin' deal. He'll still have five lifes. Think they'll let 'im out? They got us, an' they ain't lettin' us go. We're all dyin' in here. I'm the only one who knows it."

Aldo hardly left his cell except to eat. He and I usually talked in the chow hall after the other guys left.

Every week I'd ask Aldo to watch a movie with us, but he wouldn't leave his cell.

Then one night, he showed up at the door. "I was a movie buff on the street," he said to me, "guess I'll try it out."

He had a blast.

After that, he'd run over to me in the chow hall. "What's showin' t'night?"

He'd wait at the door for Latham to turn the key. He'd stuff his pockets with popcorn and candy bars. He'd set up two chairs and recline. He thought he was at the drive-in.

One night, a fly got in the room. Jimmy Doyle swatted at it. Aldo got all bent out of shape.

"No, Jimmy, don't kill it!" he screamed. "Free it!" He opened a window and was hopping over chairs to shoo the fly out.

"Take it easy," said Jimmy, "it's a fuckin' fly. They only live a few minutes."

Aldo stopped and looked at Jimmy. "So a giant who lives a million years can come along an' step on us, an' say, 'Big deal, they only live a few years.'"

I was almost taken in by Aldo's reasoning, until Fritzi said, "Aldo, shut the fuck up an' watch the movie. You killed fifteen men, now you're gonna bitch about a little fly?"

Aldo was nuts. We all were. You have to be nuts to end up behind walls, more nuts to survive it.

The day before I left Lewisburg, I went to the yard to say good-bye to everyone. Aldo showed up at the bocce courts where we hung out, first time he stepped outside in years. His face was pale. His pants had creases that could slice bread. He had a comb-over hairdo. When the wind blew, his hair flipped over to one side and hung to his shoulder.

"I had no idea he was bald," I said. "It looked pretty good to me."

"You kiddin' me?" said Gaetano. "He's got one fuckin' hair a mile long."

When the guys went in, I stayed behind to walk the track.

"I'll hang out wit' you," said Aldo.

"Go in," I said, "I'm all right alone. I got the knives in the tomato patch."

"I came out to say good-bye."

"Thanks, I'm honored."

We walked.

"I don't like leavin' my cell," he said, "but I figured, shit, I'm never gonna see this kid again. I wanted to spend a little time, tell you thanks."

"For what?"

"For givin' dead men happiness. That movie thing was great, gave us all a chance to laugh. An' I loved them movies."

"I talked to Latham. He might give youse the room three nights a week. An' he's orderin' more flicks. I sat down wit' 'im, picked some real winners, Academy Award stuff."

Aldo shook his head. "When you leave this place, it's done. We all been here ten, fifteen years, an' never done shit. We needed someone to start things up."

"Now that I did, keep it goin'."

"Nah, it's done," he said. "But I'm glad you're leavin', I really am."

I didn't know what to say; Aldo would never leave prison.

"You should come outta your cell a little more, get some fresh air."

"I like to be alone, don't care too much for the people in here. I used to be a people person, threw a lotta parties, I even danced. You know wiseguys don't dance, gotta keep up that tough guy image. Well, that's bullshit, I danced up a storm." He drew a long breath and exhaled. "Now all I have is the memories. I sit in my cell an' reminisce. . . .

They're supposed to double up C Block. I can't live wit' nobody for the resta my life."

"I know what you mean. I like my own cell, too."

"Yeah, but it's different for you. You can put up wit' some guy fartin' all over you, knowin' you're gonna leave someday. It's harder when you got life. I was away wit' lifers who killed their bunkies. One guy cut off his bunkie's head an' held it up to the glass when the hack counted them."

We walked until the guards cleared the yard, just before dusk.

Inside, Aldo gave me a hug before he walked through the metal detector and into his tier block.

After a few steps, he turned back and gave me a sad, pathetic wave, then disappeared into the chaos: rap music blasting, bare-chested men covered in tattoos, screaming and cursing, hanging from the tiers. Scar faces. Gangs huddled close, planning evil. Drug dealing. Punks looking to suck someone off. Hell on Earth.

A year later, I was in another prison when a Boston Irishman from Lewisburg landed on the compound.

"How's everyone doin' in the pen?" I asked.

"Hangin' in there."

"They still do movies?"

"No," he said, "it ended two weeks afta you left."

Aldo predicted this; I was still surprised to hear it.

Months later, a Harlem gangster was transferred from Lewisburg. He walked up to us in the yard.

"I got bad news," he said, "one of your peeps in the pen died, his name was Aldo."

"How?" asked Gussy.

"The single-man cells in C Block were switched over to double bunks. Whoever refused to double up got bum-rushed an' dragged to the hole. Knowin' they was comin' for him, Aldo crushed his inhaler on the floor, coupla guys seen 'im do it. Later in the hole, he had an asthma attack, sat in the corner an' suffocated. He didn't wanna live wit' nobody."

I thought of that wretched hell, the stink, the filth, rapes, stabbings, and murders. Maybe Aldo had the right idea.

CHAPTER 29

Imagine coming home from work at the end of a long day. You turn on the TV to watch the news. Murder, rape, arson, kidnapping, torture, all part of the six o'clock show.

You cringe, might even get a cheap thrill. But you're so far removed from it that it's not real. The following day you might talk about it at work, and then it's done. That's entertainment.

Now, imagine every one of those bastards gets dropped off at your house. You're not allowed to leave your house. You must live with them for years, possibly the remainder of your life.

When you're hungry, you go to your kitchen for something to eat. Murderers sit at the table. They stare at your food, ask you if you're done eating before you've begun. They'd easily kill you for your dessert. You look up from your plate and the man who chopped up his children is sitting across from you. Do you feel like eating? Well, you must, or you'll starve. To escape the kitchen with your life is a relief.

When you shower, you must strap a steak knife to your waist because there are naked men in your shower who would love to fuck you in your ass.

After you shower, you decide to watch TV and retire to your den. Over the years, men have been killed in your den. In fact, several murderers have taken control of your TV. They're sprawled on the couch, scratching their balls and smelling their fingers, sharpening their knives, cursing and yelling.

You get up and leave, walk past your closet, and from inside you hear the whimpering of a man being rammed in his ass.

You need to get away from all this. You walk out to your backyard for a breath of fresh air. There are ugly men on your patio who'd like to kill you. You think about escape, climb the wall and run away from this madness, but there are sharpshooters in gun towers at the corners of your yard. Nothing would please them more than shooting someone.

You return inside to go to bed, a one-inch-thick mattress with no pillow. Your bedroom window is barred, and creepy men stare in at you day and night. You can't scratch your ass without an audience.

The guards are part of some far-off world you like to remember, the real world. Why not talk to them about all this craziness, let them know that you're not as bad as the rest. They might sympathize with you. Instead, they mock you. They're paid for, and express great delight in keeping you confined to this torture chamber, only adding to the insanity of it all.

And this is maximum-security prison. This is what a person must get used to to survive in this house, the Big House.

I thought about my life. Why did I end up here, living with animals? I beat men up. I shoved guns in their mouths. I even bit people. I lived like an animal on the street. I didn't realize it until I was placed in this zoo. I hated myself for being one of them. I know why people don't like to admit the truth—it fucking hurts.

I was worn down by these thoughts when the hack said, "Counselor wants to see you."

I went to his office.

"Your security level dropped," he said. "You're going to a medium. Pack your shit."

I was leaving Lewisburg on a bus. Not in a pine box.

CHAPTER 30

The night before my transfer a hack leaned into my cell. "Hey, Ferrante, wanna check into Protective Custody for the night?"

"No, why?"

"Guys aroun' here don't like seein' nobody leave, lotta jealous creeps. Jus' lookin' out for you."

"I'll take my chances, thanks anyway."

He left and I picked up my book.

A little while later, I wrapped my machete in a T-shirt and buried it in the garbage. I packed my belongings in a cardboard box. I had a few things I wasn't allowed to take: a desk fan, an extra sweat suit, a reading light.

Cube slept in the cell across from me. He was a quiet kid, kept to himself. I walked over and gave him my stuff.

"Thanks," he said. "What can I do for ya?"

"Nothin'. When you leave, pass it on."

"I ain't never leavin'," he said.

"You got bodies?"

"No, I ain't never raised a hand to no one in my life."

"I don't get it, how'd you catch life wit' no violence?"

"I grew up in the projects, sold a lotta drugs."

"You got life for drugs?"

"Yeah."

"How old were you?"

"Eighteen."

"Any appeals?"

"Lost 'em all. I'm dyin' in here."

"That sucks."

We banged knuckles and I walked away.

Americans are very forgiving about drugs—when it comes to actors and musicians, even politicians, not young black kids from the projects.

The next morning I was chained, wrists and ankles, and put on a bus. Giant steel doors swung open and we pulled out of Hell.

All around me I saw rolling meadows, flowers and trees, singing birds on branches, peace and serenity. I looked back at the high stone walls, battlements, and gun towers. Strange, like a medieval fortress was dropped on the Pennsylvania countryside. Rapes and murders on a sweet patch of farmland. A fucking madhouse in the center of paradise.

As the bus picked up speed, I heard voices and saw faces of those I'd left behind, so many who'd die alone inside those damp walls.

I twisted my neck until we rounded a turn and Lewisburg was out of sight.

It will never leave my mind.

CHAPTER 31

A few hours later I arrived at Otisville, a medium-security federal prison in upstate New York.

As the bus pulled in I saw chain-linked fences, coils of razor wire glistening in the sun, but no stone walls, and only one gun tower that looked like traffic control for a small airfield, and I think the guard was sleeping.

Before being released onto the compound, I was led into the counselor's office.

I sat across from a young man, smooth shave, new suit; he looked fresh out of college. He tidied some papers on his desk, slid them aside, and looked at me.

"I know where you just came from. Where you were, men kill each other. Not here. Guys might try you. If you're real stupid, you'll get yourself cut, or you might have to cut somebody. But nobody here is looking to kill you, so you don't have to kill anyone first. Take my advice, and do easy time. One fuckup, and you're going straight back to the pen. This is a nice place, don't blow it."

I was released onto the compound in time for lunch.

The chow hall's floor-to-ceiling windows had a view of the Catskill Mountains. Everywhere men laughed and patted each other on the back. Strange, you don't touch another man in the pen unless you want to fuck him.

I got a tray and fell in line. I wasn't on line long before two wiseasses slipped in front of me.

You don't cut the chow line in the pen. And you don't let someone get away with cutting you. My mind raced.

I had a plastic knife on my tray—snap it in half and jig one of them, the other will run. The guy behind me had a pencil in his pocket—snatch it and jam it in one of their eyes.

What the fuck am I thinking? I'm not in the pen. I smiled a sigh of relief.

I got my food and sat wherever the hell I wanted. Nobody was killing me over a seat in Otisville. And who cares if someone cuts the line, they could even step on my foot.

I don't know if the food was delicious or I just thought so, but it was the best meal I had in years.

CHAPTER 32

I went to the yard to walk off lunch, and bumped into a guy I knew from the pen who'd arrived a couple of months before me.

"This joint is sweet, like a college campus," he said.

"You went to college?" I asked.

"No, but if I did, I'da went here. Get your cell yet?"

"No. I heard they ain't bad, 'cept for roaches."

"Shee-it, I grew up in Bed-Stuy, we had roaches for pets."

I looked around the grounds. "I can't believe they got rose gardens."

"Some ole dope dealer plants flowers. He doin' twenty, keeps 'im busy."

"Is that him?" I nodded toward an old man on one knee, poking around behind a bush.

"Yeah, but don't look now, that's where he plants his ganja. Prob'bly checkin' on it."

"Wow, this place *is* sweet."

"You get high?"

"No, but I think I'm in heaven."

CHAPTER 33

The Italians showed me around Otisville—tennis courts, bocce courts, horseshoe pits, even an Italian TV room.

Gussy said, "Nex', we'll show you the pool room."

"We can swim too?"

"No." He laughed. "We shoot pool."

"This joint's better than the resorts my family went to when I was a kid."

"You can roam anywhere you want wit'out worryin' 'bout crossin' someone's turf," said Gussy, "but you're not allowed near Unit One, where they keep the snitches about to go into the Witness Protection Program."

Unit One was a heavily guarded fortress with a boundary we weren't allowed to cross. Windows were barred and blacked out, but sometimes open a crack. Whenever cons from the general population noticed this, they'd get as close as they could and yell something like, "Drop dead, you fuckin' snitches!"

A voice would always yell back, "I'll be fuckin' your wife b'fore you get home" or "I can't wait to snatch your daughter's pussy while daddy's away."

Hacks are rotated to different units. A hack who'd worked Unit One told us how well the snitches live. "They got color TVs in their cells, an' can borrow videos from the counselor's office. An' they eat better than me an' my family."

A year or so before I got to Otisville, Anthony "Gaspipe" Casso, the infamous Lucchese family snitch, had a fight with Fat Sal Miciotta, a

Colombo family snitch. They were housed together in Unit One, and were always arguing:

"You're a bigger rat than me."

"My family was tougher than yours."

"I killed that guy, why'd you say you did?"

On New Year's Eve, during one of these arguments, Casso rolled up a magazine and rapped Fat Sal over the head. Fat Sal covered up, then realized it was only a magazine. He beat the shit out of pint-sized Casso.

The hack who broke it up told us the two were pointing at each other, yelling, "He started it."

In prison, idleness leads to trouble, so everyone must work. In Otisville, Italians had good connections; "no show," "sign in sign out," or "do-nothing" jobs.

"I gotta hook in the pool room," Gussy told me. "All you gotta do is change the chalks once a week."

"I'll pass," I said. "I wanna see if they're hirin' at Education."

I found the woman in charge of the Education Department. "I'd like to make a curriculum an' teach a class on American history."

"Sure, go ahead," she said.

Otisville had a handful of men interested in learning. The class went well. A couple of months later, I taught European history. Then world history. After that, the works of Shakespeare. I was trying to pass on a little of what I'd learned.

Was I a good teacher? Who knows? I had a captive audience.

Renaldo Rizzo was known as the cheapest mobster in the underworld, the kind of guy who'd file a loss with the IRS, claiming a slow year in the rackets. He owned a dozen supermarkets. He was also a convicted capo in the Gambino family, serving an eight-year sentence.

Rizzo introduced himself to me. Big shots usually wait to be introduced by a third party. What's this guy want? I soon found out.

Before I was able to go to the commissary, Italians gave me what I needed: soap, toothpaste, shower shoes. . . .

As soon as somebody gave me something, Rizzo would walk up behind me and ask for it, "Can I borrow a Q-tip?" "A pen?" "Got a nail clipper?" "A teaspoon of sugar?"

Besides being cheap, Rizzo was bitter.

On the street, John Gotti ruled the Gambino family with an iron fist. With John locked away in a super-max, jailed wiseguys finally complained about him.

"He ruined Our Thing," Rizzo told me, "too flashy, brought too much heat."

Another time, Rizzo bitched, "I sent Castellano an envelope once a month, an' that was that. Not good 'nough for John, he wanted us to show up at his club every fuckin' week, so we could wave to the cameras. Who needed that shit? Before John took over, they snapped one photo of me in thirty years. After John, they took thirty thousand of me in one year."

John Gotti was diagnosed with throat cancer in prison, in '98. We all heard about it through the grapevine. Not long after, Nicky No Luck came to Otisville from a prison hospital.

"I jus' left John," said Nicky, after greeting us in the yard.

Pappy was an old-timer who got ninety years. To help convict him, the government used taped conversations in '91 between John and other mobsters. Pappy was about to roll a bocce ball down the court when he looked up at Nicky. "So, how's John doin'?"

"Not too good," said Nicky. "They took out his larynx, he can't talk no more."

"They're seven years too late," said Pappy as he bent over and rolled the ball.

The Otisville commissary sold one gray cotton sweat suit. Everyone wore it.

The Italians took me to the tailor, a Colombian drug smuggler with a sewing kit. He was creative with a sweat suit. He'd add pockets, make cuffs on the arms and legs. He'd cut the sleeves off, make you a hat with one sleeve, wristbands with the other.

We all sported this one stupid sweat suit a thousand different ways.

Whenever the Colombian came up with something new, like a V-neck, whoever sported it first would strut along the tier like a runway model. A minute later, everyone was banging on the Colombian's cell door.

Besides our Colombian fashion designer, we had a Peruvian fag who gave us manicures.

Officer Hardy worked my unit. He'd doze off, twiddle his thumbs, stare at his walkie-talkie, or scribble on a pad. Bored to death. When Hardy made his rounds, he'd stare into everyone's cell, then go back to his desk and sit like a lump.

One day, Hardy poked his head into my cell while I was reading.

"I read lots when I was a kid," he said, "got any good books to pass the time?"

I gave him *Moll Flanders* and *Robinson Crusoe*.

Hardy got so into the books he stopped making rounds altogether. Cons started smoking pot in the trash room. B-Train turned his cell into a tattoo parlor; he used the motor from a Walkman, a guitar string for a needle, and ink smuggled in on a visit.

Inmates are free to roam the prison, but aren't allowed to enter other housing units. Otherwise, a con can slip into a unit, pipe someone over the head, and split.

When Christmas came around, the Italians needed a hack to look the other way while we all snuck into one unit to get together for dinner. Everyone knew I got along with Officer Hardy.

"See if he'll let us do Christmas dinner by you," said Gussy.

By now, I did my own thing, kept some distance from the Mob. But these were good guys who looked out for me when I arrived.

I talked to Hardy.

"Okay, Ferrante, but not too many guys, I don't need a problem."

On Christmas Day, we took over the rec room in my unit. We pushed together the Ping-Pong tables and threw sheets over them for tablecloths.

Earlier in the week, Patty Paresi stole two buckets from the paint shop. With a homemade heating rod called a "stinger," we boiled five pounds of macaroni in one bucket, a fish sauce in the other. Ralphy the Bandit made garlic bread and caponata. We even had a plate of finocchio and olive oil.

I gave Hardy *A Christmas Carol* by Charles Dickens. His nose was an inch off the page as a dozen Italians from other units trickled in during the 6:00 p.m. move.

Old-timers sat on chairs, the rest of us on plastic crates. Patty filled the bowls. During dinner everyone was whispering to the guy next to him about old crimes. Finally, Patty said, "What the fuck we whisperin' about? We're already in jail." Everyone nodded and started to speak out loud.

After dinner, Gussy rigged up a swag Walkman, used paper cups for speakers, and played Frank Sinatra. Everyone got sentimental when Frank sang "My Way." We hugged and sang along, "I faced it all . . . and I stood tall . . . and did it myyyyyyy way."

Joe C. cried. Everyone thought the song touched him. I had an idea he was going sour; I think it was guilt.

Halfway through our meal, Officer Hardy tapped on the glass.

"Oh, shit, I forgot the hack," said Patty, putting on his apron. He made up a bowl, walked out, and handed it to Hardy.

Patty came back with the bowl. "He don't want it. He's lookin' for you." Patty nodded toward me.

I wiped sauce off my chin and breadcrumbs off my shirt, stepped out, and closed the door behind me. "What's up, chief?"

"What's up?" he said nervously. "You said a few guys. I got every top mobster in the world in my unit. What the fuck are you doin' to me?"

"Take it easy, it's jus' a little get-together."

"Little? It's bigger than Apalachin!"

That was the last holiday we shared together while I was in Otisville.

CHAPTER 34

Over the years, family and friends sent me hundreds of books. After finishing a novel, I'd pass it on or donate it to the prison library. But I saved history and biography books. I dreamed of one day owning a home with a library, so I boxed them up and sent them home to my father to store.

Between reading my own books, I wiped out the library at Otisville. I'd just finished Martin Gilbert's *Churchill*, about to return it, when I fanned the pages, and ran a hand over the cover. It was written so well.

"I'm keepin' it. It'll look better on my shelf than theirs."

I opened the back cover, ripped out the book pocket, and tossed it in the garbage. I put the book in my locker, lay on my bunk, and folded my arms across my chest.

I lay there a minute before I got up and took the book out of my locker. I threw it on the desk, sat down and stared at it.

I felt like a fucking lowlife. How could I learn so much and still be a thief? Churchill's grumpy smirk on the cover looked like he didn't approve of this either.

I reached into the garbage and pulled out the book pocket.

I went to the library during the next inmate movement.

I placed the book on the front desk and said to the inmate librarian, "This fell out." I held up the book pocket. "You gotta glue it back on."

"How did it fall out?" he asked, like a smart-ass.

I shrugged my shoulders. How do I explain that only moments ago I was wacky enough to rip a book pocket out of a book so I could steal the book and put it on a shelf in a home I didn't yet own?

"It fell out, I dunno how."

He opened the book to inspect, and ran his hand over the back inside cover. "It shouldn't have fallen out."

I lost my patience. "I ripped it out, okay? Jus' glue it the fuck back!"

I pushed the book at him and walked out.

Halfway back to my cell, I picked up a spring in my step. For the first time in my adult life, I realized that stealing was wrong.

CHAPTER 35

Reading and contemplation helped me to understand the world. I also wanted to understand myself.

Where did I go wrong?

Why did I do the things I'd done?

Was there a problem in my upbringing?

Growing up, my family fought and screamed a lot. I got a good crack here and there—isn't that a normal home? No excuse for my behavior.

Was the problem my environment? There's no Mafia in Cow Creek, Kentucky, but I think I'd have found bums to run with anywhere. I might've headed a gang of cattle rustlers.

We had no luxuries in a material world. Did this affect me? It affects a lot of kids. They don't all go around sticking up armored cars.

Was there something inside me that moved me to do the things I'd done? Was the trouble in my genes?

My father's parents were hardworking Italian immigrants. They came to America, broke their asses, and raised seven kids who did the same, all incapable of breaking the law.

My mother's family was different. They busted their asses, but took chances on the side. My mom's dad ran a bulldozer during the day. At night, he took numbers. When he wanted to get rid of his car, he dug a big hole with a backhoe near the Whitestone Expressway, drove the car in, and buried it. It's probably still there.

My mom's brother was known as the best bulldozer operator in New York. He did the work of three men, and could pick up an egg with a two-ton bucket. He did time in Sing Sing for hijacking.

Their blood was in my veins. Was this the problem?

In Otisville, I met a chiropractor, a corporate attorney, a banker, a broker, even a shipping magnate. On my first visiting day, I introduced my father to some of these cons, also on visits with their families.

"See, Dad," I said, "I listened to you an' Mommy after all. Youse always told me to hang out wit' doctors an' lawyers."

I looked for these men in the unit, and asked them to teach me about their professions.

Hamil was a chemistry teacher. I asked him to teach me chemistry.

"Sure," he said.

One day, after a lesson in Hamil's cell, I told him about my own chemistry.

"I was doomed from the start," I told him, "since my mother's family took chances and would break the law. . . . But my father's side worked hard, went home every night, an' minded their own business. . . . I gotta learn to be more like my dad's side, less like my mom's."

Hamil nodded along, probably thought I was nuts.

A few days later, I was reading in my cell when I heard someone holler.

Another fucking loudmouth, I said to myself.

All day long, from lights on 'til lights out, they don't stop cursing at each other. Imagine trying to read physics or philosophy over this shit?

I tried to ignore it and only dropped my book when I heard Hamil pleading. Then I heard a hard smack. I ran over to Hamil's cell.

Pugo, head of the Latin Kings, had his hands around Hamil's neck. Hamil's face was blue, he couldn't breathe.

"What's up in here?" I stepped into the cell, fists clenched and ready for action.

"Nothin', nothin'," said Pugo, startled. He let go of Hamil and slid by me.

Hamil was relieved, but embarrassed. I didn't ask what happened.

It didn't matter. I knew it somehow boiled down to the fact that Pugo was strong, and Hamil was weak. I walked back to my cell and picked up my book.

Minutes later, Hamil stopped by my cell and said, "Thanks. That was your mom's blood."

"Whatta ya mean?"

"You could've minded your own business. You said your mom's family wasn't afraid to take chances. Well, her blood just saved my ass. You have free will, don't curse your chemistry, put it to good use."

That was the best chemistry lesson Hamil ever taught me.

A few years later, when I came home from prison and settled into an apartment, my sister came by with a manila envelope. "Auntie wanted you to have this, some stuff about Poppy."

Poppy was my mother's father; he died when I was eighteen. Auntie was his sister; she died while I was in jail.

I opened the envelope and slid out an old frayed newspaper clipping and some yellowed papers. On one paper, a battleship captain commended my grandfather "For Excellent Service in the Line of Duty during an Air Attack on 12 April 1945, in which a Japanese suicide plane crashed into his ship." Twenty-two men were killed instantly, some so mutilated they were shoveled into canvas bags. One hundred injured.

Another paper was addressed to my grandfather from the Chief of Naval Personnel who "takes pleasure in forwarding, with his congratulations, the following award made to you for outstanding heroism in action against enemy Japanese forces."

My grandfather, who hung out in a bar for as long as I could remember, was awarded eight Bronze Stars in the Asiatic Pacific, and never once spoke about the war. The hair on my arms stood up as I thought about Poppy and remembered what Hamil had said to me: "They weren't afraid to take chances. Free will. Don't curse your chemistry, put it to good use."

CHAPTER 36

Richard Messina was a corporate attorney with an education from the University of Virginia.

First time I saw Richard he was in the yard reading A. Scott Berg's *Lindbergh*.

"Good book," I said, leaning down to look at the cover. "I also read Berg's bio on Max Perkins, another good book."

Richard looked me up and down, stared at my tattoos, then looked back at his book, sort of dismissed me.

Fuck him, I said to myself.

I was walking away when he asked, "What else have you read?"

I turned back, introduced myself, and took a seat on the bench beside him. He and I spent the rest of the day bullshitting about literature. We'd enjoyed many of the same books. I was blown away by his awesome memory; he could name minor characters from novels he'd read thirty years before, and quote opening lines.

Richard was a breath of fresh air. He quickly became my closest friend, my only real friend in years.

Richard loved language. He'd studied the origins of English and its development. Until I heard Richard speak, I hadn't realized that I pronounced so many words wrong; I'd learned most of my vocabulary through reading and had never heard the words spoken.

Richard took up the task of polishing up my speech. He'd interrupt me in the middle of a sentence, "If you're going to use lofty words, then pronounce them correctly!" Once in a while he'd throw in "Damn it!" or "For God's sake!"

I also used words slightly out of context, giving Richard a heart attack. "No, no, no," he'd say, "not quite." Or he'd throw up a hand, pinching his thumb to his index finger, saying, "Just missed, try again tomorrow."

In time, my speech improved. Family and friends noticed the change in my vocabulary.

"You soun' like the professor from *Gilligan's Island*," my sister told me on a visit.

My father once said, "You sound fulla shit. You sure everythin' you're sayin' makes sense?"

"I think so."

CHAPTER 37

Sometimes I felt like a higher court had passed judgment on me, and the more I accepted my punishment and tried to change myself, the better things went for me. So, this same higher power, this mysterious judge, was also capable of mercy. This led me to finally contemplate the existence of God, until now, a God who seemed to constantly think up new ways to make me not believe in him.

I read the Gospels, the Koran, the Bhagavad Gita, and studied Buddhism. But the Old Testament (the Torah) was the book for me.

I decided to take a close look at the Jewish people, the Torah's trustees. They were the first to receive the Bible. After all, could God have picked the wrong horse?

I read the history of the Jews, their philosophers, and the Torah over and over; each time it spoke to me anew.

Eventually I went to see the prison rabbi, asked him to put me on his Jewish inmate list so I could learn more. He ignored me, thought I was a phony, maybe after some special treats for Jewish inmates.

"Listen," I said, "I'm not interested in your bagel and your rugelach on Saturdays. I'm lookin' for conversation."

He gave in and we talked. He found out I was for real, even looked for me when I didn't show up at his office.

In jail, most American Jews aren't considered dangerous. The dozen or so I did time with were all there for nonviolent crime. I don't think anybody ever checked into protective custody saying, "I'm scared for my life, the Jews are after me." Putting on a yarmulke and a tallis was asking for trouble. Fuck it. I did it anyway.

When other inmates thought I made a final break from the Italians, they tried to get smart with me. A few times, I threw down my yarmulke, put up my dukes, and said, "Let's get it on, muthafucka!" They got the idea and things got back to normal.

The Italians made friendly jokes.

"A Jew?" said one. "Why you wanna turn cheap?"

"Can you represent me on my tax case?" said another.

One said in all seriousness, "Why'd you give up God?"

"I pray to God."

"Not Jesus?"

"Jesus is a middleman. Jews pray directly to God. Even on the street, I went straight to the boss."

He understood it in these terms.

Richard Messina came to my cell when he heard. "Do you think the Jews will accept you?"

"Why wouldn't they?"

"Are you kidding me? You may be the only man single-handedly capable of wiping out two thousand years of intellectual supremacy."

One Friday night, I was in my cell reciting a Hebrew prayer when a black inmate leaned in. "Shee-it, that Jew act even better than Vinny the Chin's bathrobe skit. You one slick muthafucka."

When I finally left the feds and went to state prison, I was allowed to receive a fifty-pound food package once a month. I called a friend. "Can you send me a package of kosher food?"

"Sure," he said. "I'll call my buddy at Ragtime."

Ragtime was a supermarket in Howard Beach.

A week after the phone call, I received my box of food: dry sausage, sopressata, pepperoni, pickled herring, and gefilte fish.

I called my friend that night. "I got your package, thanks."

"Good stuff?"

"Yeah, but I can only eat the kosher food, I gave the Italian food away. What did you tell the guy at the store?"

"I tole him you're halfa guinea, halfa Jew. I guess he sent you half an' half."

I decided to live by the Torah; it works for me. But I know that whichever religion you follow, or none at all, the bottom line is to behave kindly toward others—especially those who aren't so nice to you. I'm still working at this.

CHAPTER 38

As I flipped through the radio one night, I came across a classical music station. The music was a soothing escape from the chaos. From then on, I'd close my eyes every night to Mahler, Rachmaninoff, or Vaughan Williams.

The somber pieces moved me to think: Where I was and where I wanted to be. The people I hurt. The many mistakes I'd made, and how I wanted to live from here on.

Since the reception in my cell sucked, I asked the house electrician for a long strip of wire. I smuggled it to my cell, hooked one end into my radio, and tied the other to the bars for an antenna. I ran the wire along the wall, tucked it into the cracks between the cinder blocks, and covered it with toothpaste so the hacks couldn't see it. All this bullshit to listen to a concert airing that night.

I finally lay down, tuned in, and asked God, "What do You do when You're in the mood for music?"

In 1685, Domenico Scarlatti, Johann Sebastian Bach, and George Frideric Handel were all born. This is what God does when He's in the mood for music.

CHAPTER 39

I went through seven attorneys, all bums. Nearly every one of them said, "I can't take cash."

"But that's all I have."

"Okay." And they cleaned me out.

When I was broke, I studied law. I became friendly with the inmate law librarian. His name was Markos. I got him moved into my cell. He was a real legal eagle, and could spot any error. For months, he and I worked throughout the night filing briefs with the court of appeals. We reversed one of my cases on a technicality.

When I received news of my reversal, Markos and I danced around the cell like I was F. Lee Bailey and he was Johnnie Cochran, until I realized I still had a state sentence to serve. I may have saved a year or two, but I was giving up a sweet fed prison to finish my time in some scummy state joint.

In short, I was still tied up. Tied up a lot tighter and a lot longer than anyone I'd ever tied up—the ironies of natural justice continued to haunt me.

I sent the final chapter of my novel home. I hugged some friends good-bye. I was put in handcuffs, leg irons, and a waist chain, "a three-piece suit," and left Otisville. I was shipped to Nassau County Jail, where I'd stay until a bunk opened up for me in state prison.

CHAPTER 40

Thomas Pizzuto was serving a ninety-day sentence in Nassau County Jail for driving under the influence. He was a heroin addict, kicking without drugs. He begged the hacks to send him to the infirmary for methadone. They told him to shut the fuck up. When he didn't, one hack stood lookout while two others opened his bars, went into his cell, and smashed his brains in. One hundred billion neurons capable of change fell dead on the cement. Cause of death: "Blunt force trauma."

It's not uncommon for hacks to gang up on an inmate. I saw a man handcuffed and thrown headfirst down a flight of stairs. He lived but I don't know how. The incident was covered up; all convicts are liars.

But stiffs don't lie.

A commanding officer told the murderers of Thomas Pizzuto, "I'll write a report to cover you guys up." Sometimes this works. This time, it didn't.

I landed in Nassau County Jail shortly after Pizzuto's murder. I briefly lived in the same block where Pizzuto died, maybe even slept in his cell. But it wasn't because of this that I felt his ghost.

I was there a week when goons woke us with dogs, barking and snapping.

My grill was cracked and I was driven from my cell with no time to dress. I was searched, my gums checked with the same stinking fingers that spread apart my ass cheeks.

"Get against the wall an' stay there!"

The goons raked through my few possessions, throwing everything outside my cell.

"That's a picture of my mother."

"Shut the fuck up! File a grievance."

"That's a card from my sister."

"Shut the fuck up! File a grievance."

A minute later, I was shoved back into an empty cell. Bars slammed behind me. All that I had moments before was wheeled away in a big waste bin.

The goons moved from cell to cell. Men not yet searched were meek, hoping a small item of sentimental value might be overlooked. Men already searched had nothing left to lose; they pressed their faces against the bars, cursing the goons.

Now and then, a convict was cuffed up and dragged away.

Some went easy, others kicked and screamed.

A tall, thin African American threw himself at the goons with kamikaze courage, getting beat down for the entertainment. Their clubs thrashed against his skull. The block silenced to listen to the thud of wood on bone. Blood encouraged his attackers like wolves on the kill. He fell to his knees, then crumpled to the floor. A boot crushed his cheek.

A man beaten down in the real world might have his day in court, or seek his own vengeance. This con sucked at the air with a blank stare of utter defeat without hope of reprisal. He'd already lost in court, and was no match for Goliath. Cruel men in a hidden cavern of society beat him where no one can see but those of us whose testimony is forever branded lies. And because we must live among them, they can rely on our silence.

Four goons cuffed his wrists and ankles, and lifted him by his limbs. They walked him facedown past my cell, like pallbearers carrying a coffin. Their jeering laughter expressed the ecstasy of violence without accountability.

Except for a smear of blood, he was completely forgotten by the rest of us as the shouting resumed. Our voices banged off the concrete like jackhammers breaking up a sidewalk. The noise is deafening. It's impossible to understand anything but "motherfucker" this, and "motherfucker" that, like an atomic "motherfucker bomb" was dropped on the tier. (I still hear this in my sleep.)

After the shakedown, the goons left the block. Everyone tired out, except the usual loudmouths, who again had the stage to themselves.

They cursed the hacks. The hacks got pissed and kept us locked in. Locking us in our cells when we're normally permitted to roam the tier block should shut everyone up, but one or two always run on, insisting how little they give a fuck about the threat of indefinite lockdown.

These mouth-runners are full of shit. They can't bear the absence of human interaction and childlike recreation, such as television, checkers, and Ping-Pong. I can practically measure how much the threat of being locked in their cells torments them by how much they bitch that it doesn't.

Soon, they beat the walls, bang and pull at their bars like chimps gone berserk at the zoo. After a while of this, their threats weaken into menacing talk without conviction. Still, they don't stop, believing the guards who are dangling the keys will unlock us if convinced their punishment isn't working. Torn between this ridiculous assumption and a bit of logic that counsels them otherwise, their mouths bark while their tones beg.

Besides being the cause of our punishment, in turn pissing us off, the loudmouths have exposed their fear of confinement, bringing upon themselves a new crisis—their standing in the eyes of fellow prisoners.

In prison, daily survival depends on being thought of as dangerous, rather than afraid. Just as a dangerous person in society is one who is unmoved by the threat of jail, a dangerous person in prison is one who doesn't give a fuck about going to the hole, a jail within a jail.

A prisoner afraid of being confined to his own cell is surely afraid of going to the hole, the penalty for fighting or stabbing another con. If a con fears the hole, and his cover is blown, everyone on the block, in time, will be blown by him.

They curse the guards, and keep us all confined, prolonging their agony and asking for trouble with the rest of us. Sadly, their mouths cause them intolerable suffering, but they can't stop.

I wrote this piece immediately after a shakedown, long before I ever imagined writing this book. Writing was my way of dealing with crazy shit. I was sitting in my underwear, shut in my ravaged cell, violence teeming around me. Outside my cell, an orderly mopped up the blood from the man who'd been beaten and dragged away.

At one time, I'd get twisted over little things I'd lost, like a book or a pen, a letter, sneakers, a homemade nightlight, or a picture of my family.

At some point, I'd lost something or another and was pushed over the edge. I no longer gave a fuck about small possessions.

Time and again, I'd lose everything, sit in my cell naked and shivering, and repeat my sanity-saving maxim, "Fuck you, you can't take my mind! Fuck you, you can't take my mind! Fuck you, you can't take my mind!"

I'd then use what they couldn't take to think about inhumanities far worse than I'd ever known, inhumanities I learned about through reading.

I'd reason away my own hardships as mere bullshit when compared to the hardships endured by innocent people throughout history.

After all, what's a little shakedown compared to the Gestapo invading your home in the middle of the night?

Innocent Jews, adults and children alike, lost everything, asses and gums checked like common criminals. Unlike me, they never again saw their homes.

I could well imagine the faces of those wicked fucks who dragged them off in the dead of night. The same faces who beat Thomas Pizzuto to death in his cell. The same faces who beat the African American to the ground and stomped on his cheek with a boot. Every so often I awoke to those faces, then returned to sleep to awake again, and pick up the pieces of my shattered life.

During the Holocaust, the little two-year-old girl with ringlets and a bonnet awoke to those faces once—then slept forever.

God forgive mankind.

CHAPTER 41

I spent several months in Nassau County Jail before I was chained and squeezed into a sealed unmarked van on my way to Downstate maximum security state prison. Blacked-out windows, pitch dark, and packed. Like being thrown into a smelly closet with strangers.

We drove for hours. I was dizzy and squinting when we finally arrived and the van doors swung open. We were led into a cold bullpen. No heat. No coats. Early January.

Without warning, my final possessions were taken from me and thrown into a garbage pail. The pail was stuffed with the personal belongings of a hundred men. I saw pictures: families, girlfriends, wives, children. When they posed for these pictures, they had no idea they'd end up in the trash. The state didn't allow us to bring "garbage" over from the feds.

Next, I was stripped naked and given a plastic cup filled with disinfectant soap for lice, ticks, and fleas. I was directed into a dark shower room. My bare feet were in a puddle of ice water. I shook like I was being zapped with electricity.

A large naked man stood beside me, holding a chain that hung from a showerhead. He was wet and shaking. The guards laughed at him. "Get that soap off, boy!" He was a man, but cried like a baby, playing into their cruel humor.

He finally mustered the courage to pull the chain, releasing a rush of cold water on top of his head. He cringed, screamed, and pleaded.

"More water, boy!" was all they said. "Still got some soap on ya!"

While the guards enjoyed his suffering, I scooped out most of the soap from my cup and wiped it on my leg, knowing they'd want every last sud washed off me.

One turned toward me. "Soap up!" he said.

I rubbed the dab of soap into my scalp and braced myself for freezing cold water, in a freezing cold shower, in the freezing month of January, in a hell with no heat.

I clenched my teeth and yanked the chain without being told—Fuck you—I wouldn't give them the satisfaction.

Ice water poured over me. My head went numb, a total brain freeze. I looked at the man beside me, stomping his feet in his own shit. He wanted to get out but the guards blocked the door, so he stomped and cried.

Some men had been in transit for weeks and arrived stinking like pigs. This poor bastard must've soaped himself up really good, believing the water would be hot, and he'd finally take a refreshing shower. He was so fucking wrong.

Every time I yanked at the chain, I told myself this would end, that it wouldn't last much longer.

As I walked out of the shower, I looked up toward the ceiling. "Why, God?"

I wasn't questioning my own situation. I was already leaving these scumbags behind. I was thinking about those filthy lowlife motherfuckers who couldn't add or spell, and had shoved professors and scientists into the showers at Auschwitz and Dachau.

When I embraced the Torah, I became a Jew in mind. When I put on a tallis, I became a Jew in body. When this thought entered my mind and tormented me, I knew I'd become a Jew in spirit.

CHAPTER 42

I was assigned a cell. I told a hack, "My window's broken an' it's freezin' in here."

He looked in and said, "Go fuck yaself," then walked away.

I went to sleep fully clothed, even crawled under the mattress for warmth. I shivered all night. By morning, my body was blue. Somehow, I survived a week like this.

Downstate was my first stop on my way up north.

I was bused upstate to my next stop, Clinton Dannemora.

Known as Little Siberia, Clinton has a Death Row, and a death look. High rotting stone walls, and the sun never shone; Dracula's Castle.

I spent a week here in a transit dorm. Convicts usually keep dorms and tier blocks where they live as clean as they can. But transit dorms are disgusting; we move through them too quickly to care.

At night, roaches covered my body. In the morning, I'd strip naked and shake them out of my clothes. Mice were in our shoes. One con bitched about this. The hack said, "Maybe your feet smell like cheese."

From Clinton I was bused to Adirondack Prison, my final destination.

I was told that the prison was once a tuberculosis hospital, with a crematorium still in the basement. The sick came here to spend their final days.

On my block, the hacks' station was the old nurses' station, and our rooms were where patients died. The building was condemned to house the condemned, whether terminally ill or prisoners.

Early one morning, just after dawn, the mountains began to rumble and my bunk shook.

"What the fuck's goin' on?" I asked my cell mate, who was lying on his bunk.

He shrugged his shoulders. "Don't know an' don't care."

I stumbled out into the corridor.

"What's goin' on?" I asked the hack, who was white as a ghost.

"How the fuck should I know?"

When the building settled, everyone walked out of their rooms; I walked back into mine. My cell mate's bunk had moved a few inches from the wall. He lay there, hands clasped behind his head, legs crossed.

"You feel that shit?" I asked.

"It shoulda fell," he said. "We coulda walked out."

He turned over and faced the wall.

I was imprisoned eight years when an earthquake centered in upstate New York shook the eastern seaboard from Maine to Maryland. I'd become hard. My bunkie had fourteen in, eleven to go. He cared about nothing. Dead numb.

Prison makes you harder than the stone and steel around you.

I often wondered if the damage could be undone.

CHAPTER 43

I wasn't in the prison long when I received news that I was eligible for parole. Since my state sentence ran concurrent with my federal sentence, I'd already served the minimum time needed to see a parole board.

I called home to tell my family the good news.

I saw no reason for the board to hold me. My disciplinary record was spotless. I educated myself and taught others. A model inmate.

A month later, I went in front of a "triumvirate" who cared nothing about how hard I'd worked to change myself, and what I'd done to help others. They "hit" me. Just like that. "Come back and see us in two years."

That same day, a child molester who'd served less time than I had was sent home.

I was bitter. But bitterness could only harm me and affect others around me, so I quickly licked it. Back to the books.

Six months later, I got a surprise letter in the mail informing me that I was eligible for Work Release.

Again, I called home to tell my family, even read the letter over the phone. The door seemed so close.

I practically skipped to the hearing and was led into a room with three serious faces. A different triumvirate.

"Your case is violent," they told me, "you're hereby denied."

They never let me speak, tell them how hard I'd worked. I never got to show them my commendations, all tucked under my arm. They didn't care. I was told to leave.

"May I ask a question?"

Someone nodded yes.

"You knew all about my case before you sent me this letter telling me I'm eligible for Work Release. If I'm being denied because of my record, then I was never eligible to begin with, since my record existed long before that letter."

"You were eligible, but because of your record, you're ineligible."

This should've been enough for me to quit, but I continued for the hell of it, "When do you overlook my record?"

"Never!" said the hag who sat between two monsters.

That word. That moment. Their faces. I'll never forget any of it. It made me wonder what I was working so hard for.

On the walk back to my block, I reminded myself that I didn't work hard for them. I did it for me, my family and friends, the half of this world who cares, and to honor my mother's soul.

CHAPTER 44

In the feds, lifers die in jail, there's no parole.

State law is different. Lifers have a chance at parole, usually after twenty-five years. But their minds are burnt out, and most are better off left inside.

If the prison gates swung open, some wouldn't leave. To go where? And do what?

When one con's mandatory release date approached, he walked into the TV room and stabbed the closest man to the door. New charge = No release = Happy con.

They are conditioned, and can't cope with free will.

An inmate down the hall from me once hollered, "On the chow." It was two a.m. My bunkie got up and began getting dressed for breakfast.

"Go to sleep," I said, "that was someone fuckin' aroun'."

After eight years in prison, I may have fallen for it, too, if I hadn't been awake reading.

You lose your sense of time in prison, since every day is the same.

On a visit, my buddy asked me how old I was. I paused, had to ask him what year it was. You ignore birthdays in jail, a sad day, a reminder of how long you've been locked up, and how much of your life you've wasted. I felt this way no matter how industriously I used the time.

Cons who've been away a while are stuck in time. I was able to tell when a man was put away just by listening to his stories.

One con ran on and on about how great Woodstock was. He'd been in since '69.

Another talked all day about his red '84 Camaro.

"How long you got in," I asked, "'bout fifteen years?"

"Yeah, how'd ya know?"

I was away with a forty-five-year-old man who'd never driven a car or been with a woman; he came in when he was seventeen.

These men, whose lives have been cut short, exist in a fantasy world. They dream of life in the real world. But prison is all they know.

I had a bunkie who told me, "When I get out, I'll be chillin' in my Benz wit' my Rolly. Then I'ma sit down at a five-star restront an' eat me some rice an' beans, french fries, an' fried Jack-mac [canned mackerel]."

They have little sense of time and no sense of reality.

CHAPTER 45

Even after I finished my novel, I kept writing. I wrote a Torah commentary. I recorded my dreams, which led to a theory on time, and wrote thousands of pages of notes on every subject.

One day, another con saw me writing and asked if I could write a letter to his wife. "She 'bout to leave me." I wrote one, then another, and another until I patched up his marriage.

Word spread.

Another con asked, "Can you write a poem for my girl?"

I did. This also got around.

Soon, I was writing poems and love letters for just about everybody. I'd sit a guy down in my cell and try to get a handle on his feelings to keep the writing real.

I helped some write their own letters.

While I was held in the county jail, I met a fifty-something man named Bruce. He was slow, probably mildly retarded. He'd been arrested for graffiti, locked up for ten months, and never taken to court.

Bruce asked me for help. I called his court-appointed attorney, who wouldn't get on the phone with me. I wrote to the court clerk as if I were Bruce, demanding a court date. No response.

When I left Bruce, I'd accomplished nothing for him; it was almost a year since he'd been arrested.

Months later, I'd just sat down with my tray in the Adirondack chow hall when a black kid yelled from across the table, "What up, Lou?"

"I don't recognize you," I told him.

"It's me, Dreads, from the county."

I pictured a mop-full of dreadlocks around his bald head.

"I didn't know ya head was that small."

"Po-lice shaved my shit in Downstate," he said. "I'll grow 'em back."

"What's up?" I asked.

"'Memba Bruce?"

"Yeah, he's still locked up?"

"No, your shit cut 'im loose. He lef' 'bouta week afta you. Went to court, came back, an' bounced. He tole us all to look out for you in the system, tell you 'Thanks.' "

That moment was the best I'd felt in years, maybe my entire life.

CHAPTER 46

One night, I tuned in to a lecture on public radio. At the end, the announcer told listeners how to purchase the tape. Unlike the feds, the state allowed cons to have a cassette recorder, so I asked my family and friends to send in lectures on cassette.

From then on, I gave my eyes a break from reading every few hours and listened to university lectures while staring out at the snowy Adirondack Mountains.

One day, a squirrel hopped onto my window grating from the ledge below. He appeared so suddenly, it looked like he was thrown at the grating. I broke off a piece of the granola bar I was eating and put it on the sill. He ate it then and there.

My bunkie had been in the prison for years. "They come around all the time," he said. "If you feed 'em, they'll never stop."

I bought nuts, and more came. All day, squirrels traveled in and out of the surrounding woods to my window, navigating coils of barbed wire. They'd pop up with an inch of snow on their heads.

I named them. Scars had a deep gash on his back from the razor wire. Rusty had spots of reddish brown. And then there was Balls; I didn't know they had any until he showed up. He was nice, except when he'd pee on my window. After the females gave birth, baby squirrels came too. They'd hang upside down on the grating and eat. I petted their bellies. They relieved my solitude.

CHAPTER 47

I was chained to Slim on the bus ride from Clinton to Adirondack. Slim was serving a six to twelve for robbery, which would probably amount to the max because of his record.

Slim's parents were junkies. He and his brother were taken away by the state and placed in foster homes. In one home, they slept in the attic. They weren't allowed downstairs at night, even to use the bathroom.

One night, Slim couldn't hold it and took a leak in the corner. He was covering it up with newspapers when he heard someone stomping up the stairs. His urine leaked through the ceiling. His foster dad beat him until he pissed blood.

Slim's brother was in another jail serving twenty-five to life for murder.

Slim and I were housed in the entry dorm at Adirondack together. As soon as I arrived, I had commissary money sent in. Slim had nobody outside to send him money.

On our scheduled store day, I asked if he needed anything, figured I was chained to him for two days.

"No," he said, "I'm good. I been goin' wit'out my whole life. Thanks anyway."

I bought Slim some necessities anyway, soap, shampoo, and some ten-cent soups, for nighttime hunger.

A few days later, Slim noticed me reading the Torah on my bunk, a yarmulke on my head.

"You're a Jew?" he asked, surprised.

"Yeah."

"I thought you was Italian."

"I'm an Italian Jew."

It wasn't necessary to give him the whole conversion story. I just said, "Jews come in all flavors, Spanish, Italian, American."

He narrowed his eyes, bothered.

That day, he and I were assigned to different housing blocks.

Later that week, I saw Slim in the yard with some young white kids. They huddled together for about five minutes until the hacks broke them up. On my way back to my block, I overheard someone say that Slim was an Aryan leader, and the huddle was an initiation.

Slim was tattooed up, but no swastikas or lightning bolts, at least that I could see. Either way, I went my way, he went his. We wouldn't mix well.

A couple of weeks later, Slim snuck into my block, walked into my cell, and dumped some music cassettes on the bunk. "Some dude who knew my bro went home an' lef' 'em to me. You can keep 'em. My brother's an Aryan, too. I wrote him a letter, tole him the only guy who ever helped me in my life is a Jew. I feel fucked up."

He opened his shirt and showed me a swastika tattooed across his chest. "Some dude in my block's gettin' ink on the visit. I'm coverin' this up nex' week."

A ten-cent soup can change someone's opinion of an entire race; the power of a good deed.

CHAPTER 48

I lived in C Block.

Men serving time in the hole were allowed an hour of outdoor rec a day. The men were put in small iron cages right beneath the windows of our second-story housing block. They'd yell up to us and ask if we'd relay messages to other prisoners on the compound.

As long as the messages were harmless, I'd help if asked. I'd been doing this for several months before it dawned on me how insane it was to speak to men in dog cages and think nothing of it.

I'd been jailed too long.

Exactly how long didn't hit me until I was walking to chow and someone yelled, "Hey, Pop."

I looked around and saw a kid behind me. "Who the fuck you callin' Pop?"

"You. What's on the menu?"

"Pop? I'll break your fuckin' neck!"

"Easy, ole-timer, I ain't mean to offend you."

When I came to prison, everyone referred to me as "Kid." I now had some grays, a receding hairline, and lines on my forehead.

Pop. That hurt.

CHAPTER 49

After two more years of study, I received a letter for another parole hearing. A few weeks before, I noticed a crowd in front of a cell, laughing. Some guy was on his bunk in violent convulsions. He was lying on his back, and had bitten his tongue. I ran into his cell. After I wrestled him onto his side, I pried his mouth open to drain the blood. When I carried him to the infirmary, the nurse told me he'd had a diabetic seizure and I'd saved his life.

The next day, the guy thanked me. A few guys on the block told me to ask the prison parole officer to put it in my report for my parole hearing. I still have the letter that I received in response to my request. It reads: "Parole will not solicit a letter of commendation from medical or your dorm officer."

Odd, since they never had any problems scraping up stuff to keep me in jail.

Anyway, I went to see the parole board.

If they hit me, I'd have less than six months left before my mandatory release date.

I was in prison over eight and a half years. What's another six months?

This was the attitude I took to the parole hearing. They don't tell you their decision on the spot. I remember walking back to my block, certain that I'd lost.

Jupiter was a 250-pound gorilla, known for raping cons.

I slept across from Jupiter's cell. He bunked with a kid from Trinidad, nicknamed "Trini." Every night, Jupiter laid it on Trini hard, fucking him for a good half hour before falling asleep on top of him. I'd hear Jupiter snoring and Trini trying to squirm out from under him.

One day, Trini must've "dropped a note" behind the hack's desk, snitching on Jupiter. Trini had no idea Jupiter was also the hack's inside man.

I was on my way back from the phone when the hack was reading the note for everyone to hear.

The hack hollered for Jupiter.

Jupiter walked up to the desk, rubbing his eyes like he just woke up from a nap. "What up?"

"Your cellie says you been reamin' him in his ass every night. Is that true?" The hack held up the note; Jupiter snatched it and read it with difficulty, then ripped it up and threw it to the floor. He stomped back to his cell and disappeared inside.

First I heard, "You tellin' the po-lice I been doggin' your ass!" Then I heard a loud slap. What I heard next reminded me of cartoons when the door is closed and the characters are banging around inside.

A minute later, Jupiter walked out of his cell and said to the cop, "My cellie clocked me." He didn't have a mark on him.

The hack hit the alarm and had the goons lock up Trini for assault. Trini was dragged off, his eyes swollen shut, a fat lip, and his shirt ripped and soaked with blood. Jupiter went back to his cell. I heard him snoring ten minutes later.

Every month, a list of new parolees is posted on the wall for everyone to see. I found out I made parole when my name appeared on this list. Predators love this list; they know a release date can soften up an otherwise tough con. Most cons don't want to risk a fight, and in turn a new charge, when freedom is so close.

Jupiter was always first to run up and see the parole list.

When I called home to tell my family that I'd made the list and would soon have a release date, I noticed Jupiter over my shoulder; he'd been eyeing me all day.

By this time, I wore glasses and a yarmulke. I looked more bookish than crookish. He had the wrong impression.

When I hung up the phone, Jupiter stepped to me. "I want the phone at eight o'clock!"

"Why tell me?" I asked. "I don't run the phones."

"You gettin' smart wit' me, Jew Boy!"

The hack, his hack, poked his head over the desk and looked down the corridor at us, then ducked back in.

A dozen witnesses. The hack's on his side. My release date. A no win.

I went back to my cell and sat on the edge of my bunk, my body trembling from adrenaline. I wanted to smash his brains in, but I kept telling myself he wasn't worth it.

Unfortunately, jail isn't that simple. If I let him get away with this today, tomorrow he'll try to rape me.

As soon as this thought entered my head, I was convinced he was after my ass. Can you blame me?

My mind-set shifted.

"I don't give a fuck," I said to myself. "I'll blow my date!"

I went looking for him.

I found him alone in a stall in the communal bathroom, his big tugboat sneakers tapping on the floor, cigarette smoke rising over the door.

I kicked open the door. He was taking a shit with his hand around his prick, a cigarette hanging from his lip.

He tried to pull up his pants. I hit him in the jaw with a right, but it didn't faze him, so I kicked him in his balls.

"You want this ass, muthafucka?"

He couldn't answer, couldn't catch his breath.

"I don't give a fuck if I'm leavin' this joint in five days, or five minutes, you fuck wit' me again an' I'll cut your fuckin' balls off! You hear me?"

I slammed the door on him and walked away.

Back in my cell, I tried to cool down, but I still had a big problem.

At this point, I didn't care if Jupiter ratted me out to the hack. But the whole tier block saw him shout me down. No one saw me even the score in the bathroom. As far as they knew, I'd turned soft since I got my release date. I'd have to deal with five more Jupiters before leaving if I didn't fix his ass on Front Street.

I was thinking about different ways to get him again when some con named G-Money walked into my cell, a towel around his waist.

"You one crazy muthafucka," he said. "Ev'ybody be talkin' 'bout it."

I scrunched up my face. "Talkin' 'bout what?"

"How you jus' punked out Jupiter in the bat'room. Yo, yo, I jus' stepped out the shower nex' to the shitters when you blew big boy's cover. I tole ev'ybody he a fake."

Jupiter avoided me until the day I left.

The Head Honcho upstairs had watched over me for years. I'd leave prison without a mark on my face and my ass as tight as a tie.

CHAPTER 50

Iwas required to attend a two-hour class to help cons readjust to the outside world. The guy seated next to me had been in a cell for twenty years. They stuck him in this same two-hour class and believed he was suddenly ready for New York City.

After years of incarceration, some men were given fifty or sixty dollars in "gate money," a canvas jacket, and tossed out into the street. They gave one man back the pants he was locked up in. He held the pants up to his waist; they hung to his knees.

Watching these men stuff underwear and toothpaste into a brown paper bag saddened an otherwise happy day.

They asked directions to a shelter. Some trembled. One cried.

They had no home. No family. No job. No driver's license. And no car. And a week later, they must report to parole, or be violated and sent back to prison. How do they get to parole?

The money given them should last a day or two, then what?

There's your high rate of recidivism.

CHAPTER 51

I was feeding a squirrel on my windowsill when the hack tapped my shoulder. "Turn in your linens, you're outta here." He asked me if I wanted to take the window with me, "since you haven't moved from it in two years." He wished me luck.

With the exception of a couple of real assholes, the hacks in Adirondack were supercool.

It was finally time to leave.

My vision was blurred from years of reading and writing in the dark. I couldn't see three feet in front of me. I read through splitting headaches, missed countless meals, and wrote until my fingers would cramp up and I'd drop the pen.

I wondered why I'd worked so hard. Why, when I could never erase my record? Why, when statistics say the rest of my life should be a downward spiral? Why'd I read over a thousand books? Why'd I listen to over a thousand lectures? Why'd I write a twelve-hundred-page novel I couldn't get anyone to read? Why care when even today people walk away from me when they hear about my past?

I looked out of my cell window at the Adirondack Mountains. I longed to be high up on one of those peaks, on the other side of that razor wire, far away from gun towers, without a number on my chest.

I thought about the subjects of all those great biographies I'd read, and I wondered why each of them had worked so hard.

The people I admired didn't do it for money; some never saw any. They never posed for a portrait or a bust. Many never stood before an admiring crowd or experienced the thrill of thunderous applause. Then why had they given themselves over to such painstaking effort?

For a moment, I knew their secret. I felt it somewhere inside me. Before the feeling had passed, I sat down on my bunk and wrote these thoughts:

It's all for that quiet moment on a remote mountaintop at twilight when all of the world's glory passes before the lonely heart of man. When Rodin's trusty chisel has fallen to rest beside the stone flakes. When the quill of Montaigne has dried and drifted to Earth. And the last gloom and glee has been masterfully fondled from the orphaned keys of Chopin's piano. When the tragic wanderings of an incorrigible seeker are at last acquainted with the great beyond. When any personal struggle, endured with brilliant tenacity, lifts up the chin, and the ominous void that man has always, terror stricken, infused with grunts, syllables, words, then talk, is now the faithful confidant to whom he turns, when the triumphs of his mighty soul, and all that ever was, and all that ever will be, the infinite power and majesty of creation, are momentarily fused and finely balanced between the frail lips of a mortal stranger who scratches into the wind the bulk of his bounty, the infinite depth of his determination, and the ultimate sum of his glory . . . bound up in a simple phrase ordinarily fashioned by the bouncing lips of a small child in need of hurrah, "I did it."

These were the last three words I spoke before I walked out of prison, a place I'd called home for nearly a decade.

EPILOGUE

One day I was in a cell, the next day I was on the street.

Just like that. No longer a danger to society. No more walls. No barbed wire. No leg irons. No guards. Such a strange feeling, just as strange as captivity had felt when I first went in.

Life had been so slow in my cell that I felt like I was now thrown into the middle of a tornado. Cars speeding by. Planes overhead. People racing in every direction. I experienced psychological bends. What to do? Where to go? What to eat?

I know how "the Ice Man" would feel if awakened and led through the streets today; the world had changed. The last Italians and Irish had moved out of Flushing, hardly anyone spoke English. Cars were different, and my clothes were ten years out of style. Everyone, including little kids, had cell phones, and I'd never seen the Internet.

My sister took me in. The first night was overwhelming. Before bedtime, I showered, looked down at my feet, and couldn't believe I was showering without shoes. Piss, shit, and semen no longer floated around my ankles toward the drain. I stayed in there forever, scrubbing prison off my body.

She set up a bed, but I slept on the floor. I wasn't used to a soft mattress; cold and hard was what I knew.

I awoke all night thinking I was still in jail, and each time, it took a minute for reality to sink in. It happens even today. I awake hearing screams and curses, and think I'm still there.

When my sister called my name in the morning, I said, "Right here," and shook my blanket. I thought she was a hack; if you have a blanket covering you, they need to see you move. Over the years, I'd been counted over twenty-five thousand times, it was my automatic reaction.

Before I brushed my hair, I banged my brush against the sink, to shake out the roaches. But there were none. I still do this today.

The first few times my sister drove me around, I held on to the seat. After being stationary for so many years, fifty miles per hour in the front seat of a car felt like I was being hurled around in a rocket.

I moved into an apartment, two small rooms on the first floor of a two-story house. I was disorganized and I constantly lost things: my keys, my wallet, the TV remote, the house phone. In the little box where I'd lived, everything was right at my fingertips, and I wasn't used to carrying anything.

At first, I wouldn't leave my apartment unless I had to.

You see, in prison, the more you hate confinement, the faster the walls close in, crushing your spirit. So I convinced myself that I loved confinement, and stayed inside my cell even when we were allowed to leave. Believing it was my choice gave me a sense of free will.

I'd conditioned myself so well that now I had to learn to leave my apartment, one step at a time.

My family took me to dinner. My table manners had just about vanished from years of rushing to eat against the clock. It was also the first time I'd held a knife in years without having to defend my life with it. When I got up, I banged my knuckles on the table, like cons do in the chow hall. It was our way of excusing ourselves from the table when we weren't allowed to talk. It took time to lose the habit.

My cousin Don noticed I was having a tough time adjusting. He knew I liked the beach and offered to take me, thought it might help.

The beach was beautiful but reminded me of jail.

Seagulls flew around some of the prisons I'd been in. I used to stuff sliced white bread in my pants and smuggle it from the chow hall to my cell, where I'd feed the seagulls from my window. Watching them fly and swoop, listening to them haw, put a smile on my face, reminded me of the beach.

But memory works both ways; just as the seagulls were able to take me away from the hell of prison, they now returned me there.

I wanted to go back to my apartment.

I had to report regularly to federal probation and state parole. Sometimes, they'd drop in on me. The first time my parole officers knocked at the door, I scrambled to the kitchen to hide my knife set, then laughed to myself. "What am I doing? I'm allowed to have knives."

When my father came to my apartment, I was washing clothes in a bucket.

"What are you doing?" he asked. "There's a washer and dryer at my house, and a Laundromat on the corner."

One by one, I broke jail habits, usually when someone close to me pointed them out.

My driver's license had expired while I was away. I was slow to renew it, probably leery to drive after so long. But my sister was on my back, since she was my taxi. I found out that I had to start all over, and enroll in driver's ed.

My father dropped me off at my first class. I kissed him good-bye, got out of his car, and walked off. I was a few steps away when I turned back and opened the car door.

"What's the matter?" he asked.

"I just kissed you good-bye after you dropped me off at driver's ed. I'm a grown man. Next I'll ask if you can drive me around on a date."

He laughed.

I couldn't even go on a date. I had a 7:00 p.m. curfew as a condition of my parole. How do I tell a woman, "I don't have a car, I'll pick you up on my bicycle and have you home before dark."

Before I was locked up, I dated girls in their late teens and early twenties. Time stopped when I went to jail, so when I came home, I was still looking at young girls.

Talking to a woman my own age felt weird, like I was flirting with an older woman. They seemed old to me back then. But now I was older, too. I was confused. Sometimes, when I looked in the mirror, I didn't recognize the person staring back at me.

I was halfway through life. I didn't have a driver's license. I never had a job, never paid taxes, never had my own credit card, and would never have had a bank account if the lawsuit from my car accident could've been settled with cash. I couldn't even keep track of time without bells, locks, and clocks. I was a mess.

You find your place in life over the years. You struggle, you grow, you meet new challenges. You find a place to live, to work, and a group of friends. When you lose eight or nine years, your old friends, and your old way of life, it feels like you've been tossed into the unknown.

I couldn't find my place. Everywhere I went, I was a stranger.

I became friends with a rabbi and asked him to convert me. After my official conversion, I wanted to purchase tefillin. The rabbi scribbled off an address to a Hebrew store in College Point, Queens. I didn't realize exactly where it was until I pulled up at the corner. I was less than a block from where I'd hijacked a truck more than a decade before. I got out of my car to look around. From where I stood I could see the scene of the crime and the Hebrew store, a stone's throw from each other.

Everything that happened to me between that hijacking and now flashed before my eyes. I was blown away. I could never have imagined this fate on that day. I felt like God led me to this spot, to show me my entire journey in the space of a breath.

A few weeks later, I was in a kosher restaurant out east, far from Brooklyn and Queens, when I noticed the acting boss of the Colombo family at a table across from me. He and his tattooed bodyguard were slurping down matzoh ball soup.

I said to my cousin Enzo, "Could this guy have turned Jew, too? I mean, what are the odds? What should I say to him, 'Come stai, paesan,' or 'Shalom, gazi gazun?' "

My cousin asked, "Is he on your list?"

The feds gave me a three-page list when I came home, two hundred Gambino mobsters I couldn't be seen with, or I'd be sent back to jail.

"I don't think he's on my list," I said, "he's not a Gambino. But I can't be seen with a felon either, and I know he's a felon 'cause I did time with him."

Just as I asked the waitress for the check, he noticed me.

"Hey, Louie."

I got up and gave him a hug.

"We shouldn't be seen together," I told him. "If they snap a shot of us, we're fucked. You being watched?"

"Sure, they're probably outside now." He looked around at the tables. "If they didn't come in to eat."

I said good-bye and ran out the door.

The first three years I was home, I lugged around *Aleesa,* my twelve-hundred-page novel, trying to get a literary agent to read it.

I made a million phone calls. I nudged my way into buildings and offices, even struck up conversations with complete strangers trying to find that one person who could help.

One day, I met the screenwriter David Black.

"Your story is more interesting," he told me, "write it."

"I'd rather forget my past," I said. "I want to be known as a writer, not a gangster."

David never quit on me. He encouraged me, calling me at all hours of the day and night. He sent me to agents, but no one was interested in my novel, they all asked for my story.

As stubborn as always, I wouldn't give in. I refused to write about the streets. It was depressing to recall a wretched life of brute force and cunning, a life that scarred victims, disappointed loved ones, and burdened good people with jury duty. I wasn't ready to examine myself and deal with the past.

But David was also stubborn and never stopped hounding me. "Don't regret your past, make peace with it, and go on."

I knew he was right. I was torn. But everything was still too fresh.

I needed more time to come around. It took three years before I broke down and wrote a chapter. Finishing this book, I made peace with my past. I'm finally free.

Looking back, I see my past as tragedy mixed with comedy. Our way of thinking was ridiculous.

I once went to a wake for a mobster. A little boy, maybe four or five years old, sat down beside me. He asked me questions, "What's your name?" "Where are you from?" Typical things children ask.

His father was talking to somebody a chair away. When he noticed his son asking me questions, he leaned over and said to him, "What are you, a fuckin' cop? Leave the man alone!"

I laughed and saw nothing wrong with this. That's how mobsters raise kids.

In my early twenties, I had a friend who liked the Mafia glitter. He made street money, and hung around social clubs, but he was harmless. His killers knew this when they put a bullet in the back of his head and stuffed him into the trunk of his BMW. He rotted in his parked car about a week until the postman smelled his corpse and called police.

In prison, I played cards with his killers for a month before I found out they were charged with his murder. They were his close friends, and they killed him over a buck. And that's the Mafia.

No more honor. No secret society. No glamour. Any honorable men left over from the old days are strangers in their own world—the way I felt when I came home to Flushing.

Today, life drags. The weeks and years pass uneventfully. No one bangs at my door with a tip. I haven't held a gun in years; I'd probably shoot myself in the foot.

No more fast money, no fast cars, or fast women.

I don't know nobody, got no connections. I buy retail, and get robbed like everyone else. I wait to be seated at restaurants. And I wait in line at the DMV. I even got yelled at by some gung-ho security guard who thought I cut the line.

With nothing going on, I just sit and think. But life is better this way. I'm getting older, and I feel at least ten years older than I am.

When I think about the past, I try to remember good times.

I see my mother when she was alive and shining, with her long black hair and healthy glowing skin. She made people laugh, even while she was dying, courage I'll never forget.

I see my grandmothers, my aunt and uncle, and my cousin Joseph. I didn't get to be with them again, they passed on while I was away.

I see the women I've loved; Cindy rubbing my forehead in her warm caring way, and Angela squeezing me with sudden love.

I see Juney with all of his restless energy spilling over in his smile.

I see Funzi shaking my hand, excited to see me. And Tony the Twitch laughing behind the wheel. I see the natural beauty in his twitch, when he'd just let go and not try to control it.

I see Tony Pork Chop taking a break from his workhorse lifestyle for a few months, to live the fantasy life of a gangster.

I see Barry the Brokester's serious face with five kids at home. He was determined to send them to college, and give them a better shot than he had. Back then, I wasn't able to see him in this light.

I like to remember the smiles. Even as prisoners, we laughed when life was horrible.

When I was young, I saw a kid slash at an old woman and take off with her purse.

I was driving a stolen car. I left the car in traffic, jumped out, ran the kid down, and tackled him to the pavement. I wrestled the razor out of his hand and recovered the woman's purse.

The whole thing happened in front of a bank. The bank president's office was all glass, with a view of the street. He came outside, told me he'd seen the whole thing, and asked for my name and address. A few days later, I got a letter from him in the mail:

> *I wanted to personally thank you . . . seeing young fellows like yourself is very refreshing, and I hope that our future will be filled with cleaner streets and a better country.*

All in the same moment, I jumped out of a stolen car and risked my life to defend an old woman. Mario would rob a bank, but risk his ass to beat up a rape-o, and avenge a girl he didn't even know. I watched the Twin Towers fall from a prison TV room. Some of the hardened thugs around me were close to tears. I later heard that an old friend of mine, Augie, who'd become a made man, and eventually went to jail, was one of the first volunteers at Ground Zero. He suffers from illnesses caused by breathing toxins at the site. He'll probably die for his heroism.

Sometimes the heart is good, but the mind is mixed up. Good people usually come around, and everyone deserves a chance. That's why life isn't lived in a day. If there's one thing you learn in prison, it's that everything takes time.

ACKNOWLEDGMENTS

Special thanks to my friends and family, who wrote to me, visited me, sent me books, and accepted my collect phone calls while I was in prison. I know the pain of solitude, but nothing would've hurt more than to feel I'd been forgotten; thank you all for never letting me feel that pain.

Especially to my dear father; my sister, Lisa; Uncle Anthony; Aunt Clo; cousins Don and Denise; my stepmom, Betty; and my stepsister, Debra.

To George, Rita, Norma, Jerry, Louis, Richie, Donna, Alex, Mario, Peter Trip, Ronnie, and Elizabeth.

To pals from jail: Basil Whelan, Lorenzo Musso, Danny Breslau, Markos Pappas, and Vic Orena Jr.; and to the memory of Richard Messina, who died in prison. Thank you for everything you taught me, Richard.

Upon my return to the world, thanks to special people like David Black, Tommy Gallagher, Barbara Weisberg, Robin Shamburg, Maya Casagrande, Ruda Dauphin, Harry Stein, Richard Abate, Joe Lamberta Sr. and Joe Jr., John Brunetti, Paul and Karen Dawson, Kieran and Sarah McLoughlin, Jean and Howie Silverstein, Jerry Bauer, Rabbi Arthur Rulnick, and Bill Yosses, a caring man who introduced me to my dear friend and agent, Lisa Queen. Thanks for everything, Lisa. Thanks also to Jonah, Eleanor, Jessica, Ann, and Spencer from Lisa's office.

To my state parole officers, Lionel Lauture and Ms. Brown; and my federal PO, Edward Kanaley.

To Claire Wachtel, Jonathan Burnham, and Brenda Segel of Harper-Collins: thank you for believing in me. You three were able to envision the whole book at our first meeting, when only a couple of chapters had been written. Claire, you're the best. Thanks also to Julia Novitch, Katherine Beitner, Kathy Schneider, Christine Boyd, Kevin Callahan, Tina Andreadis, Nina Olmsted, David Koral, Michael Morrison, and Jane Friedman.

To Jacqueline Remmers, at Luitingh-Sijthoff, my Dutch publisher.

To Brenda Kimber and the whole team at Transworld. I feel as though I know you forever, Brenda.

To my mother's dearest friend Rhoda Pobliner and her daughter Beth Birnbaum, who I've known since I was five, when I introduced myself as "the boy from aroun' the torner." You listened as I read my manuscript aloud; your guidance was invaluable.

And to my angel, Gabriella, who accepted my past and commented on every chapter. I'll never forget the long nights you sat in front of the keyboard typing my handwritten drafts into the computer. How many times you fell asleep mid-sentence, and I shook you awake to continue. You are beauty, inside and out.

And to God, who opened my eyes.